# LANGUAGE, COMMUNICATION, AND CULTURE

# INTERNATIONAL AND INTERCULTURAL COMMUNICATION ANNUAL

**Volume XIII**                                                              **1989**

**Editor**
Stella Ting-Toomey
*Arizona State University*

**Coeditor**
Felipe Korzenny
*San Francisco State University*

**Editorial Assistant**
Lauren Gumbs
*Arizona State University*

**Consulting Editors for Volume XIII**

Robert Arundale
*University of Alaska*

George Barnett
*University of New York at Buffalo*

Richard Brislin
*East-West Center*

Donal Carbaugh
*University of Massachusetts at Amherst*

Howard Giles
*University of Bristol*

William B. Gudykunst
*Arizona State University*

Beth Haslett
*University of Delaware*

Brooks Hill
*University of Oklahoma*

Geert Hofstede
*Institute for Research on Intercultural Cooperation
The Netherlands*

Robert Hopper
*University of Texas at Austin*

C. Harry Hui
*University of Hong Kong*

Tamar Katriel
*University of Haifa
Israel*

Thomas Kochman
*University of Illinois at Chicago*

Cheris Kramarae
*University of Illinois at Urbana*

Margaret McLaughlin
*University of Southern California*

Tsukasa Nishida
*Nihon University
Japan*

Barnett Pearce
*University of Massachusetts at Amherst*

Gerry Philipsen
*University of Washington*

Susan Shimanoff
*San Francisco State University*

Robert Shuter
*Marquette University*

Lea Stewart
*Rutgers University*

Deborah Tannen
*Georgetown University*

Karen Tracy
*Temple University*

INTERNATIONAL AND INTERCULTURAL COMMUNICATION ANNUAL
VOLUME XIII                                                    1989

# LANGUAGE, COMMUNICATION, AND CULTURE

## CURRENT DIRECTIONS

edited by

## Stella TING-TOOMEY
## Felipe KORZENNY

Published in Cooperation with
The Speech Communication Association
Commission on International and Intercultural Communication

**SAGE** PUBLICATIONS
*The Publishers of Professional Social Science*
Newbury Park   London   New Delhi

*For information address:*

SAGE Publications, Inc.
2111 West Hillcrest Drive
Newbury Park, California 91320

SAGE Publications Ltd.
28 Banner Street
London EC1Y 8QE
England

SAGE Publications India Pvt. Ltd.
M-32 Market
Greater Kailash I
New Delhi 110 048 India

Printed in the United States of America


Library of Congress Cataloging-in-Publication Data


International Standard Book Number 0-8039-3449-1
International Standard Book Number 0-8039-3450-5 (pbk.)
International Standard Series Number 0270-6075

**FIRST PRINTING, 1989**

# Contents

**PART III: LANGUAGE AND INTERGROUP COMMUNICATION**

# Preface

This is the thirteenth volume of the *International and Intercultural Communication Annual*. The *Annual* is sponsored by the International and Intercultural Communication Division of the Speech Communication Association. The series presents theme-based publications that aim at promoting better understanding of the international and intercultural communication processes.

The theme of Volume XIII is the relationships among language, communication, and culture. The volume is divided into three parts. Part I deals with the critical issues related to language acquisition, context, and cognition. Part II presents an array of perspectives in analyzing the role of language in comparative cross-cultural communication settings. Part III examines the role of first-language and second-language usage in intergroup communication contexts.

On both conceptual and methodological grounds, this volume reflects multiple orientations to theory and research concerning the relationships among language, communication, and culture. Each orientation is distinctive, yet complements another orientation. Volume XIII should appeal to scholars, researchers, and students who are intrigued and enticed by the fascinating, multifaceted aspects of language. The volume reflects the current ideas and approaches of scholars working in the disciplines of psychology, linguistics, sociolinguistics, intergroup relations, and communication.

Many individuals made this volume possible. First, I want to thank my colleagues, graduate students, and the staff of the Department of Communication, Arizona State University, for providing a supportive environment in which to work. Second, I want to extend my special appreciation to the editorial board members for generously offering their time and expertise in reviewing the submitted manuscripts. Third, I want to acknowledge the help of Lauren Gumbs, for spending countless hours proofreading each manuscript, and for serving as a superb editorial assistant to this volume; Paula Trubisky, for her good cheer and support throughout the editing phase; Peter Ehrenhaus and Michael Hecht, for serving as ad hoc reviewers in times of need; and the staff of Sage Publications, for providing professional support in the publishing of this volume. In addition, I want to thank the two previous editors, Bill Gudykunst and Young Yun Kim, for laying a solid foundation for the development of this series. Their guidance and encouragement in the development of this book are gratefully acknowledged. Felipe Korzenny, my coeditor, has also been most supportive in every phase of the editing process. It has been a delight to work with him. This volume also owes its worth to the talent and intellectual commitment of the authors. Without their labor and creative ideas, this book would not exist.

Finally, it is Charles and Adrian to whom I owe the greatest debt. I thank them for their enormous patience and understanding during the many Saturdays and Sundays I have spent away from them.

*Stella Ting-Toomey*
Arizona State University

# 1

## Language, Communication, and Culture
### *An Introduction*

STELLA TING-TOOMEY  •  *Arizona State University*

*This chapter presents an overview of this volume by providing a synopsis of each chapter and by explaining the underlying logic of the arrangements of the chapters. Three approaches characterize the overall content of the eleven studies in this volume: developmental, interactional, and social psychological. Finally, current directions for the study of language, communication, and culture are assessed and specific directions for future research are recommended.*

This volume brings together multiple conceptual and methodological orientations to examine the relationships among language, communication, and culture. Conceptually, the authors in this volume have utilized approaches such as developmental language acquisition, cultural communication, pragmatics, and intergroup communication in analyzing the linkages among language, communication, and culture. Methodologically, approaches such as ethnography of speaking, rhetorical analysis, conversational analysis, and quantitative analysis have been employed. Each chapter in this volume provides a slightly different angle from which to look at the critical role of language in cross-cultural or intergroup communication settings, yet, at the same time, the chapters complement one another.

The volume is divided into three parts: Part I is concerned with language, context, and cognition; Part II addresses the relationship between language and communication styles across cultures; and Part III discusses language and intergroup communication. The chapters are arranged in such a way that the two chapters in Part I deal with general, but critical, issues concerning the relationships among language acquisition, cultural function, and cognition. The authors of the six chapters in Part II examine either culture-specific or culture-universal dimensions of language across different speech communities. Finally, the three chapters in Part III focus on first- versus second-language usage in intergroup interaction contexts.

## THE STUDIES

The volume as a whole is more theoretical than methodological. Haslett (Chapter 2) argues that children in a specific cultural context acquire tacit knowledge of the cultural system via the language socialization process. Specifically, she proposes that while there exist universal stages of language acquisition, researchers should pay close attention to the socialization norms of language acquisition in different cultural settings. She emphasizes the importance of understanding the language development process in conjunction with social knowledge acquisition and cultural knowledge acquisition. Steinfatt (Chapter 3) discusses the important notion of understanding the impact of language on human perception and cognition. The central question of his chapter asks: To what extent does language influence our thought processes? Through an exhaustive analysis of the existing evidence on interlanguage and intralanguage studies, he concludes that only the subtle form and not the strong form of the linguistic relativity hypothesis holds in different cultures and subcultures.

Part II contains six chapters that utilize an interpretive orientation to the study of language in comparative cross-cultural communication settings. Philipsen's (Chapter 4) work provides the contextual frame for the two chapters that follow. Philipsen argues for the importance of understanding "speech" via the communal function of communication. The *communal function* refers to the creation, affirmation, and negotiation of shared identity among the interlocutors in a given cultural community. After comparing the role of speech in four cultural communities, he concludes by emphasizing the importance of studying speech in conjunction with personhood construction in different cultures. Carbaugh (Chapter 5) extends Philipsen's thesis and develops a structural model of speech that organizes speech and the meanings of speech in terms of performance level and meaning level. The performance level concerns how different "cultural terms of talk" can be classified into speech acts, speech events, and speech styles. The meaning level of "talk" refers to the metaphorical functions of talk in reflecting the implicit cultural models of communication, sociality, and personhood in different cultural settings. Griefat and Katriel (Chapter 6) analyze the folk-linguistic term *musayara* as used in the discourse of Arabs in Israel. Using data gathered between 1982 and 1986, they examine in detail the interaction ethos of *musayara* (which refers to "going with" or "accompanying" one's partner in conversation) from a variety of ethnographic sources. They conclude by comparing how the *musayara* code and the *dugri* ("talking straight") code of native Israeli Jews can create potential miscommunication in intercultural encounters between Arabs and Jews in Israel.

Johnstone (Chapter 7) explores the ways in which culture, language, and rhetorical situation come together to shape persuasive strategies used in the European West and the Iranian East. She distinguishes the difference between persuasive styles and persuasive strategies, and argues that while persuasive style is a facet of the culture, persuasive strategies enable speakers in different cultures to make choices, based in immediate rhetorical situations, among "available means of persuasion." Hopper and Doany (Chapter 8) take a slightly different approach to studying the interrelationships among language, communication, and culture. They offer universalist descriptions of some practices in telephone conversations. By analyzing conversational speech events in English, French, and Arabic, they argue for the importance of studying linguistic universals that transcend cultural boundaries. From a contextual perspective, Banks (Chapter 9) proposes a model of language for intercultural communication based on linguistic pragmatics. Two interdependent dialectics undergird the model: competence dialectic and practice dialectic. Banks uses the model to analyze the canonical forms of pronouns in English and Mandarin Chinese, and the interpretations of the pronoun choices are cast in terms of their power and solidarity implications. The critical relationship between cultural ideology and language practice is emphasized.

Part III focuses on the theme of the relationship between language usage and ethnolinguistic identity. Garrett, Giles, and Coupland (Chapter 10) extend Giles and Byrne's (1982) intergroup model of second-language acquisition, presenting revised propositions that incorporate outgroup as well as ingroup factors and factors that pertain to dominant as well as minority group language learners. In addition, specific sociolinguistic factors that promote second-language acquisition are discussed. The revised intergroup model adopts a broader stance toward the relationship between language and ethnolinguistic identity. Gudykunst (Chapter 11) examines the influence of Hofstede's (1980) dimensions of cultural variability on ethnolinguistic identity of sojourners in the United States. His results reveal that three out of Hofstede's four dimensions have a significant multivariate effect on the five components (ingroup identification, multiple group memberships, group boundaries, intergroup comparisons, and ethnolinguistic vitality) of ethnolinguistic identity. He urges that future research should address the specific boundary conditions of ethnolinguistic identity theory and test the theory in diverse interethnic linguistic communication settings. Finally, Bourhis (Chapter 12) explores the critical factors that influence language choice strategies in bilingual organizational contexts in Canada. He identifies five factors (linguistic skills, speech accommodation, organizational position, group vitality, and the linguistic work environment) that influence the linguistic code-switching process in the bilingual work environment. The rest of the chapter details a new method to evaluate the linguistic work environment of speakers and their communication processes in bilingual organizational systems.

## DIRECTIONS

The major approaches presented in this volume follow the three-part development of this book: developmental, interactional, and social psychological. The *developmental approach* (Chapters 2 and 3) of language and communication involves theorizing about language developmental acquisition in relationship to acquiring tacit knowledge structures of the culture. The emphasis is on the importance of acquiring language and cultural communication practices simultaneously in the linguistic development stages of the child. Developmental theorists attempt to understand the linkages between language and the cognitive processing in a culture.

The *interactional approach* (Chapters 4 through 9) emphasizes how speech is codified through interactional routines and sequences in different cultural communities. The focus is on exploring what people are doing with speech as they interact face to face in a specific interactional context. This approach, then, emphasizes the dynamics of *languaging* as individuals come together and communicate. Interactional theorists are interested in delineating the appropriate styles and norms of communication practices in different cultural milieus. The approach follows closely Ochs's (1986) argument that most cross-cultural differences in language are differences in "context and/or frequency of occurrence" (p. 10). She summarizes:

What is different across societies is the extensiveness of these routines in terms of the semantic-pragmatic content covered (e.g., politeness phenomenon, role instruction, teasing, shaming, insults, language correction), the number of interlocutors involved (dyadic, triadic, multiparty), the social relationship of the interlocutors (e.g., caregivers, peers, strangers), the setting (e.g., inside/outside household dwellings, private/public, formal/informal distinctions in setting), the length of the imitative routines (e.g., number of turns, length of time), and the frequency of occurrence in the experience of young children. (p. 10)

At different language socialization stages, individuals do not learn language *per se;* rather, they learn the various patterns and styles of language interaction that enable them to function as competent communicators in different situational contexts.

Finally, researchers using the *social psychological approach* (Chapters 10, 11, and 12) examine the underlying factors that influence language choices in multilingual communication settings. Group comparison factors, identity salience factors, and attitudinal and motivational factors are some of the variables that have been identified as critical to the language accommodation process in intergroup communication situations. Social cognitive theorists map out a set of specific social psychological conditions that account for first-language or second-language usage among majority groups and minority groups in different worldwide cultural communities.

Taken together, the three approaches in this volume reflect the current trends and directions of the multidisciplinary nature of studying language, communication, and culture. The three themes that emerge out of this volume include the importance of studying (1) the relationship between language and context, (2) the relationship between language and identities (i.e., personal identity, social role identity, and cultural/ethnolinguistic identity), and (3) the multiple functions and meanings of language and communication in relationship to culture.

Almost all authors in this volume voice the importance of understanding language, communication, and culture *in situ.* Almost all contributors to this collection discuss the critical role of language usage through communication to assert and negotiate different facets of identity. Finally, all researchers in this volume are interested in somehow relating the different levels and functions of language usage to the collective life of a culture.

## CONCLUSION

The eleven essays in this volume, as a whole, provide a sounding board for further theorizing about the processes of language, communication, and culture. While many excellent volumes have been compiled on the topic of language and culture (see, for example, Crystal, 1987; Forgas, 1985; Gumperz, 1983; Holland & Quinn, 1987; Philips, Steele, & Tanz, 1987; Schieffelin & Ochs, 1986; Shweder & LeVine, 1984), this volume brings together multiple theoretical perspectives that examine language *and* communication as a focal point in the context of either cross-cultural or intergroup interaction settings.

Many authors in this volume have sketched out frameworks or models for further empirical testing. Several researchers have utilized diverse methodological tools such as ethnographic analysis, rhetorical analysis, conversational analysis, and case study method to capture the relationship between language and communication in conjunction with the communal life of a culture. Multiple theoretical and methodological developments are healthy for the inquiry into language, communication, and culture at this stage. The different perspectives presented in this volume complement, rather than oppose one another. Many functions and dimensions of language and cultural communication style are proposed. Each author has opted to discuss the interlinkage between language and communication based on his or her points of research interest and orientation. While no singular definition has been offered for language *per se,* most researchers will agree that language is part of a symbolic system that is governed by sociocultural norms and rules.

In synthesizing the basic ideas in this volume, it appears that multicultural team efforts are urgently needed in the theorizing phase concerning language, communication, and culture. Methodologically, both "insider" and "outsider" modes of inquiry are necessary so that cross-cultural comparative studies can be conducted with functional, conceptual, linguistic, metric, and/or sample equivalence (Lonner, 1979; see also Gudykunst & Ting-Toomey, 1988). Finally, issues such as language, cognition, *and* affect, language *and* nonverbal communication, and language *and* communication competence in different cultures need to be addressed more fully by intercultural communication researchers who are interested in the dynamic process of communication via language. Language is the *sine qua non* of human symbolic communication process. It should hold a central place in any human communication study.

A well-rounded theory of language *and* communication should focus on the influence of cultural variability, social cognitive variability, and affective variability upon the situated use of language as part of the larger communication system. Competence and performance levels of language usage and language code-switching abilities should be accounted for. Finally, linguistic communication or miscommunication through the different cultural ethos of style variation in different cultures should also be carefully delineated and examined.

# REFERENCES

Crystal, D. (1987). *The Cambridge encyclopedia of language*. Cambridge: Cambridge University Press.

Forgas, J. (Ed.). (1985). *Language and social situations*. New York: Springer-Verlag.

Giles, H., & Byrne, J. (1982). The intergroup model of second language acquisition. *Journal of Multilingual and Multicultural Development, 3*, 17–40.

Gudykunst, W., & Ting-Toomey, S., with Chua, E. (1988). *Culture and interpersonal communication*. Newbury Park, CA: Sage.

Gumperz, J. (1983). *Discourse strategies*. Cambridge: Cambridge University Press.

Hofstede, G. (1980). *Culture's consequences: International differences in work-related values*. Beverly Hills, CA: Sage.

Holland, D., & Quinn, N. (Eds.). (1987). *Cultural models in language and thought*. Cambridge: Cambridge University Press.

Lonner, W. (1979). Issues in cross-cultural psychology. In A. Marsell, A. Tharp, & T. Cibrowski (Eds.), *Perspectives in cross-cultural psychology*. New York: Academic Press.

Ochs, S. (1986). Introduction. In B. Schieffelin & E. Ochs (Eds.), *Language and socialization across cultures*. Cambridge: Cambridge University Press.

Philips, S., Steele, S., & Tanz, C. (Eds.). (1987). *Language, gender, and sex in comparative perspective*. Cambridge: Cambridge University Press.

Schieffelin, B., & Ochs, E. (Eds.). (1986). *Language socialization across cultures*. Cambridge: Cambridge University Press.

Shweder, R., & LeVine, R. (Eds.). (1984). *Culture theory: Essays on mind, self, and emotion*. Cambridge: Cambridge University Press.

**I**

**LANGUAGE, CONTEXT,
AND COGNITION**

# 2

## Communication and Language Acquisition Within a Cultural Context

BETH HASLETT  &bull;  *University of Delaware*

*This chapter argues that young children acquire communicative abilities within a distinct cultural context: Both communicative abilities and cultural norms are thus simultaneously acquired. The tacit knowledge ingrained in one's culture provides an interpretive frame of reference for understanding and evaluating communicative behaviors of members of a particular cultural group. Cultural variability influences the types of communicative behaviors acquired and the context in which they are acquired.*

### COMMUNICATION AND LANGUAGE ACQUISITION WITHIN A CULTURAL CONTEXT

Exploring how young children develop their communication skills is a complex task, especially since scholars must account for the acquisition of very different languages and the diverse communication skills within different cultural contexts. Various theoretical explanations of communication development stress different factors as being very important, and in each perspective the importance of culture also varies. Generally, developmental theorists have explored universals of acquisition, such as the linguistic universals proposed by Chomsky (1965), or differences in acquisition, as does sociolinguistic research (Schieffelin & Ochs, 1986). In what follows, we shall examine both facets of communication development—universal aspects as well as differences. Culture plays an important role in both respects, since both universals and differences must be assessed in cross-cultural comparisons. Our discussion will also cover basic definitional issues surrounding culture and communication.

The chapter proceeds in three sections. The first section discusses some basic definitional issues. The second section looks specifically at cultural influences in the acquisition process and, finally, some implications for future research are discussed.

## WHAT IS BEING ACQUIRED?

Before we begin, it is necessary to establish working definitions of the terms *communication* and *culture*. A very useful definition of *communication* has been articulated by Scheflen (1974): Communication is an organized, standardized, culturally patterned system of behavior that sustains, regulates and makes possible human relationships. Scheflen's view emphasizes that communication is a shared, structured, conventional, culturally patterned, and multichannel act (Haslett, 1987).

Culture can be viewed as an "inherited system of ideas that structures the subjective experience of individuals" (LeVine, 1984, p. 20). Geertz (1973) views culture as shared ways of life, with sharing on both the concrete level (e.g., artifacts) and the cognitive level (e.g., language, symbols). Both views emphasize that culture is a shared, consensual perspective within a social group, although members may not share that perspective equally or in every facet of experience.

### *Communication and Culture*

LeVine (1984) notes the integral relationship between communication and culture. He argues that culture represents a consensus in a community about the meaning of symbols, both verbal and nonverbal, and that this consensus is "substantially related to the importance of communication in social life" (p. 68).

For humans, culture and communication are acquired simultaneously: Neither exists without the other. Culture, by definition, is a shared, consensual way of life, and that sharing and consensus are made possible only through communication. In turn, humans communicate in a cultural milieu that constrains the form and nature of communication. Thus when one asks about cultural influences on the acquisition of communication, one needs to acknowledge that culture constrains both *what* is acquired and *how* it is acquired. In turn, communicative processes shape the culture that is transmitted from generation to generation.

Culture provides the shared tacit knowledge that enables members to understand and communicate with one another. As LeVine (1984) notes, every culture has an underlying rationale—"a collective value, arbitrary in itself, that is taken as an absolute requirement in a rational explanation of a customary practice" (p. 81). This cultural rationale—a culture's tacit or background knowledge—provides the basis for interpretive practices followed by group members. Members use this tacit knowledge to communicate. Such tacit knowledge surfaces in the form of pragmatic presuppositions, conversational implicatures, judgments of relevance, interpretive procedures, and the like. When communication scholars fail to acknowledge the role of culture as tacit knowledge in communication, only the *form* of communication is analyzed, while its *function* remains obscure.

Different cultures also have differing degrees of openness with respect to communication. As LeVine (1984) points out:

> Reflective discourse refers to conventionalized formats for commenting on cultural beliefs and norms in themselves and in their influence on social behavior. Cultures vary enormously in the development and elaboration of such formats. (p. 81)

He further notes:

> Culture cannot be reduced to its explicit or implicit dimensions. It would be fallacious to take what is given by informants at face value and assume that the rest of behavior and belief is untouched by culture. It is equally fallacious to discount explicit rules, beliefs, and labels as lacking social or psychological reality or as mere reflections of, or disguises for, implicit cultural orientations. In culture, as an organization of shared meanings, some meanings are more explicit than others, for reasons having to do with the pragmatics of social life and their history for a given society. (p. 77)

The maturational, developmental context, however, presents unique difficulties of its own in exploring the relationship between culture and communication. Developmental processes are no longer assumed to be progressive, linear steps toward reaching some adult standard of behavior (Bruner, 1975; Isbell & McKee, 1980; Shweder & LeVine, 1984). Rather, development seems to occur as a function of the different types of knowing and experiencing that children encounter. None of these differing experiences is ever lost; rather, their meanings become layered upon one another and form a rich composite of information and knowledge (LeVine, 1984, pp. 80–85). Thus at any developmental point in time the meanings of the child for events and experiences will be distinct from any prior point and from any adult model. LeVine uses the analogy of appreciating and understanding one's house in very different ways as one grows up to illustrate the different layers of meaning an individual develops. In effect, we switch from frame to frame, with each frame reflecting a new understanding.

Thus far, we have established working definitions for communication and culture and their interrelationships. In looking at the developmental process specifically, it seems clear that cultural and communicative practices are being acquired simultaneously. Indeed, neither is possible without the other. In addition, given the complexities of different cultures, it seems reasonable to assume that the acquisition process will vary from social group to social group. Finally, some cultures will be more open to analysis than others as a function of their communicative practices. Some cultures will be relatively open in their communication, whereas other cultures may be very closed and protective of their privacy.

In what follows, we will look more specifically at the acquisition process. First, we will distinguish between language and communication. Next, we will explore some universals in acquisition. Finally, we will deal with some differences in communicative practices and in what is viewed as communicative competence in different cultures.

## ACQUIRING COMMUNICATIVE SKILLS

### Distinguishing Language and Communication

Distinction between language and communication is needed given that we are focusing mainly on communication processes. Language can be viewed as the symbolic code that underlies verbal communication (Haslett, 1987). Verbal communication is the *use* of language to create and maintain human relationships. Another communication system is that of nonverbal communication—gestures, eye gazes, proxemics, and the like—which may accompany verbal communication or may be used as a solitary communication system.

In this discussion, we shall not be concerned with the acquisition of language, but rather with how humans acquire the use of language. This presupposes, of course, that necessary language skills must be acquired before certain communicative strategies, such as questioning, can be developed. These remarks, however, should not be interpreted to mean that language is a necessary precursor to communication. Evidence suggests that nonverbal communication skills are the earliest communicative system in use; some scholars have argued that an infant's pointing and reaching are precursors to subsequent verbal commands and request (Bates, 1979; Bruner, 1975). Paralinguistic elements, like stress and pitch, are present during the prelinguistic stages of development as well (Reich, 1986).

## Some Universals in Acquiring Language and Communication

Very briefly, with respect to language learning, infants appear to go through the following stages (Reich, 1986):

### Prelinguistic Stages

(1) *Birth cry:* Occurs at birth.

(2) *Vocalizing:* This production of random sounds by the infant is generally believed to reflect sounds of any language, not just the culture's language.

(3) *Babbling:* The infant's production of sounds that begin to approximate the sounds of his or her native language begins at approximately 6–9 months.

(4) *Single words:* The production of single words, usually representing important people or objects in the infant's environment, begins at 12–18 months.

### Linguistic Stages

(1) *Simple sentences:* The child, approximately 18 months, produces two-word utterances called *telegraphic speech*: content words (such as verbs and nouns) are spoken, while function words (such as articles) are generally not spoken. The function words that may sometimes be included are personal pronouns, demonstratives, and verb particles. This telegraphic speech stage appears to be universal, since function words vary between 6% and 16% of the speech content during the two-word stage. This lack of function words has been documented in at least 12 different languages, ranging from French to Mandarin to Swedish, thus reflecting diverse languages and cultures.

The sentence types being acquired appear to be ordered in the following way: expressions of reference, expressions of events, expressions of attribution, location and possession, and expressions of experiencing and instrument (Reich, 1986, p. 83).

(2) *Three-term sentences:* The child begins to produce utterances containing three terms (e.g., subject-action-object, as in "John hit ball").

These sentences begin to show a more distinct structure, seemingly based on the underlying semantic organization of agents, objects, action, instruments, and the like.

(3) *Sentences of greater length and complexity:* This stage progresses as the child's cognitive and linguistic capacities grow.

These stages appear to be universal, although how particular relationships (such as possession) are expressed varies across different languages.

The issue of what abilities underlie these stages and language itself is hotly debated. Explanatory views emphasize humans' biological capacity for language, their cognitive capacity for language (i.e., information processing capacity), or how social interaction facilitates language acquisition.

In his seminal book, *The Biological Foundations of Language* (1967), Lenneberg argues that humans are uniquely "prewired" for language acquisition. In support of this position, he reviews data from aphasic patients and suggests a critical learning period for language acquisition up to puberty. After puberty, Lenneberg argues, brain plasticity is lost and thus an injury to the left hemisphere (the dominant hemisphere controlling language) results in a permanent language deficit, the severity of which is determined by the severity of the aphasic injury. Other evidence supporting an innate human predisposition for language includes (a) a universal age of onset for language at approximately 2 years, (b) special cortical centers for speech production and interpretation, (c) the emergence of language in children of very low intelligence or children experiencing severe environmental deprivation, and (d) the ability of humans to transfer hemispheric brain functions. Considerable research has been done attesting to the robustness of language and modifying the critical period from birth to approximately 6 years of age.

Cognitive explanations have focused on speech perception and production as well as memory limitations in language acquisition. Generally, those linguistic structures having more complexity, either grammatically or semantically, take longer to acquire and are more difficult to process. Considerable work has been done on children's understanding of different linguistic concepts and the order in which linguistic structures are acquired.

Other explanatory models focus on how social interaction makes possible and facilitates language acquisition. One point generally

agreed upon is that interaction with a speaker is necessary for language acquisition: The speaker does not necessarily have to be an
adult, but that is the general rule. Learning language via interaction
with an adult caretaker seems to be a very common cultural practice,
and the language addressed to young children is termed ACL (adult-
child language). Adults talk very differently to young children, compared to the way they talk among themselves, and they *simplify* their
speech by making shorter utterances, speaking more slowly, making
fewer errors, pronouncing words more clearly, using a distinct vocabulary, using less complex syntax, and discussing the here-and-now
(Reich, 1986, pp. 89–93).

Outside of ACL, no general set of social practices seems to be
followed. A wide range of divergent cultural practices seem to permit
and facilitate language acquisition. The scope of the present chapter
prohibits discussing these widely differing acquisition strategies, and
there are, of course, other complex issues involved when we discuss
the simultaneous acquisition of two languages or the delayed acquisition of a second language.

In conclusion, it seems reasonable to say that no one model satisfac-
torily explains language acquisition. It seems likely that innate, cognitive, and social factors play complex, interactive roles in language
acquisition. For different cultures, the balance of innate, cognitive,
and social factors in language acquisition may well vary, given that
different languages are being learned.

While we have discussed some general stages in language acquisition, no comparable general stages of *communicative development*
can be detailed. The variability of communicative and social practices
across different cultures is such that one can generalize only about
very broad principles and not about specific strategies. I believe the
following set of principles can be viewed as culturally invariant or
universal:

(1) *Communication is viewed as an important basic need in all cultures.*
Very young infants are able to respond uniquely to the human voice
(Reich, 1986). The research of Trevarthen (1977, 1979) and Lenneberg
(1967) suggests that humans may be "prewired" to recognize the communicative importance of language. This innate recognition may, some
suggest, account for the rapidity of language acquisition. In addition,
the eye gaze synchrony between adult and infant is regarded as a
primary communicative strategy (Stern, 1977). In acknowledging the

importance of communication, humans recognize that messages have effects, that humans send messages intentionally, and that communicators mutually influence one another.

(2) *Communication is recognized as a multichannel phenomenon.* That is, all cultures use verbal and nonverbal communication systems. Most use dress, adornment, and architecture as well to communicate.

(3) *Communication has three general purposes: to express thoughts and desires, to establish communion with others, and to share knowledge.*

(4) *All cultures appear to use communication to mark status and social identity and to maintain face (i.e., politeness).*

## Cultural Differences in Communication

At the outset, scholars have clearly demonstrated strong differences in verbal and nonverbal communication across cultures and subcultures. These differences determine how messages are sent, interpreted, and responded to. Indeed, a voluminous research literature documents critical differences in nonverbal communication (Scherer & Ekman, 1985), social identity and judgments (St. Clair & Giles, 1980), intergroup communication (Gudykunst, 1986), communication development (Ochs & Schieffelin, 1984; Schieffelin & Ochs, 1986), and values (Hofstede, 1980). The work of Sapir and Whorf is especially relevant, with their view of strong linguistic determinism (Whorf, 1956). Although linguistic differences create different conceptualizations of the world, clear communication across cultures is accomplished daily in a multitude of ways, even though subtle nuances in meaning may be lost (Glenn, 1981). Although the specific relationships between preverbal (prelinguistic) stages and verbal stages need further study, most scholars agree that these two stages are not independent of one another (Sugarman, 1983).

Since communicative practices vary cross-culturally, clearly what is being acquired varies as well. Furthermore, the process of acquiring communicative skills varies cross-culturally. If there is any generalization possible in this domain, it clearly is the principle that *what is acquired is valued by the culture.* For example, silence is valued by Quakers, deference is valued by the Japanese, and openness is valued by North Americans. Each of these cultural values is reflected by different communicative practices. As Gardner (1984) observes:

> After the first year or two of life, the individual enters into negotiations not merely with physical or social objects but also, and increasingly,

with sets of symbols and discourses of meaning with words, pictures, gestures, numbers, ritualistic activities, and other "mediators of significance"; and it is here that the differences across cultures become most manifest, increasingly profound, and sometimes irremediable. (p. 270)

In the context of development, cultural practices and communicative practices are inextricably tied. Cultural knowledge and communicative practices mutually influence one another. Ochs and Schieffelin (1984) suggest that:

> The capacity to express intentions is human but which intentions can be expressed by whom, when, and how is subject to *local expectations concerning the social behavior of members* [italics added]. With respect to the acquisition of competence in language use, this means that societies may very well differ in their expectations of what children can and should communicate (Hymes, 1967). They may also differ in their expectations concerning the capacity of young children to understand intentions (or particular intentions). (p. 307)

Ochs and Schieffelin (1984) suggest that cultures have very different expectations concerning the young child's competence, and thus patterns of interaction between adult caretakers and children vary widely. On the basis of their own anthropological studies, they contrast Anglo-American middle-class caretakers, Samoan caretakers, and Kaluli (Papua, New Guinea) caretakers. Anglo-American acquisition strategies involve the following patterns: (a) Dyadic adult caretaker-child interaction is stressed, (b) children's utterances are assumed to be meaningful, (c) adult caretakers accommodate children, and (d) adult utterances are simplified when directed to children. In contrast, Samoan practices are such that (a) multiparty interactions are stressed, (b) children's first utterances consist of defiant and angry words, (c) caretakers are ranked hierarchically, with lower-ranking caretakers actually taking care of children, and (d) adult caretakers do not try to interpret children's utterances, as children are expected to clarify any problematic utterances. Finally, the Kaluli practices involve (a) emphasis on triadic interactions among adult, child, and sibling, (b) infants being viewed as having no understanding, (c) explicit modeling of what to say, and (d) no expansion of children's utterances or any attribution as to their state of mind.

From these brief characterizations, it can readily be seen that both cultural values and communicative practices vary widely. Communicative practices are based upon and convey cultural values, and such values, as well as practices, will vary across cultures. There appears to be considerable diversity in *what* communicative practices are required, and in *what contexts* practices are acquired.

### Dimensions for Assessing Communicative Differences

One way to analyze cultural variation is to look at universal human needs or demands—such as the need for survival, health, or affiliation with others—and examine how cultures satisfy these needs. From this perspective, we can look at some universal requirements for acquiring communication and explore how different cultural practices meet these needs. The work of Ochs and Schieffelin (1984) reflects such an attempt.

Ochs and Schieffelin suggest several underlying dimensions on which to assess differences. First, one can look at whether sociocultural practices demand that the child adjust to the situation or the situation be adapted to the child. In the former case, multiparty interactions and noticing others' behaviors help the child adapt to the situation. In the latter, situations may be clarified or simplified for the child. Second, one can examine the social organization of the early childhood environment created for the child. How many adults, for example, act as caretakers? How much peer contact is facilitated? Third, one can carefully assess the negotiation of meanings between caretakers and young children. How much intentionality and understanding, for example, is credited to the young child? And, finally, how much participation in social situations is expected of the young child? As Schieffelin and Ochs (1984) cogently conclude:

> Children's strategies for encoding and decoding information, for negotiating meaning, and for handling errors are socially organized in terms of who does the work, when, and how. Further, every society orchestrates the ways in which children participate in particular situations, and this, in turn, affects the form, the function, and the content of children's utterances. Certain features of the grammar may be acquired quite early, in part because their use is encouraged and given high priority. In this sense, the process of language acquisition is part of the larger process of socialization, that is, acquiring social competence. (p. 310)

In my analysis of communicative development, I have stressed the importance of social knowledge (Haslett, 1984, 1987). This social knowledge involves knowledge of self, knowledge of others, and knowledge of situations. In the United States, knowledge of self involves the acknowledgment of the self as separate from others, animacy, independence of action by agents, and a recognition of mutual influence between animate agents. Knowledge of others involves growing awareness of the roles others play as friends, brothers, teachers, and the like. Finally, knowledge of situations involves an understanding of appropriate behavior in particular settings and the expectations for participation in these contexts. These three knowledge components appear to be universal in that they reflect salient features of how cultures are organized. Of course, the cultural values that determine sociocultural knowledge in each domain will vary widely, as we have seen in the cases of the Anglo-American, Samoan, and Kaluli acquisition contexts.

Considerable research suggests that cultures mark power, social identity, and politeness/respect communicatively. Power may be marked through the use of power pronouns (Brown & Gilmour, 1960), topic initiation and changes (West & Zimmerman, 1985), and interruptions (Zimmerman & West, 1975). Social identity has been marked in dialects, language choices, vocabulary, and the like (St. Clair & Giles, 1980; Tajfel, 1978). Social identity is particularly important from a cross-cultural perspective since linguistic and communicative differences mark ethnic, social class, and social group (ingroup versus outgroup) differences (St. Clair & Giles, 1980). Politeness or maintaining face has been well-documented across a number of cultures (Brown & Levinson, 1987). Politeness seems to be an indispensable practice since it permits societies to solve problems cooperatively and to maintain social cohesion. These three dimensions often interact with one another. For example, the individual with the most power can often set rules for interaction, such as politeness norms, and choose the social identity being used (e.g., language choice between two bilinguals). An understanding of these social needs, and the varying communicative strategies pursued in satisfying them, will aid our efforts in understanding communicative differences.

Issues such as universal principles and culturally diverse practices, of course, reflect deep-seated values as to the nature of life itself and the values individuals or cultures choose to follow. The main underlying criterion for judgments about communicative practices depends upon standards for competent communication. Some communicative needs appear universal—the need for communion with others and the need for information itself appear to be universal. However, who knows specific types of information, to whom they convey it, and under what circumstances may be quite different across cultures. We next turn to the issue of similarities and differences in light of the notion of becoming a competent communicator.

## Defining a Competent Communicator

The one feature of communicative competency that can be assumed is that the individual is being cooperative in Grice's sense of cooperation. That is, according to Grice (1975), the cooperative communicator makes his or her contributions, as and when needed, according to the social purposes of the interaction. In other words, when establishing standards of communicative competence, one assumes that an individual is "playing by the rules" in his or her given cultural milieu. Whatever the message content, it is expressed in culturally understood and recognized ways, even though the speaker's intent may be to confront or argue. Even rule violations must be accomplished according to the cultural rules.

Although competency seems to require that communicators be cooperative (at least insofar as their knowledge and skill allow them to be), what counts as cooperation depends upon the social practices of a given culture. Thus the notion of competency, like those of communication and of culture, is a diverse one. From the research already reviewed, one can argue that communicative competency varies as a result of differing levels of expected participation, different beliefs as to the cognitive capabilities of young children, different social situations, different types of knowledge, and different values and standards.

Gardner (1984) suggests some general domains of competence that members of a culture must meet in order to survive as a social entity. He suggests that all individuals, regardless of cultural membership, must be able to handle the physical, artifactual, and social aspects of life. In order to accomplish this, individuals develop competencies in the linguistic, spatial, logicomathematical, kinesthetic-bodily, musical, interpersonal, and intrapersonal domains. Of these, the most relevant competencies for communication appear to be the linguistic, kinesthetic-bodily, interpersonal, and intrapersonal domains. Each domain includes both practical skill and formal knowledge. Finally,

Gardner (1984) suggests that these domains are differentially available to children as a result of both cognitive and cultural constraints:

> Not all domains of knowledge are readily available to youngsters. Some, such as logical reasoning involving abstract propositions, may prove relatively difficult to master and relatively easy to forget, once the supporting contexts are no longer present. . . . Other forms of knowledge, such as the ability to adjudicate among different value systems or sensitivity to the motivations behind individual utterances, are readily accessible to most adults but prove surprisingly opaque to preadolescents. Finally, moving away from the notion of cognition *sensu strictu*, there are predictable progressions in the area of moral development (Kohlberg, 1969), social development (Selman, 1980) and ego development (Loevinger, 1976) that cry out for validation, or alteration, in the light of work in cultures with different end states of competence in these person-oriented domains. (p. 272)

In summary, what acquiring communicative competency requires is, first, a willingness to be a cooperative speaker/listener. In other words, the young child is open and accessible to communication with others. Beyond this, acquiring communicative competence requires that (a) sociocultural knowledge about cultural practices be available and displayed for the child; (b) the *linkages* between sociocultural knowledge and communicative practices be displayed for the child; (c) the child experience the situations in which he or she can learn these linkages; (d) the child's experiences enable him or her to learn both the *what* and *how* of communication (Gardner, 1984); (e) the child's early social experiences enable him or her to express feelings and needs, to relate to others, and to share information; and (f) the child be evaluated on how well he or she is understood.

## RESEARCH IMPLICATIONS

The most important implication following from this overview is that culture cannot be ignored in any analysis of communication. As has been amply demonstrated, communication and culture are simultaneously acquired and mutually dependent. In particular, sociocultural knowledge provides the basis for message interpretation: Studying communicative processes while ignoring underlying interpretive premises is foolhardy as well as fatally flawed. One then studies form rather than function, and ignores the interpretive linkages between them. Thus culture is *always* an issue and should not be a taken-for-granted concept in our analysis of communication.

This perspective suggests several useful research approaches. First, ethnographic approaches would provide an analysis of communication from the participants' viewpoints and thus incorporate sociocultural knowledge. Such knowledge, of course, would need to be examined and its relevance to the particular situation documented. As LeVine (1984) has pointed out, this type of knowledge is often tacit, and thus difficult to uncover. Additional richness could be added to research through the use of multicultural research teams, in which cultural bases are represented. Ethnographic analyses are emic rather than etic, and are motivated by the sociocultural constraints on communicative behavior. Second, scholars could look at communicative practices across cultures in a comparative sense. All cultures appear to mark power, status, and identity. Comparable settings might be selected in which these characteristics are displayed and the different communicative strategies used to display them analyzed. Research on differences in communicative development have been approached along these lines in the volume by Schieffelin and Ochs (1986). For example, attachment between caretaker and infant is a universal developmental accomplishment, yet it is achieved in a variety of ways. Third, the bilingual child presents a unique opportunity for studying communicative development cross-culturally, especially in light of the child's acquisition of two languages as well as two sociocultural systems. Careful attention must be directed to the context in which the two languages are being acquired (both learned simultaneously in the home, one language learned at home and the other at school, or whatever).

Finally, diversity must be emphasized. There is diversity in *what* is acquired, as well as in *how* it is acquired. There is diversity in both cognitive and communicative demands placed on the child. For common human problems, such as the need to express feelings or influence others, there is a diverse array of communicative strategies that address these concerns on both individual and cultural levels.

As our knowledge concerning communicative development expands, so must our appreciation of its diversity and richness. For our own survival, strategies for accommodating this diversity must be sought. Our challenge as developmental communication researchers is to begin to understand this diversity.

# REFERENCES

Bates, E. (1979). *The emergence of symbols*. New York: Academic Press.

Brown, P., & Levinson, S. (1987). *Politeness*. Cambridge: Cambridge University Press.

Brown, R., & Gilmour, A. (1960). The pronouns of power and solidarity. In T. Sebeok (Ed.), *Style in language*. Cambridge: MIT Press.

Bruner, J. (1975). From communication to language: A psychological perspective. *Cognition, 3*, 255–287.

Chomsky, N. (1965). *Syntactic structures*. The Hague: Mouton.

Gardner, H. (1984). The development of competence in culturally defined domains. In R. Shweder & R. LeVine (Eds.), *Culture theory*. Cambridge: Cambridge University Press.

Geertz, C. (1973). *The interpretation of cultures*. New York: Basic Books.

Glenn, E. (1981). *Man and mankind*. Norwood, NJ: Ablex.

Grice, H. (1975). Logic and conversation. In P. Cole & J. Morgan (Eds.), *Syntax and semantics: Vol. 3. Speech acts*. New York: Academic Press.

Gudykunst, W. (1986). *Intergroup communication*. London: Edward Arnold.

Haslett, B. (1984). Communicative development. In R. Bostrom (Ed.), *Communication yearbook 8* (pp. 198–267). Beverly Hills, CA: Sage.

Haslett, B. (1987). *Communication: Strategic action in context*. Hillsdale, NJ: Lawrence Erlbaum.

Hofstede, R. (1980). *Culture's consequences: International differences in work-related values*. Beverly Hills, CA: Sage.

Isbell, B., & McKee, L. (1980). Society's cradle: An anthropological perspective on the socialisation of cognition. In J. Sant (Ed.), *Developmental psychology and society*. London: Macmillan.

Kohlberg, L. (1969). Stage and sequence: The cognitive-developmental approach to socialization. In D. A. Goslin (Ed.), *Handbook of socialization theory and research*. Chicago: Rand McNally

Lenneberg, E. (1967). *The biological foundations of language*. New York: John Wiley.

LeVine, R. (1984). Properties of culture: An ethnographic view. In R. Shweder & R. LeVine (Eds.), *Cultural theory*. Cambridge: Cambridge University Press.

Loevinger, J. (1976). *Ego development: Conceptions and theories*. San Francisco: Jossey-Bass.

Ochs, E., & Schieffelin, B. (1984). Language acquisition and socialization: Three developmental stories and their implications. In R. Shweder & R. LeVine (Eds.), *Cultural theory*. Cambridge: Cambridge University Press.

Reich, P. (1986). *Language development*. Englewood Cliffs, NJ: Prentice-Hall.

St. Clair, R., & Giles, H. (1980). *The social and psychological contexts of language*. Hillsdale, NJ: Lawrence Erlbaum.

Scheflen, A. (1974). *How behavior means*. Garden City, NY: Doubleday.

Scherer, K., & Ekman, P. (1985). *Handbook of methods in nonverbal behavior research*. Cambridge: Cambridge University Press.

Schieffelin, B., & Ochs, E. (Eds.). (1986). *Language socialization across cultures*. Cambridge: Cambridge University Press.

Selman, R. (1980). *The growth of interpersonal understanding.* New York: Academic Press.

Shweder, R., & LeVine, R. (Eds.). (1984). *Cultural theory.* Cambridge: Cambridge University Press.

Stern, D. (1977). *The first relationship.* Cambridge: Cambridge University Press.

Sugarman, S. (1983). Empirical versus logical issues in the transition from prelinguistic to linguistic communication. In R. Golimkoff (Ed.). *The transition from prelinguistic to linguistic communication.* Hillsdale, NJ: Lawrence Erlbaum.

Tajfel, H. (1978). *Differentiation between social groups.* London: Academic Press.

Trevarthen, C. (1977). Descriptive analyses of infant communication behavior. In H. Schaffer (Ed.), *Studies in mother-infant interaction.* London: Academic Press.

Trevarthen, C. (1979). Communication and co-operation in early infancy: A description of primary intersubjectivity. In M. Bullowa (Ed.), *Before speech: The beginnings of human communication.* London: Cambridge University Press.

West, C., & Zimmerman, D. (1985). Gender, language and discourse. In T. van Dijk (Ed.), *Handbook of discourse analysis: Vol. 4. Discourse analysis in society.* New York: Academic Press.

Whorf, B. L. (1956). *Language, thought and reality: Selected writings* (J. Carroll, Ed.). Cambridge: MIT Press.

Zimmerman, D., & West, C. (1975). Sex roles, interruptions and silence in conversations. In B. Thorne & N. Henley (Eds.), *Language and sex: Difference and dominance.* Rowley, MA: Newbury.

# 3

## Linguistic Relativity
### Toward a Broader View

THOMAS M. STEINFATT • *University of Miami*

*This chapter attempts to summarize what is currently known concerning the Sapir-Whorf linguistic relativity hypothesis. It includes many studies and areas of study which bear upon the hypothesis but have not previously been discussed as studies of linguistic relativity, such as language acquisition, bidialectism, bilingualism, aphasia, and deafness.*

Linguistic relativity is a reaction against the nominalist position originating in Platonic and Aristotlian philosophy and popular through the 19th century, that knowledge of reality is not affected by language (LR-NO). The nominalist position regards language as an arbitrary outer form of thought, contending that any thought can be expressed in any language and that translatibility is not a problem. Early conceptions of the relationship between language and thought may be found in Mandell (1931). A list of reviews of experimental work on thought and concept formation may be found in Diebold (1965). As proposed by Sapir (1921), Whorf (1956), and Cassirer (1953), *Weltanschauung* thesis was very generalized and thus almost impossible to test. Greenberg (1956), Lenneberg and Roberts (1956), Henle (1958), Fishman (1960), and Osgood and Sebeok (1965, pp. 192–203), have each suggested ways of organizing the hypothesis. Slobin (1979) distinguishes between two forms of the linguistic relativity hypothesis: a "strong" form in which language structure *determines* the logic of thought itself, and a "weak" form where language structure *influences* cognitive structure. Drawing on these views, but modifying them substantially, I believe linguistic relativity implies that there is a set of independent variables (a), based on differences between languages in phonology, grammar, or semantics which must be the *basis* for the proposed difference, which must influence a dependent variable set (b), composed of logic (LR-LO), or cognitive structure and world-view (LR-GCS), or perception, individual cognitions, or areas of cognition (LR-CA), each manifested in observable behavior. This has the effect of proposing three linguistic relativity hypotheses corresponding to LR-LO, LR-GCS, and LR-CA, where at least one of these areas must be influenced by one or more of the independent variable areas for linguistic relativity to be said to occur. Most theorizing and research concerned with linguistic relativity has examined comparisons between languages. If linguistic relativity actually occurs, if language differences are a powerful influence on modes and processes of thought, then language differences should produce thought differences regardless of language labels such as English and Hopi.

## LANGUAGE LEARNING AND LINGUISTIC RELATIVITY

Consider the question of when, and by what process or mechanism, linguistic relativity would have to occur, if it does occur. This question has received little attention from previous writers, yet it is a question regarding not just the probability but the *possibility* of the truth of linguistic relativity. Linguistic relativity holds that language structures thought. This would seem to presume that language is acquired before thought or at least before thought patterns are set and ingrained. If thought were acquired and fixed first, before the acquisition of language, then it would have to be argued that thought is used in the process of acquiring language, but that the process of acquiring language then changes the thought that helped to acquire it. While this is possible, it is a far more complex process than language simply being acquired before the logical processes of thought. Another possibility would be language structuring the way we *think about* or conceptualize something (LR-GCS), rather than structuring logical thought processes (LR-LO).

### The Process of Acquiring Language

The history of psycholinguistics is discussed by Blumenthal (1970). Theories of language acquisition in the nineteenth and early twentieth centuries generally followed the psychological school of Wundt and his theory of the sentence, as expressed in *Die sprache* (1900). Much early theorizing was based on very limited observation of the process being described. Empirical research, the careful observation of children's early language behavior, begun by Stern in the late 1800s, has resulted in several modern views. The schools of thought presented below represent major thrusts of current thinking in language acquisition. Research and theory in the area of language acquisition is extensive, and no attempt has been made to survey the entire field.

## Piaget

The work of Piaget bears directly on linguistic relativity. Piaget (1951, 1961, 1962; Piaget & Inhelder, 1966; Sinclair-de-Zwart, 1967, 1969) makes a clear distinction between the beginning of intellectual operations in the child, which he views as internalized sensorimotor actions (things to react to) and the beginning of representational thought (objects as known out there). Representational thought involves the substitution of a symbol for objects-as-known. Piaget holds that intellectual operations, the fundamental logic of thinking, are present *before* the acquisition of language and the beginning of representational thought, and are not changed by language and representational thought. Representational thought is formed at the same time as language acquisition. As the shift from "things to react to" to representational thought occurs, the child moves from a concern with success in object manipulation to satisfy personal desires and a reaction to objects and events, to a concern with communicating newly discovered knowledge about objects and events to others.

Piaget argues that language does not cause the change to representational thought, but results from it. The overall conclusion of Sinclair-de-Zwart (1967, 1969) regarding her research on Piaget's theories, together with the studies of Furth (1966) and Oléron (1957), is that the studies confirm Piaget's view that *language is not the source of logic but rather is structured by it.* If language is structured by intellectual operations formed before the acquisition of language, the possibilities for linguistic relativity should be limited to its influence on representational thought (LR-GCS or LR-CA), which is formed at the same time as language acquisition. If Piaget's position is correct, it should not be possible to find evidence for linguistic relativity within the scope of basic, fundamental logical functioning between native speakers of different languages (LR-LO), no matter how great the variations between the languages.

## Skinner

While most language theorists hold that language and thinking are two different mental processes, Skinner (1957) and the behaviorists, together with Merleau-Ponty (1945), a phenomenologist, treat language and thought as *identical processes*. "If thinking is a wholly verbal activity, only human beings past infancy should be able to think" (Church, 1961, p. 148). Yet we know that many animals produce behaviors in solving simple problems that apparently result from some form of thought; for example, an ape using a stick to reach a banana. People also appear to be able to think without the use of language, as in solving certain problems involving geometric shapes (Steinfatt, 1977, pp. 77–79).

## Vygotsky

Vygotsky (1962) argues that in order to communicate a thought a person must be familiar with a generalized concept representing a category. There are thoughts that cannot be communicated to children, even though the children are familiar with the words necessary to express those thoughts, because the children do not possess the generalized category that would be necessary to interpret the thought intended by an adult.

According to Vygotsky (1962), it is an "indisputable fact of great importance" that "thought development is determined by language, i.e., by the linguistic tools of thought and by the sociocultural experience of the child. Essentially, the development of inner speech depends on outside factors; the development of logic in the child, as Piaget's studies have shown, is a direct function of his socialized speech. The child's intellectual growth is contingent on his mastering the social means of thought, that is, language" (p. 51). Vygotsky argues that the early development of speech and of intellect progress along separate lines and are biologically driven. The later development of inner speech and verbal thought does not result directly from the earlier forms and, in fact, is driven by a different process, experience with the world.

In Vygotsky, we find the notion of speech as a *vehicle* for understanding. His emphasis that understanding speech is not the same as understanding thought implies a lessened role for any form of linguistic relativity, for it implies that there are many ways of representing a thought in any language, and hence a lessened role for any specific representation in any given language. Yet Vygotsky believes that later thought development is determined by language, suggesting a role for any of the three forms of linguistic relativity, especially LR-GCS and LR-CA.

## Chomsky, Pinker, Anderson, and Wexler and Culicover

Chomsky (1965) proposes the existence of an innate schema of grammar in humans as a necessary postulate to account for language acquisition in children. As partial evidence, he cites the general ungrammatical character of common everyday speech samples available to the child (p. 58). The child's problem as language learner is "to determine which of the (humanly) possible languages is that of the community in which he is placed. Language learning would be impossible unless this were the case. The important question is . . . how detailed and specific is the innate schema (the general definition of 'grammar') . . . ?" (p. 27). While the barrier to linguistic relativity proposed by Chomsky seems contradicted by certain classes of observations (Sinclair-de-Zwart, 1969), other theorists such as Anderson (1974, 1975, 1976), Pinker (1984), and Wexler and Culicover (1980) start from quite different theoretical perspectives, but each claims to have been forced to a nativist position when attempting to construct a precise theory of language acquisition.

## Langer

Langer (1957) states that "language is primarily a vocal actualization of the tendency to see reality symbolically" (p. 109). While the most obvious manifestation of language, and the one that receives the most attention, is communication between persons, Langer argues that *internal symbolic behavior*—the attaching of *significance* to certain objects, events, or sounds—comes before and gives rise to between-person communication. According to Langer (1957), "The essence of language is the formulation and expression of conceptions rather than the communication of natural wants" (p. 118). Attempts to teach animals and wild children language through using language for *requests* are failures, according to Langer, because they do not provide for intrapersonal symbolic representation as a necessary prior condition. Though Itard (1802) tried to teach Victor the wild boy to use words to obtain things, Victor would constantly babble the word he had learned rather than use it in a utilitarian fashion to obtain what he needed. Langer (1957) observes that "young children learn to speak, after the fashion of Victor, by constantly using words to bring things *into their minds,* not *into their hands*" (p. 121).

### Summary of Language Acquisition and Linguistic Relativity

If language and thought are conceived of as the same process, one cannot speak of one influencing the other except in the trivial sense of language influencing language or thought influencing thought. Thus Skinner is forced to the nominalist position (LR-NO). With the exception of Vygotsky, if *any* of the currently popular reconstructions of children's language acquisitions are correct, the possibilities for a strong linguistic relativity effect on the logical processes of thought itself (LR-LO) should be severely restricted. If Vygotsky is correct, then any of LR-LO, LR-GCS, or LR-CA should be possible. If Pinker, Chomsky, and the nativists are correct, then most of the force of linguistic relativity is muted since all languages are products of the same initial innate grammar (anti-LR-LO, anti-LR-GCS, anti-LR-CA). How could it be argued that language differences, especially grammatical differences, produce major differences in thought, if those languages all have a common innate origin? Any effects of linguistic relativity would then have to be due to semantic or phonetic differences, differences that would seem to provide far less in the way of explanatory mechanisms for linguistic relativity effects than would mechanisms based on grammatical differences. Langer's (1957) position deals mainly with semantics and has important implications for LR-CA.

## LANGUAGE DIFFERENCES AND COGNITION

### The Interlanguage Evidence: Does Language Affect Thought?

The basis of the argument commonly cited in favor of linguistic relativity is presented in Whorf (1956). It consists of several groups of examples of phonological, semantic, and grammatical interlanguage differences, plus Whorf's interpretations of the effects of these differences on the processes of thought. I will not review this entire set of evidence but will select two examples that represent it well, one from Whorf's work with the Hopi and one from Hoijer's (1956) work with the Navaho.

## Whorf

Whorf (1956) discusses the Weltanschauung implicit in the verb forms of Hopi and of English. English has past, present, and future tenses as well as some subtenses such as past-perfect. This corresponds to the Western view of time as a "smooth flowing continuum . . . [proceeding] . . . at an equal rate, out of a future, through a present, into a past" (p. 57). In contrast, Hopi has no way of making reference to time. Verbs have no tense and there is no way of implying tense. Yet Hopi is able to account for all observable phenomena of the universe, just as is English. While English verbs contain reference to one of two cosmic forms in Western thought, *time,* distinguishing it as a concept totally orthogonal to the other cosmic form, *space,* Hopi verbs reflect the two grand cosmic forms of Hopi thought, the *manifested* and the *manifesting*, wherein no distinction based on time can be made. The *manifested* consists of all of that we call past and most of present events of the historical physical universe. The *manifesting* is a combination of a small part of our present, our notion of future, our notion of phenomenological cognitive and emotional events, our notion of hoping for, and our notion of "heart" in the sense of the "nature" of things, struggling to get out and be made manifest. The beginnings of a future event, part of what we call the present, such as starting to wake up, is included in the manifesting. The future is interlocked with a notion of the nature or heart or spirit or predestined essence getting out to the manifest world, and cannot be referred to apart from the process of manifesting. Time and space are combined. The future is already with us in the manifesting, not advancing toward us. The past cannot be distinguished from the present since both are manifested. Death and broken relationships clearly have different meaning for the Hopi.

In discussing a Hopi verb form that isolates the small "present" portion of manifesting, at least three different "begins doing it" usages can be distinguished in Hopi speech. Whorf (1956) asks, "Why should a pattern ('begins doing it') which appears to us to be perfectly uniform . . . in all cases, present itself to the mind of the bilingual English-speaking Hopi informant as a meaning which switches back and forth between two (or more) fundamental meaning categories of his own language?" (pp. 103–104). Whorf suggests that the only way to understand this usage shift is in believing that "the Hopi observer conceives the events in a different manner from the one whose native language is English" (p. 104). The examples are evidence for LR-GCS.

*Hoijer*

The color spectrum is an objective, publicly observable property existing in physical reality. Glucksberg and Danks (1975) review much of the research on color spawned by Whorf's observations. Hoijer (1956) uses examples to point out that not all languages separate the continuous spectrum of color into the same divisions, or even into as many divisions, with languages such as Navaho (and Shona and Bassa; Gleason, 1961) using break points different from English. The inference is that because the color categories of the languages are different, thought about color must be different for speakers of different languages (LR-CA). Experimentally, *memory* for color has also been shown to be affected by the availability of *a name for the color*.

Consider an arbitrary point on the color spectrum which is recognized by a language as a break point between two color categories, say blue and green in English. Recognizing and discriminating a color chip previously seen but not present from two other same-color-category chips currently present is difficult, as anyone who has been to a paint store and forgotten to bring a chip knows. Yet discriminating this absent chip from two others, which are exactly as far apart on the color spectrum as the first pair, but where one of the pair is in the same color category as the absent chip while the other is in a different color category, is quite easy (Brown & Lenneberg, 1954; Lantz & Stefflre, 1964; Stefflre, Castillo Vales, & Morley, 1966). This is clearly pro linguistic relativity (LR-CA) evidence. If two color chips are present at the same time, it is easy to discriminate between them for speakers of any language regardless of color category or the language of the perceivers, an anti-linguistic relativity finding. Heider and Oliver (1972), studied the Dani of West New Guinea, who divide all colors into only two words, corresponding roughly to *light* and *dark*. Heider and Oliver showed Dani and American subjects a color chip for 5 seconds, and 30 seconds later showed subjects an array of 40 color chips including the first one shown. Americans made slightly fewer errors than Dani in selecting the correct chip, probably due to greater experience in color discrimination tasks as well as to a more differentiated color vocabulary. But the *kinds* of errors made by both groups were very similar. Heider and Oliver produced cognitive maps of the color space of both sets of subjects and found them to be virtually identical. Given even this radical difference in language for color, the cognitive processing of color did not seem to be affected—an anti-linguistic relativity finding (anti-LR-GCS).

*Henle*

Henle (1958) provides one of the better summaries of the interlanguage arguments in favor of Whorf's hypothesis and the mechanism by which it should work. First, he suggests that *vocabulary* is related to perception and conception. Citing Bruner and Goodman's (1947) proposal that perception can be conditioned as easily as a salivating response, Henle points out the plausible connection between the sound of a word taken as stimulus and the conditioned perceptual response set. The evidence offered for this is the example of differences in color perception categories between Hopi and English (LR-CA).

Second, Henle proposes that *inflections* are relevant in producing *forced observations*. He argues that a verb form that contained a suffix indicating a particular tense might be abbreviated by using the stem of the verb in place of the suffixed form, thus "depriving the language of any word having the old meaning of [the verb stem itself]" (1958, p. 9). The speaker is thereby forced to observe his variation in language, though perhaps unconsciously. Different observations are forced in different languages, hence, different mental sets should occur. He offers as evidence that time must be specified by English verbs but not by Wintu, thus time should be called to attention in English more than in Wintu. Additionally, Wintu requires a statement of how one claims to know what one claims to know. It is not possible to claim knowledge without stating the evidential basis for the claim in Wintu. This is an LR-CA claim.

Third is sentence structure. English and its language family recognize two basic types of sentence: actor-action (John hit Mary) and subject-predicate (John is tall). The subject is an enduring object in both types, "recognizable through time." As Henle says, a mechanic in English speaks of fixing the timing of an engine (a process) in the same way he would speak of fixing a tire (an object), but not so a person speaking in Hopi, an LR-GCS claim. The metaphor of a stable physical object represents a processual relationship between events. Classic logic assumed the subject-predicate form to be basic and attempted to force all statements into this form, a notion that is currently rejected by most logicians. Metaphysics from Aristotle through the 19th century assumed this subject-predicate form, arguing that the world was composed of *substances* and their *attributes,* substance as subject and attribute as predicate. Twentieth century Western philosophy has rejected this view, with Russell (1945) arguing that "substance" was a "metaphysical mistake."

### Summary of the Interlanguage Evidence

Whorf's analysis of the relationship between the verb structure and the metaphysics of Hopi and of English illustrates the parallels between the two. While Whorf's discussions are strongly suggestive of a relationship of language and thought, they cannot show a causal direction. Thinking in terms of *manifested* and *manifesting* could lead to the existence of the corresponding verb forms in the language, rather than language producing the thought. The introduction of the notion of time into Hopi thought should lead to a way to express time in the Hopi language. If so, language would appear to be structured by thought rather than structuring it. Whorf's examples show a clear relationship between the metaphysics of the culture and the structure of its language. They do not establish the causal direction. If one argues that language influences thought, a minimum condition should be independent demonstrations of the existence of a level of language, the existence of a level of thought, and a connection between them that produces a result. Examples can suggest such conditions but cannot demonstrate them.

While the examples imply a language-induced thought difference regarding color, linguistic relativity could affect *perception of* color, *memory for* color, *cognitive organization of* color, and/or *ease of communication about* color. The examples are not specific with respect to a prediction of exactly what is to be affected. Thus if it could be shown that language does *not* affect any one of these, the others could be raised as the important consequences of linguistic relativity, opening linguistic relativity to the charge of being nonfalsifiable. Language affects memory for color, but not perception of nor cognitive organization of color (anti LR-GCS). Cognitive organization would seem more closely related to "thought" than would simple memory.

In Wintu, it is not possible to claim knowledge without stating the evidential basis for the claim. One need only read scholarly journals, let alone listen to common conversation, to observe that it is quite possible to do so in English. Perhaps graduate courses, at least, should be taught in Wintu. Yet since Russell spoke English it is clear that thinking in English is no barrier to perceiving the subject-predicate problem in logic and dismissing it (anti LR-LO and LR-GCS). And while it would be nice to think that teaching in Wintu would produce students more aware of the evidential basis for their statements, it is clearly possible in Wintu as in any language to propose generalized causes for many classes of dissimilar events, the explanation for which is unknown. The reasons for the falling of the rain, the shining of the sun, love, hate, and misfortune may all be given as "because God has willed it to be so." A language which forces a reason does not necessarily force a right or a good reason.

## The Intralanguage Evidence

Previous authors have concentrated on the interlanguage view of differences in thought produced by different languages. Yet differences of the type that linguistic relativity argues should produce thought differences—that is, differences in language structure, semantics, and phonetics—also occur among dialects within a given language community. If linguistic relativity works based on such differences between languages, it also ought to work in the intralanguage sense when such differences occur between dialects of a single language.

Considerable research has focused upon the question of intralanguage differences as a basis for difference in thought, though the relationship of this research to linguistic relativity has not been emphasized. Church (1961) did consider the question of intralanguage differences in asking how Whorf would explain the intracultural differences within a language, à la Pygmalion (LR-CA), which are often greater than cross-cultural differences such as those between upper-class French and upper-class English.

Much of the research on intralanguage differences is summarized in Williams (1970a). More recent updates are available in Roy (1987), Hall and Nagy (1987), and Stewart (1987), but the positions on these issues have not changed substantially since Williams (1970a). Since many of those who advocate the deficit position reference Bernstein's (1958, 1959, 1960, 1961a, 1961b, 1962, 1964a) notion of elaborated and restricted codes, a brief explanation of that distinction is in order.

## Elaborated Versus Restricted Codes

Restricted codes are context bound. Elaborated codes are relatively context free—one does not need the context, publicly observable or phenomenological within the speaker, in order to make sense of the message.

The importance of this distinction to linguistic relativity is made clear by Bernstein's belief that different codes create different orders of relevance and relation. The speaker's experience is affected by the relevance selection parameters of different speech systems. Children learn their culture's social structure, according to Bernstein, through the social structure embedded in speech, an LR-GCS position. Bernstein (1970) comments:

> Every time the child speaks or listens, the social structure is reinforced in him and his social identity is shaped. The social structure becomes the child's psychological reality through the shaping of his acts of speech. . . . Children who have access to different speech systems or codes—that is, children who learn different roles by virtue of their families' class positions in a society—may adopt quite different social and intellectual orientations and procedures despite a common developmental potential. (p. 30).

The similarities to Whorf's LR-GCS views are striking. Evidence for and against Bernstein's linguistic relativity position is discussed below.

## The Deficit Position

At the heart of the deficit position is the observation that many children, especially lower-class Black children, use a dialect of English that seriously impairs both oral and written communication in school, due to the difference in structural (grammatical) features of the dialect. Blank (1970) states: "In all enrichment programs . . . language has emerged as a common denominator of the learning deficit. This has led many investigators to the belief that while other handicaps may exist, *language is at the core of the difficulty for the disadvantaged child*" (p. 69; italics added).

Williams (1970b) discusses the *deficit* and *difference* positions on Black language, in reference to the poverty cycle. The *deficit* position argues that both employment and economic disadvantages lead to developmental disadvantages, including a deficit in language development, and that deprived language in turn leads to continued employment and economic disadvantages. Foeman and Pressley (1987) discuss the ways Black language and cultural values may interact with corporate cultures in a more positive fashion.

The deficit position takes a clearly pro-linguistic relativity (LR-GCS) stance. Supporters of the deficit position often reference Bernstein's notion of elaborated and restricted codes, with the claim that children in poverty exist in restricted code environments. Bernstein (1970) states that use of his work to equate a restricted code to linguistic deprivation is erroneous. It is a pervasive error. Supporters of the deficit position include Bereiter and Engelmann, (1966); Jensen, (1969); Olim (1970), and Whiteman and Deutsch, (1968).

*The Difference Position*

The difference position argues that no natural language is any less developed or more primitive than any other. "The linguist takes it as basic that all humans develop language. After all, there is no reason to assume that black African bush children develop a language and black inner-city Harlem children do not! . . . ( . . . there are no primitive languages). The linguist assumes that . . . no language is structurally better than any other language" (Baratz, 1970, pp. 13–14). Thus any performance deficit by poor children must be explained in terms of forcing them to work within a second language or, at least, a second vernacular. Supporters of the difference position include Baratz (1968, 1970), Labov (1970), Labov, Cohen, and Robins, (1965), Roy (1987), Shuy (1970), and Stewart (1970, 1987). While the deficit position argues that some languages produce thought inferior to others, a clear linguistic relativity stance, the difference position says that all languages are capable of producing thought of equal quality, and that observed differences result from difficulties caused by the second language interfering with the first, not the first alone. "Thought of equal quality" does not necessarily imply the equality of thought processes, so the difference position does not take a clear linguistic relativity stance, either pro or anti.

*An Extended Argument for the Deficit Position:*

*The Mother-Control Position*

Olim (1970), expanding on part of Bernstein's restricted code notion, argues that the behavior that leads to poverty is learned in early childhood, through language, from the mother, the primary socializing agent, during mother-child communication. According to Olim (1970), "The mother's first words, when she shows her child objects and names them, have a decisive influence on the formation of the child's mental processes. The word isolates the essential features of an object or event and inhibits the less essential properties (Luria & Yudovich, 1959)" (p. 217). The form of control used by the mother is a major variable in Olim's conception.

Olim employs Hess, Shipman, Bear, and Brophy's (1968) three types of family control (status or position appeal, subjective states-feelings of individuals, and rational consequences-situation), stating that deprived families tend to use input control techniques to limit the probability of a response and they *inadvertently* use input control due to "the disadvantaged mother's *inability to provide the symbols and patterns of thought and communication necessary for developing the cognitive potential of the child*. This is because *she has a limited fund of ideas and information on which to draw in her attempts to cope with the environment*. The result is the oft-noted paucity of linguistic and symbolic interaction in culturally deprived families" (Olim, 1970, pp. 221–222; italics added). Olim also suggests that mothers in the other two categories are more likely to be upper class and thus use elaborated codes "because these orientations not only permit but demand an elaborated code to deal with *the wide range of alternatives of behavior and thought that are involved*" (1970, p. 223; italics added).

Hess and Shipman (1965a) studied Black mother-child dyads from four socioeconomic groups and found maternal teaching style to be as predictive of children's language performance as a combination predictor composed of mother's IQ and social class. They propose that mother-child interactions shape language and communication abilities, which in turn shape cognitive style and patterns of thought (LR-GCS). Hess and Shipman (1965b) suggest that cultural deprivation leads to a lack of shared cognitive meaning in mother-child communication. Family control systems that offer a range of alternatives in both thought and action foster greater cognitive growth than systems with predetermined solutions and little freedom for alternatives. Black families ranging from welfare cases to college-educated fathers were studied. Low status led to restricted codes. Hess and Shipman (1965b) conclude that "the meaning of deprivation is a deprivation of meaning."

Olim (1970) uses the linguistic relativity notion to argue for the

importance of concept formation through language in human development, that concept formation must be socially and linguistically mediated as through restricted and elaborated codes (pp. 217–220). This
portion of Olim's argument is a non sequitur, since linguistic relativity
is not a necessary condition for concept formation to be socially and
linguistically mediated.

## Examples of Studies Supporting the Deficit Position

Examples of studies often cited in support of the deficit view are
Hill and Giammatteo (1963), who found White third-grade children
of high socioeconomic status to be superior to those of low status on
all measures including vocabulary, reading, arithmetic, and problem
solving; Ivey, Center, and Tanner (1968), who studied 40 first-grade
children using the Illinois Test of Psycholinguistic Abilities, and
found a relationship between cultural deprivation and language development but not between race and language development; Jackson
(1944), who compared 600 mostly White students representing the
upper and lower quartiles in reading skills in grades two through six,
finding that socioeconomic status, parental education, and father having a professional occupation were all related to better reading
scores; John and Goldstein (1964), who suggest that the lower-class
child has less opportunity for both stability of word-referent relationships and corrective feedback and that this potentially affects cognitive functioning; and Deutsch (1965), who studied 292 children and
found that membership in minority and lower-class groups was associated with reduced levels of language functioning. This reduction was
more pronounced in the fifth than in the first grade, leading Deutsch
to postulate a "cumulative deficit phenomenon." Similarly, Peisach
(1965) found no difference in first graders' ability to replace words in
a sentence based on social class, but did find such a difference in fifth
graders. Bernstein (1960) compared the verbal language ability scores
of working-class and middle-class school-age children. Using a nonverbal measure of IQ, Bernstein found a general relationship between verbal scores and IQ scores for middle-class children across the
entire IQ range, and a similar relationship for working-class children
in the low to middle ranges of IQ. But in the upper IQ ranges,
working-class children's language ability scores were lower than
would have been predicted by their IQs. Additional support may be
found in Bernstein (1958); Bernstein and Henderson (1969); Caplan

and Ruble (1964); Carson and Rabin (1960); Clark and Richards (1966); Connors, Schuette, and Goldman (1967). DeBoer (1952) reviews the literature on the relationship between language and social class up to 1950.

## An Extended Argument for the Difference Position

Labov (1970) has produced a strong statement of the difference position, beginning with a critique of the common methods used in studying multilingual processes, as in many of the studies cited in the previous section. Labov notes that interviews with children who are not native speakers of SAA often seem to produce *no* language. He suggests that we interpret these interviews as attempts to avoid harassment by speakers of a different dialect. Labov's (1970) examples and analysis of those examples are classics of methodological criticism and interpretation. A Black child may respond "Nope" or a variant of it to a series of questions posed by an interviewer attempting to assess the child's language abilities. The child is likely to be labeled "nonverbal" as a result. Hurst and Jones (1967) report the difficulties of getting 3- and 4-year-old Black girls to talk even to Black interviewers, especially when compared with the speech they generate when with other young Black children. But Wood and Curry (1969) found that Black school-age girls were able to change their speech systematically, through stylistic and grammatical changes, when asked to use "school talk" as opposed to "home talk." By controlling interview factors such as atmosphere (potato chips and presence of the interviewee's best friend), combined with height difference (the interviewer sits on the floor and is thus no taller than the interviewee) and the introduction of taboo words and topics, Labov illustrates how to change a "nonverbal" child with "no language" into a highly verbal child actively competing for the floor. The failure to use methods that provide children an equal chance to demonstrate their language skills is characteristic of many studies supporting the deficit position.

Beyond the "no language" label, differences between Black dialects, which have been termed "broken" or "corrupt" English, and White speech have been considered evidence of the mental limitations of Blacks by speakers of English since at least the early seventeenth century. While English speakers regarded the Black creole form as inferior, the Dutch who settled in Surinam taught Black creole to Dutch settlers as a formal language in formal courses in the late eighteenth century (Stewart, 1970, p. 360).

In contrast to the argument of the deficit theorists (and of Chomsky's nativist position regarding all children) that underprivileged children are deprived of the opportunity to hear grammatical speech, Labov (1970) has found that

> working-class children hear more well-formed sentences than middle-class children. This statement may seem extraordinary in the light of the current belief of many linguists that most people do not speak in well-formed sentences, and that their actual speech production, or performance, is ungrammatical. But those who have worked with any body of natural speech know that this is not the case. . . . [We have shown] that the great majority of utterances in all contexts are complete sentences and most of the rest can be reduced to grammatical form by a small set of editing rules. (pp. 170–171)

Stewart (1970) argues that Black dialects account for most of the really difficult problems of variation from SAA, as illustrated by Loban (1966). BE retains traces of creole structure, which may account for why BE is perceived by SAA speakers as more deviant than the most deviant speech of uneducated American Whites. While BE is closer to SAA than is a foreign language such as Spanish, it is easier for a Spanish-speaking child to tell where Spanish ends and English begins than for anyone to tell exactly where BE ends and SAA begins. The BE child trying to learn SAA is at a greater disadvantage than the foreign-language-speaking child for that reason. That is, a *quasi-foreign language* (Stewart, 1964) may be more difficult to learn than a completely foreign language, based on ease of boundary recognition.

Phonological differences appear to cause some of the semantic differences that lead to considerable difficulties in internal processing of responses. In first grade, Black children respond "soft," twice as often as White children when defining *allow,* confusing it with *aloud.* According to Entwisle (1970), "By third grade 'let' is the most frequent response of white suburban children to *allow,* whereas inner-city black children are still giving 'soft,' 'quiet,' and 'low' as the three most frequent responses" (p. 135). The most common third-grade Black responses to *since* are "money," "dumb," and "five." It takes until the fifth grade and beyond to get White semantic responses to *since,* which is being confused with *cents. Since* serves as a logical operator. Failure to understand the function and intent of *since* would clearly interfere with the child's ability to process the message as intended. *Allow* concerns control, and functions as a social operator. Failure to understand *allow* would seem to hinder an understanding and development of control in relationships and interpersonal understanding (Entwisle, 1970).

## The "Other Children" Position

Hockett (1950) was one of the first to point out that while we know little about the transmission of linguistic habits to new generations, the speech of other children is clearly an important factor. Stewart (1968) suggests that young children learn more of their speech from other children than from adults, and that through this process, the older dialects of any language can usually be found in the speech of children, as well as in the oldest members of a speech community. Stewart (1965) and Dillard (1967) cite evidence for this. If this is true, then any influence of a language on intrapersonal communication would seem likely to occur through its older dialect forms rather than through the more modern adult forms of the language. The older-dialect notion provides a clear rival hypothesis to the "lack of development" explanation for Black children's "poor" speech. It also is in direct opposition to the "mother/child method-of-control" hypothesis of Olim (1970) and of Hess and Shipman (1965a, 1965b) discussed above. If children learn more of their speech from other children than from parental modes of control, then the hypothesized "limited fund of ideas" of minority parents could not be used to explain a deficit position, even if evidence could be found for the "limited fund" notion.

The "other children" position provides a complication for the Sapir-Whorf hypothesis as well as for the deficit position. Not only do the children of a given culture and language apparently learn their own dialect in the form of older dialects from other same-dialect children, they combine that dialect with the older dialects of different-dialect children with whom they come in contact to produce relatively unique dialects of their own. Only after age 4 do these child dialects begin to give way to the adult dialect that the individual will eventually speak. Depending on the proportion and mix of children of different dialects, the dialect spoken by any child before age 4 should be somewhat different for different mixes and proportions of influence on the dialect. Could it be argued that each unique dialect produces a different pattern of thought? If White children learn their language through a Black dialect does that make them "think Black"? If small dialectic differences do not make a difference in thought, then what *is* the critical unit necessary to produce difference patterns of thought? Must the languages be from different language families? How different must they be, and how do we tell?

## Does Language Refer to the Situation or to Itself?

In intrapersonal processing, people may respond to the logic of the situation or to the logic of the language as expressed in the sentence. Perhaps BE speakers use logic different from that of SAA speakers, as linguistic relativity would predict. This would explain the BE use of the double negative or *negative concord,* as in "He don't know nothin'." Clearly, this sentence "has" to mean "He does know something" since the "don't" negates the "nothin'." So BE speakers must be using a different logic than SAA speakers. The problem with this interpretation is in its failure to consider the grammatical features of BE regarding negation. The use of *don't* to signal negation would be done through stress patterns, in the same way an SAA speaker would signal negation by saying "He *doesn't* know *nothing.*" Older Anglo-Saxon forms used *negative concord* in this way. Labov (1970) comments: "What is termed 'logical' in standard English is of course the conventions which are habitual" (pp. 174–175). In addition to the grammatical form, the logic of the situation makes clear the intended meaning of the BE speaker.

Is SAA still a superior form to BE since SAA has its own logic, an extended code apart from the context of what is being said? Consider English versus Japanese as languages, aside from cultures. In either language with a positively phrased question ("Do you want . . . ?"), "yes" means yes and "no" means no. In English, a yes response to a negatively phrased question ("Don't you want . . . ?") usually means yes with respect to the action and a no response means no with respect to the action. That is, in English one would respond "No" to "Don't you want to go to the movies?" if one did not want to go. Thus English retains consistency to situations and action. In contrast, Japanese retains consistency of propositional logic rather than to situation and action. In Japanese one would respond "Yes" to "Don't you want to go to the movies?" if one did not want to go. "Don't you want to go to the movies?" can be rephrased without the interrogative as "You do not want to go to the movies." Since this is a correct statement, the Japanese, responding to the English statement, would say "Yes." The English speaker, responding to the situation, would say "No," meaning "No, I do not want to go to the movies" rather than "No, it is untrue that I do not want to go to the movies," which is the strictly logical consequence of the "No" response. Now consider Japanese culture integrated with its language structure. It is impolite to refuse a request or to say no directly in Japan. One of my students, a Japanese woman who has been here from Japan less than six months, was asked to go to an on-campus bar the other night by a student from New York. She did not want to go, but when he asked, "Don't you want to drop by the Rathskeller?" politeness made her respond "No," meaning that she would go. She was surprised but relieved when he took her polite, propositional no as an intended, situational no and went without her.

In English, *SAA or BE*, one responds to the logic of the situation when answering a negatively phrased question, while in Japanese one responds to the logic of the sentence. Thus SAA operates as more of a restricted code in this case than Japanese since it is more context and action dependent. Does this mean that Japanese is a more logical language than English? Clearly not if we understand that the logic of English is often action oriented while the logic of Japanese is propositional, just as we must understand that the logic of BE is even more action oriented than that of SAA.

## Examples of Studies Not Supporting the Deficit Position

Examples of studies that found no difference based on status include the work of Noel (1953), who found a relationship between parents' language usage and their children's usage, but no difference in terms of father's occupation; LaCivita, Kean, and Yamamoto (1966), who, studying second, fourth, and sixth graders, found no differences on a task of guessing the meaning of a nonsense syllable by its position and use in a sentence based on socioeconomic status; and Ruddell and Graves (1968), who found that while low-status Black children show more errors in development of syntax than high-status White children, this difference occurs only on material likely to be more familiar to Whites. On material unfamiliar to both, the difference was not found. These studies are intended only as examples, not as an exhaustive survey of studies that would counter the deficit position.

In any interpretation of such studies that support or oppose the deficit position, one must consider not only the methodological limitations pointed out by Labov and others, but the "file drawer" or probability of publication problem posed, somewhat paradoxically, by significant differences supporting the deficit position and nonsignificant differences supporting the difference position. It is more difficult to publish the nonsignificant findings that would oppose the deficit view than the significant ones that support it, though this clearly should not be the case if adequate statistical power is present in the nonsignificant studies. Another factor to be considered is that children may also perform poorly if they are not taught efficiently or fairly. Rosenthal and Jacobson (1968) review several studies demonstrating the self-fulfilling prophecy effect of teachers' expectations on children's performance.

### Implications of the Intralanguage Studies

In summary, the difference position seems to account for the available data on intralanguage cases better than the deficit position. LR-GCS-type linguistic relativity is strongly associated with the deficit position and the restricted code notion on which it is based. Little support for either the deficit position or LR-GCS is found when the available evidence is reviewed together with critiques of the evidence. The support for the difference position discussed above does not in itself necessarily imply evidence against LR-GCS, since the difference position is not directly associated with any LR view. While the deficit position clearly implies LR-GCS, LR-GCS does not necessarily imply the deficit position.

### The Evidence from Bilingualism

If linguistic relativity is correct, the formation of thinking of bilinguals should be influenced by two different worldviews (LR-GCS). Prior to 1962 it was commonly believed that childhood bilingualism impaired intellectual development, particularly verbal intelligence (LR-LO), with arguments similar to those of the deficit position discussed above: The "pure" language (the accepted dialect without interference from other language forms) was considered superior.

Peal and Lambert (1962) set out to demonstrate this impairment in an extensive study of Montreal schoolchildren but found *no* ill effects of bilingualism and many slight but significant cognitive advantages (slight pro-LR-LO). Palij and Homel (1987) trace the history of this controversy to the present, noting that Lambert and Tucker (1972) found that cognitive skills learned in one language, such as arithmetic, can be transferred to another language and are not dependent on the language in which the skill was acquired (anti-LR-LO). Cummins's (1987) literature review found some support for Vygotsky's belief that bilingualism promotes a metalinguistic approach to language in the form of an analytic orientation toward language found in bilinguals but not monolinguals (pro-LR-CA), but no difference in awareness levels on semantic orientation or on general properties of language (anti-LR-CA).

## The Chinese-English Studies

Hockett (1950) and Aaronson and Ferres (1987) discuss many of the differences between Chinese and English. One difference is that Chinese does not contain a natural counterfactual structure, where English does, as in "If I had been going that way I would have taken you, but I was not," or "Positive evidence for the deficit position would have supported LR-GCS had it been found." Bloom (1981) developed Chinese and English stories that contained *counterfactuals* and found that most monolingual Americans understood the English stories, but few Chinese monolinguals understood the Chinese stories, implying a cognitive structure difference (LR-GCS) between Chinese and English. Bloom also tested Chinese-English bilinguals who used English as an everyday business tool. They understood only 6% of the Chinese stories. One month later, Bloom gave the same respondents the English stories, and they scored 94% on comprehension. He also studied the lack of *definite generic article* usage in Chinese, as in "The buffalo is becoming extinct," finding that the less the English experience of bilinguals, the less they were willing to grant conceptual meaning to the statements (LR-GCS). Bloom studied a third difference of *entification*, the shift from a completed sentence to an abstract nominal phrase; for example, the shift from "Bush will be elected" to "The election of Bush." He found that Chinese speakers had greater difficulty both with performing and with comprehension of the transformation than native English speakers (LR-GCS or LR-

CA). Au (1983, 1984) failed to replicate Bloom's finding of Chinese speakers' failure to understand counterfactual reasoning (anti-LR-GCS). Compared to Au's study, Bloom's subjects knew less English, his stories and counterfactuals were more abstract, and his stories used Chinese in a form unfamiliar to Chinese speakers.

Aaronson and Ferres (1987) discuss the differences in processing the meaning and structure of words and sentences between Chinese and English. They tested a *cognition hypothesis* that states that language-specific differences between L-1 and L-2 can lead to cognitive performance differences between bilinguals and monolinguals in processing sentences. Using English monolinguals and Chinese-English compound bilinguals, they found that bilinguals saw more structural significance in both function and content words than monolinguals and that the size of the differences is larger for structure than for meaning (LR-CA).

## Discussion of the Bilingual Studies

Bloom (1981) provides the strongest pro-LR-GCS and LR-CA data since Brown and Lenneberg (1954). The fact that Au was unable to replicate the crucial finding of failure to understand in her Chinese subjects suggests that unfamiliarity with a complex form rather than inability to think counterfactually due to speaking Chinese may best account for Bloom's and Au's results. The lesser English knowledge of Bloom's subjects supports Bloom's results over Au's, but his use of a less familiar form than Au proposes an alternative explanation for his results. While it is clear that the lack of counterfactual markers in Chinese would provide initial difficulties in communicating with Americans, it is not at all clear that the absence of such markers leads to an *inability* in certain areas of abstract thinking, as hypothesized by Bloom. While each of Bloom's studies is creative and his results are interesting, they seem to suggest that people unfamiliar with a task have difficulty with the task. His data may also show differences in verbal processing strategies rather than general thought differences. Since the same individuals could process stories in English but not in Chinese, thought differences can hardly be proposed as an explanation. They do not provide evidence that Chinese speakers *cannot* think in terms of counterfactuals, definite generic articles, or entifications (LR-LO or LR-GCS), but that they *do not* normally express thoughts using such constructions (pro-LR-CA).

The writing data used to support Aaronson and Ferres's (1987) cognitive hypothesis came from a study of two papers, one from each of two undergraduate bilinguals, and "the two-page menu of a neighborhood Szechuan restaurant" (p. 82). The authors' attempt to deal with this by comparison of their results with Hakuta's (1987) findings does not serve as a sufficient comparison due to potential differences in methodology between the two studies. While linguistic phenomena may demonstrate far more stability across individuals than some other communication phenomena, a study with n-2 plus a menu seems immediately suspect. An unfamiliarity hypothesis would seem to account for the data about as well as the assumption of deep cognitive performance differences. The data show that these Chinese-English bilinguals had difficulties in written performance in the same areas where linguistic differences occur between the languages. For linguistic relativity, the question would have to be, are the difficulties embedded in the cognitive structure of the individuals (LR-GCS), or simply relatively habitual ways of processing information that can be overcome (LR-CA)? The key difference in distinguishing between these two positions may be the amount of time it takes to overcome the effects of L-1 on the processing of L-2 given motivation, practice, and a correct model. This study does not provide that key. Different comprehension strategies are not the same as different modes of thought. The study does show a likely association between writing difficulties and linguistic differences between languages.

De Avila (1987) suggests that most studies of bilinguals have made little or no attempt to measure the extent of bilingualism of the subjects, who may not have been linguistically competent in *either* L-1 or L-2. He comments: "When linguistic and test demand characteristics are controlled, many of the reported ethnolinguistic group differences in cognitive functioning fail to emerge" (p. 150).

### The Evidence from Aphasics

If linguistic relativity actually occurs, we should expect that aphasics who have learned a language, lost it, and had to relearn it should show the effects of prior language learning on their thought processes, especially during the relearning process. Lambert and Fillenbaum (1959) studied aphasia among bilinguals and discuss three possible explanations for the reacquisition of language by aphasics, one of which, the "rule of Ribot," states that linguistic habits acquired early are more resistant to aphasic damage than those acquired later (LR-CA). These authors studied the records of all cases of bilingual aphasia available to them in Europe (about 23) and in Montreal, Canada (about 11). The rule of Ribot was supported for compound bilinguals, but not for coordinate bilinguals. Yet linguistic relativity should have at least as much as to say about coordinate bilinguals, whose thought processes should supposedly be formed in the first language, than about compound bilinguals, whose thought processes should be affected relatively concurrently by both languages. Thus this study provides only mild support for LR-CA.

## *The Evidence from the Deaf*

Furth (1966) suggests that the deaf can comprehend and apply a principle as well as can the hearing, once they know what it is. Their deficiency seems to be in a lessened performance in discovering what the principle to be applied is (p. 146). Furth argues: "If language is the key factor, how does language facilitate discovery of new concepts while lack of it does not impede comprehension and use of concepts? . . . conceptual comprehension and use appear to be purer aspects of intelligence than discovery. Why then should language affect a less and not affect a more important part of intelligence?" (p. 148). Compared to the possible effects, Furth asks, are not the observed effects trivial and superficial? Furth's observations support LR-CA but not LR-LO or LR-GCS.

Experiments by Oléron (1957) and Furth (1966) indicate that deaf children show only slight deficits in performance over hearing children on elementary logical operations such as the standard Piagetian tasks of seriation and conservation of liquids. The deaf-mute children have intact sensorimotor schemes, but have not acquired spoken language. In contrast, blind children tend to be four years behind normal and deaf-mute children on elementary logical operations (Hatwell, 1960). The blind children have acquired spoken language but have no intact sensorimotor schemes. Thus sensorimotor logical operations seem dependent on visual perception rather than on language, an anti-LR-LO, anti-LR-GCS finding. Furth concludes that neither logical thinking nor the organization of intelligence requires language.

Rodda and Grove (1987) agree with Furth, reviewing the recent literature on cognitive skills of the deaf and concluding that the deaf have the same semantic or categorizing competence as the hearing, and the same higher cognitive skills, but are deficient in purely linguistic skills and short-term memory storage (LR-CA) (pp. 157–183). Sign language does not transmit grammatical structure well in the sense of spoken language (p. 186). Yet sign language is neither primitive nor inefficient and is capable of communicating meaning as quickly and as efficiently as speech (p. 225). Despite their lack of grammar in the spoken-language sense, the deaf in a given culture do not seem to have a substantially different worldview than the hearing persons around them (anti-LR-GCS), nor do they have demonstrably different ways of thinking (anti-LR-LO).

## IMPLICATIONS AND FUTURE RESEARCH

### Linguistic Relativity-Logical Operations

The case for an effect of language on logical operations is weak. Vygotsky's theory of language learning might allow for it but does not predict it; Piaget's, Chomsky's, and Skinner's would not. The data on children's acquisition of language indicate that fundamental logical patterns are formed before language and do not change as a result of language. Language affects representational thought, not logical operations. Peal and Lambert's (1962) study of Montreal schoolchildren found a slight advantage for bilingual over monolingual children in both verbal and nonverbal measures of intelligence. Bloom (1981) claimed a logical operation difficulty in his Chinese subjects, but many alternative interpretations of his results are possible. These are the only positive studies. On the negative side, the results with the deaf provide strong evidence that logical operations do not suffer from a lack of language. The evidence from the deaf seems so compelling that we can essentially dismiss the LR-LO hypothesis unless and until new evidence is presented in its favor that takes into account the evidence from the deaf.

### Linguistic Relativity-General Cognitive Structure

The general cognitive structure hypothesis is at the heart of Whorf's views. Vygotsky's and Piaget's theories of language learning would allow for it, while Skinner's would not, and Chomsky's would severely limit it by removing grammar as an independent variable. The most compelling evidence for LR-GCS is Whorf's work with Hopi. It is almost impossible to read Whorf's work and dismiss it. Hopi, both language and culture, employs a view of the world different from that used by persons nurtured in European languages. The question remains, does the language cause the Weltanschauung or do the culture and Weltanschauung provide a need for language forms to support them? Hopi who encounter Western culture are capable of changing worldviews, though it is a painful and often unrewarding process. Persons of Western culture can also adopt Hopi views wholeheartedly. Whatever power language might have to induce a Weltanschauung seems fleeting at best. Heider and Oliver (1972) found the same cognitive structure for color in the Dani, who have only two words for color, as in American college students known for their preppyism and color consciousness. If language causes cognitive structure, how can this be?

Nootka and Wintu are quite different from English in structure, but these differences are only suggestive of cognitive consequences for which there is no direct evidence. Other examples can be found, such as Glucksberg and Danks's (1975) point that English has no true future tense, but creates one using modal auxiliaries that indicate degrees of hope, intention, and probability (might, shall, will, should, would, could). Since French has a proper future tense, they ask whether French and English speakers have a different conception of time. This difference does not seem to exist. Henle's forced observation notion is interesting, but is only suggestive of research to be done. And while Aristotelian subject-predicate logic may have dominated Western thought, demonstrating that it did so because of subject-predicate formulations in Western languages is another matter entirely. If strong linguistic relativity (LR-GCS) were to hold, how could Western thinkers ever have escaped it clutches? The restricted code, deficit, mother-control position argues for an LR-GCS position, but the evidence produced for it seems massively flawed. The difference position, together with methodological problems in many of the deficit studies, accounts for the deficit results without the need to appeal to deficient language as a cause. Bernstein's elaborated/restricted code distinction seems best understood as descriptions of the language of lower socioeconomic status persons as seen through the eyes of those higher in status. Bloom's (1981) results support LR-GCS, but are flawed. Peal and Lambert (1962) also offer some potential support. But the work with the deaf again suggests rather strongly that no LR-GCS effect can be ascribed to language. If the evidence from the deaf is correct, it must be the case that the correlation between language and Weltanschauung demonstrated by Whorf does not have language in a causal position.

### Linguistic Relativity-Cognitive Areas

The cognitive area hypothesis is a weaker form of linguistic relativity than either LR-LO or LR-GCS. While not as central to Whorf's views as LR-GCS, LR-CA has received considerably more empirical support. Vygotsky's and Piaget's theories of language learning would allow for it; Skinner's would not. Chomsky's would limit it to an effect produced by semantics and phonology, eliminating grammar as an independent variable. Langer's position would directly support it. The work of Furth (1966) and Rodda and Grove (1987) with the deaf indicates that language functions to allow easy discovery of new concepts, but that lack of language does not impede comprehension and use of concepts once discovery is achieved. This is similar to Langer's position. One cannot fully grasp multiple regression or factor analysis until one has a solid understanding of a bivariate correlation coefficient and the factors that affect it. One cannot understand the difference in meaning of birth, death, or marriage in Hopi versus Western culture without first understanding *manifested-manifesting* versus *time-space*. This would explain both the effect of subject-predicate logic on Western thought for over 2,000 years and the relative ease of removing this effect once the new concept is attained. It is directly analogous to the struggle of the deaf, or the struggle of any human, to understand prior to attaining the concept. It is what Vygotsky meant when arguing that in order to communicate a thought a person must be familiar with a generalized concept representing a category. LR-CA does not hold that language determines cognitive structure or even the categories of thought open to us. It holds that thought can occur without language, and without concepts, but only with great difficulty. Whorf's work with the Hopi shows this, as does Bloom's Chinese work. Bloom's studies do not provide evidence that Chinese speakers *cannot* think in terms of counterfactuals, definite generic articles, or entifications, but that they *do not* normally express thoughts using such constructions. If by *linguistic relativity* we mean that someone thinking in a particular language is not used to and does not *normally* think or use language in a particular fashion (LR-CA), Bloom's experiments illustrate this result. But if we mean that language influences thought to the extent that one *cannot* think

(LR-GCS), say, counterfactually, because of a deficit provided by a native language, then we find no evidence for that position in Bloom's results.

The evidence on color seems to support this. Color categories clearly affect memory. Storage and recall of information is easier when a category exists for it. Perception of color is not affected by language, nor is the cognitive organization of color. Aaronson and Ferres's (1987) results, based on a limited sample size, show an LR-CA effect in the increased importance ascribed to both function and content words by bilinguals. Cummins (1987) noted this same more analytic orientation toward language found in bilinguals, as predicted by Vygotsky. Lambert and Fillenbaum's (1959) study of aphasics also gives mild support.

Is a finding of LR-CA important? What does it mean for theory and research? I believe that the essence of linguistic relativity may be found in Hoijer (1956, p. 122), who rightly points out that the differences between languages are not to be found in what *can* be said, but in what it is *relatively easy* to say. Expanding on Hoijer, the difficulties of language are not that it changes our thought processes, as "strong" linguistic relatively suggests, but that we struggle with it to say what we wish to express. These struggles take different forms in different languages. For the Chinese, stating a counterfactual is difficult. For a Westerner, explaining *manifesting* is difficult. Following the path of least resistant language can lead us to misstate our intent. We do not always say what we intend, and slippage between intended and actual messages should be greater when the intended thought is more difficult to express in the language than when expression of the thought is easy in that language.

Now cognitive dissonance holds that beliefs follow behavior, that thought can follow statements. Saying something slightly different from what we mean, because it is easier to do so in our particular language or dialect, and then changing our meaning to conform with our words, away from our original intent, may be where the main truth of the linguistic relativity hypothesis lies. I intend to explain *manifesting* in English, but misstate it slightly because the exact thought is difficult to express. I then slowly come to believe in the thought *as I have expressed it*, rather than as it was in my original intent, and slowly change the meaning I have for *manifesting,* as well as the meaning of those who talk with me. The meaning of the word in my language and culture becomes different from its meaning in

Hopi, even though at one time I grasped its meaning. I *can* communicate it correctly, at least originally, but it is more difficult, so I am less likely to do so. In this way, cognitive dissonance interacts with ease or difficulty of expression in a given language to produce differences in thought between languages, or between dialects within a language.

In Hopi an explanation of *manifesting* is easy. So in Hopi we would not see the dissonance-type meaning shift regarding *manifesting* that we see in English. But in Hopi *time* is difficult. So we should see Hopi speakers fudge slightly on their intended meanings with respect to time, when putting them into words. Once fudged, the statement comes to be believed over the original meaning. The differences in ease of expression between languages should produce different types of meaning shifts in each language, as meaning moves from intent to statement to adjusted thought. The real question for future research is, of course, can the occurrence of this process be demonstrated and, if so, what are the conditions that foster or inhibit it? To what extent are the speakers, and the listeners, in a given language aware of and/ or able to compensate for this process? And to what extent does this process account for Weltanschauung differences between languages? In this regard, Osgood and Sebeok (1965) suggest that intracultural studies of linguistic relativity effects may yield better evidence than intercultural studies because the former remove culture as a rival hypothesis to language.

In closing, it needs to be pointed out that where linguistic relativity effects are found in the studies mentioned above, they are seldom in the more interesting grammatical or worldview area, but usually in the less interesting and inherently more limited area of semantic and category boundary differences, which may be overcome by learning new words and categories, though the linguistic relativity-cognitive dissonance process outlined above should make that difficult. While much of the evidence reviewed fails to give general support to any specific linguistic relativity view, the power of these studies to detect a weak effect, if it were there, is low, both because much of the evidence was not designed to test for the different forms weaker effects might take and because weak effects are less likely to appear in any given study, even when present, than are stronger effects. A strong effect, such as linguistic relativity-logical operation or linguistic relativity-general cognitive structure, should be more evident in a study designed to test for it than inherently weaker linguistic relativity-cognitive area effects (Cohen, 1977).

# REFERENCES

Aaronson, D., & Ferres, A. (1987). The impact of language differences on language processing: An example form Chinese-English bilingualism. In P. Homel, M. Palij, & D. Aaronson (Eds.), *Childhood bilingualism: Aspects of linguistic, cognitive, and social development* (pp. 75–119). Hillsdale, NJ: Lawrence Erlbaum.

Allen, R. R., & Brown, K. L. (1976). *Developing communication competence in children.* Skokie, IL: National Textbook.

Anastasi, A. (1953). *Differential psychology.* New York: Macmillan.

Anderson, J. R. (1974). *Language acquisition in computer and child* (Human Performance Center Report No. 55). Ann Arbor: University of Michigan.

Anderson, J. R. (1975). Computer simulation of a language acquisition system: A first report. In R. L. Solso (Ed.), *Information processing and cognition: The Loyola symposium.* Hillsdale, NJ: Lawrence Erlbaum.

Anderson, J. R. (1976). *Language, memory, and thought.* Hillsdale, NJ: Lawrence Erlbaum.

Anderson, J. R. (1983). *The architecture of cognition.* Cambridge, MA: Harvard University Press.

Au, T. K. (1983). Chinese and English counterfactuals: The Sapir-Whorf hypothesis revisited. *Cognition, 15,* 155–187.

Au, T. K. (1984). Counterfactuals: In reply to Alfred Bloom. *Cognition, 17,* 239–302.

Au, T. K. (1985). Language and cognition. In L. L. Loyd & R. L. Schiefelbusch (Eds.), *Language perspectives II.* Baltimore: University Park Press.

Baratz, D. C. (1968, September). *The assessment of language and cognitive abilities of the Negro.* Paper presented at the annual meeting of the American Psychological Association.

Baratz, J. C. (1970). Teaching reading in an urban Negro school system. In F. Williams (Ed.), *Language and poverty: Perspectives on a theme* (pp. 11–24). Chicago: Markham.

Bereiter, C., & Engelmann, S. (1966). *Teaching disadvantaged children in the preschool.* Englewood Cliffs: Prentice Hall.

Bernstein, B. (1958). Some sociological determinants of perception. *British Journal of Sociology, 9,,* 159–174.

Bernstein, B. (1959). A public language: Some sociological implications of a linguistic form. *British Journal of Sociology, 10,* 311–326.

Bernstein, B. (1960). Language and social class. *British Journal of Sociology, 11,* 271–276.

Bernstein, B. (1961a). Aspects of language and learning in the genesis of the social process. *Journal of Child Psychology and Psychiatry, 1,* 313–324.

Bernstein, B. (1961b). Social class and linguistic development: A theory of social learning. In A. H. Halsey, J. Floud, & A. Anderson (Eds.), *Education, economy, and society.* New York: Free Press.

Bernstein, B. (1962). Social class, linguistic codes, and grammatical elements. *Language and Speech, 5,* 221–240.

Bernstein, B. (1964a). Elaborated and restricted codes: Their social origins and some consequences. In J. Gumperz & D. Hymes (Eds.), The ethnography of communication [Special issue]. *American Anthropologist, 66*(6), Pt. 2, 55–69.

Bernstein, B. (1964b). *Family role systems, communication, and socialization.* Paper presented at the Conference on Development of Cross-National Research of Education of Children and Adolescents, Chicago.

Bernstein, B. (1965). A sociolinguistic approach to social learning. In J. Gould (Ed.), *Penguin survey of the social sciences.* Baltimore: Penguin.

Bernstein, B. (1970). A sociolinguistic approach to socialization: With some reference to educability. In F. Williams (Ed.), *Language and poverty: Perspectives on a theme* (pp. 25–61). Chicago: Markham.

Bernstein, B., & Henderson, D. (1969). Social class differences in the relevance of language to socialization. *Sociology, 3,* 2–20.

Blank, M. (1970). Some philosophical influences underlying preschool intervention for disadvantaged children. In F. Williams (Ed.), *Language and poverty: Perspectives on a theme* (pp. 62–80). Chicago: Markham.

Blank, M., & Bridger, W. (1966). Deficiencies in verbal labeling in retarded readers. *American Journal of Orthopsychiatry, 36,* 840–847.

Bloom, A. (1981). *The linguistic shaping of thought: A study in the impact of language on thinking in China and the West.* Hillsdale, NJ: Lawrence Erlbaum.

Bloom, A. (1984). Caution—The words you use may affect what you say: A response to Terry Kitfong Au's "Chinese and English counterfactuals: The Sapir-Whorf hypothesis revisited." *Cognition, 17,* 275–287.

Blumenthal, A. L. (1970). *Language and psychology: Historical aspects of psycholinguistics.* New York: John Wiley.

Braine, M.D.S. (1987). Acquiring and processing first and second languages: Comments on Hakuta, Cummins, and Aaronson & Ferres. In P. Homel, M. Palij, & D. Aaronson (Eds.), *Childhood bilingualism: Aspects of linguistic, cognitive, and social development* (pp. 121–128). Hillsdale, NJ: Lawrence Erlbaum.

Brewer, W. F. (1974). The problem of meaning and the interrelations of the higher mental processes. In W. B. Weimer & D. S. Palermo (Eds.), *Cognition and the symbolic processes* (pp. 263–298). Hillsdale, NJ: Lawrence Erlbaum.

Brian, C. R., & Goodenough, F. L. (1929). The relative potency of color and form perception at various ages. *Journal of Experimental Psychology, 12,* 197–213.

Brown, R., & Lenneberg, E. H. (1954). A study in language and cognition. *Journal of Abnormal and Social Psychology, 49,* 454–462.

Bruner, J. S., & Goodman, C. C. (1947). Value and need as organizing factors in perception. *Journal of Abnormal and Social Psychology, 42,* 34.

Caplan, S., & Ruble, R. A. (1964). A study of culturally imposed factors on school achievement in a metropolitan area. *Journal of Educational Research, 58,* 16–21.

Carroll, J. B., & Casegrande, J. B. (1958). The function of language classification in behavior. In E. E. Maccoby, T. Newcomb, & E. L. Hartley (Eds.), *Readings in social psychology* (3rd ed.). New York: Holt, Rinehart & Winston.

Carson, A. S., & Rabin, A. I. (1960). Verbal comprehension and communication in Negro and white children. *Journal of Educational Psychology, 51,* 47–51.

Casegrande, J. B., & Hale, K. L. (1967). Semantic relationships in Papago folk definitions. In *Studies in southwestern linguistics.* The Hague: Mouton.

Cassirer, E. (1932). Le language et la construction du monde des objects. *Journal de la Psychologie Normale et Pathologique, 30.*

Cassirer, E. (1953). *The philosophy of symbolic forms: Vol. 1. Language.* New Haven, CT: Yale University Press.

Cazden, C. B. (1966). Subcultural differences in child language: An interdisciplinary review. *Merrill-Palmer Quarterly, 12*, 185–219.

Cazden, C. B. (1970). The neglected situation in child language research and education. In F. Williams (Ed.), *Language and poverty: Perspectives on a theme* (pp. 81–101). Chicago: Markham.

Chomsky, N. (1957). *Syntactic structures.* The Hague: Mouton.

Chomsky, N. (1965). *Aspects of the theory of syntax.* Cambridge: MIT Press.

Chomsky, N. (1967). *Language and mind.* New York: Harcourt, Brace & World.

Church, J. (1961). *Language and the discovery of reality: A developmental psychology of cognition.* New York: Random House.

Clark, A. D., & Richards, C. J. (1966). Auditory discrimination among economically disadvantaged and nondisadvantaged preschool children. *Exceptional Children, 33*, 259–262.

Cohen, J. (1977). *Statistical power analysis for the behavioral sciences.* New York: Academic Press.

Condon, J. C. (1975). *Semantics and communication.* New York: Macmillan.

Connors, C. K., Schuette, C., & Goldman, A. (1967). Informational analysis of intersensory communication in children of different social class. *Child Development, 38*, 251–266.

Creelman, M. B. (1966). *The experimental investigation of meaning.* New York: Springer.

Cummins, J. (1987). Bilingualism, language proficiency, and metalinguistic development. In P. Homel, M. Palij, & D. Aaronson (Eds.), *Childhood bilingualism: Aspects of linguistic, cognitive, and social development* (pp. 57–73). Hillsdale, NJ: Lawrence Erlbaum.

De Avila, E. (1987). Bilingualism, cognitive function, and language minority group membership. In P. Homel, M. Palij, & D. Aaronson (Eds.), *Childhood bilingualism: Aspects of linguistic, cognitive, and social development* (pp. 149–169). Hillsdale, NJ: Lawrence Erlbaum.

De Avila, E., & Duncan, S. E. (1980). Definitions and measurement of bilingual students. In California State Department of Education, *Bilingual program, policy, and assessment issues.* Sacramento: California State Department of Education.

De Avila, E., Duncan, S. E., & Ulibarri, D. M. (1982). Cognitive development. In E. E. Garcia (Ed.), *The Mexican American child: Language, cognition, and social development.* Tempe, AZ: Center for Bilingual/Bicultural Education.

DeBoer, J. J. (1952). Some sociological factors in language development. *Elementary English, 29*, 482–92.

Deese, J. (1974). The psychology of meaning. In A. Silverstein (Ed.), *Human communication: Theoretical explorations.* Hillsdale, NJ: Lawrence Erlbaum.

Deutsch, M. (1965). The role of social class in language development and cognition. *American Journal of Orthopsychiatry, 25*, 78–88.

Deutsch, M. (1967). *The disadvantaged child.* New York: Basic Books.

Deutsch, M., Katz, I., & Jensen, A. R. (Eds.). (1968). *Social class, race, and psychological development.* New York: Holt, Rinehart & Winston.

Diebold, A. R. (1965). A survey of psycholinguistic research, 1954–1964. In Osgood, C. E., & Sebeok, T. A., *Psycholinguistics.* Bloomington: Indiana University Press.

Dillard, J. L. (1967, Fall). Negro children's dialect in the inner city. *Florida Foreign Language Reporter.*

Ebersole, F. B. (1979). *Language and perception: Essays in the philosophy of language.* Washington, DC: University Press of America.

Entwisle, D. R. (1968). Subcultural differences in children's language development. *International Journal of Psychology, 3,* 13–22.

Entwisle, D. R. (1970). Semantic systems of children: Some assessments of social class and ethnic differences. In F. Williams (Ed.), *Language and poverty: Perspectives on a theme* (pp. 123–139). Chicago: Markham.

Ervin-Tripp, S. (1964). An analysis of the interaction of language, topic, and listener. In J. Gumperz & D. Hymes (Eds.), The ethnography of communication [Special issue]. *American Anthropologist, 66*(6), Pt. 2, 86–102.

Fishman, J. A. (1960). A systematization of the Whorfian hypothesis. *Behavioral Science, 5,* 323–339.

Flavell, J. H. (1963). *The developmental psychology of Jean Piaget.* Princeton, NJ: Van Nostrand.

Foeman, A. K., & Pressley, G. (1987). Ethnic culture and corporate culture: Using Black styles in organizations. *Communication Quarterly, 35,* 239–307.

Frandsen, K. D., & Green, J. O. (1978, November). *Speech and language sciences, 1977: A review and commentary.* Paper presented at the annual meeting of the Speech Communication Association, Minneapolis.

Furth, H. G. (1966). *Thinking without language.* New York: Free Press.

Garfinkel, H. (1972). Remarks on ethnomethodology. In J. Gumperz & D. Hymes (Eds.), *Directions in sociolinguistics: The ethnography of communication* (pp. 301–324). New York: Holt, Rinehart & Winston.

Gesell, A. (1941, January). The biography of a wolf-child. *Harper's Magazine,* pp. 183–193.

Ghiselin, B. (Ed.). (1955). *The creative process.* New York: Mentor.

Gleason, H. A. (1961). *An introduction to descriptive linguistics.* New York: Holt, Rinehart & Winston.

Glick, J. (1987). Bilingualism: Cognitive and social aspects. In P. Homel, M. Palij, & D. Aaronson (Eds.), *Childhood bilingualism: Aspects of linguistic, cognitive, and social development* (pp. 171–179). Hillsdale, NJ: Lawrence Erlbaum.

Glucksberg, S., & Danks, J. H. (1975). *Experimental psycholinguistics.* Hillsdale, NJ: Lawrence Erlbaum.

Greenberg, J. H. (1956). Concerning inferences from linguistic to nonlinguistic data. In H. Hoijer (Ed.), *Language in culture* (pp. 3–19). Chicago: University of Chicago Press.

Gumperz, J. J. (1962). Types of linguistic communities. *Anthropological Linguistics, 4,* 28–40.

Gumperz, J. J., & Hymes, D. (Eds.). (1972). *Directions in sociolinguistics: The ethnography of communication.* New York: Holt, Rinehart & Winston.

Hakuta, K. (1987). The second language learner in the context of the study of language acquisition. In P. Homel, M. Palij, & D. Aaronson (Eds.), *Childhood bilingualism: Aspects of linguistic, cognitive, and social development* (pp. 31–55). Hillsdale, NJ: Lawrence Erlbaum.

Hale, H. (1887). The origin of languages and the antiquity of speaking man. *Proceedings of the American Association of the Advancement of Science, 35,* 279–323.

Hall, R. A., Jr. (1966). *Pidgin and creole languages.* Ithaca, NY: Cornell University Press.

Hall, W. S., & Nagy, W. E. (1987). Continuities/discontinuities in the function and use of language as related to situation and social class. In P. Homel, M. Palij, & D. Aaronson (Eds.), *Childhood bilingualism: Aspects of linguistic, cognitive, and social development* (pp. 243–280). Hillsdale, NJ: Lawrence Erlbaum.

Hanfmann, E., & Kasanin, J. (1937). A method for the study of concept formation. *Journal of Psychology, 3*, 521–540.

Harms, L. S. (1961). Listener comprehension of speakers of three status groups. *Language and Speech, 4,*, 109–129.

Hatwell, Y. (1960). *Privation sensorielle et intelligence.* Paris: Presses University France.

Hawkins, P. R. (1969). Social class, the nominal group and reference. *Language and Speech, 12*, 125–135.

Heider, E. R., Cazden, C. B., & Brown R. (1968). *Social class differences in the effectiveness and style of children's coding ability* (Project Literacy Report No. 9). Ithaca, NY: Cornell University.

Heider, E. R., & Oliver, D. C. (1972). The structure of the color space in naming and memory for two languages. *Cognitive Psychology, 8*, 337–354.

Henle, P. (1958). Language, thought and culture. In P. Henle (Ed.), *Language and culture* (pp. 1–24). Ann Arbor: University of Michigan Press.

Herman, S. (1961). Explorations in the social psychology of language choice. *Human Relations, 14*, 149–164.

Hess, R. D., & Shipman, V. (1965a). Early blocks to children's learning. *Children, 12*, 189–194.

Hess, R. D., & Shipman, V. (1965b). Early experience and the socialization of cognitive modes in children. *Child Development, 36*, 869–886.

Hess, R. D., Shipman, V., Bear, R., & Brophy, J. (1968). *The cognitive environments of urban preschool children.* Chicago: University of Chicago Press.

Higgens, C., & Sivers, C. (1958). A comparison of Stanford-Binet and Colored Raven Progressive Matrices IQs for children with low socioeconomic status. *Journal of Consulting Psychology, 22*, 465–468.

Hill, E. H., & Giammatteo, M. C. (1963). Socioeconomic status and its relationship to school achievement in the elementary school. *Elementary English, 40*, 265–270.

Hockett, C. F. (1950). Age grading and linguistic continuity. *Language, 26*, 449–457.

Hofstede, G. (1984). *Culture's consequences: International differences in work-related values* (abridged ed.). Beverly Hills, CA: Sage.

Hoijer, H. (Ed.). (1956). *Language in culture.* Chicago: University of Chicago Press.

Homel, P., Palij, M., & Aaronson, D. (Eds.). (1987a). *Childhood bilingualism: Aspects of linguistic, cognitive, and social development.* Hillsdale, NJ: Lawrence Erlbaum.

Homel, P., Palij, M., & Aaronson, D. (1987b). Childhood bilingualism: Introduction and overview. In P. Homel, M. Palij, & D. Aaronson (Eds.), *Childhood bilingualism: Aspects of linguistic, cognitive, and social development* (pp. 3–9). Hillsdale, NJ: Lawrence Erlbaum.

Honkavaara, S. A. (1958). A critical re-evaluation of the color and form reaction, and disproving of the hypothesis connected with it. *Journal of Psychology, 45*, 25–36.

Hopper, R. (1976). Children's acquisition of language codes. In R. R. Allen & K. L. Brown (Eds.), *Developing communication competence in children* (pp. 3–15). Skokie, IL: National Textbook.

Hurst, C. G., & Jones, W. L. (1967). Generating spontaneous speech in the underprivileged child. *Journal of Negro Education, 36*, 362–367.

Hymes, D. (1967). Models of the interaction of languages and social setting. *Journal of Social Issues, 23*, 8–28.

Hymes, D. (1972). Models of the interaction of language and social life. In J. Gumperz & D. Hymes (Eds.), *Direction in sociolinguistics: The ethnography of communication* (pp. 35–71). New York: Holt, Rinehart & Winston.

Irwin, O. C. (1948a). Infant speech: The effect of family occupational status and of age on use of sound types. *Journal of Speech and Hearing Disorders, 13*, 224–226.

Irwin, O. C. (1948b). Infant speech: The effect of family occupational status and of age on sound frequency. *Journal of Speech and Hearing Disorders, 13*, 320–323.

Irwin, O. C. (1952). Speech development in the young child 2: Some factors related to the speech development of the infant and young child. *Journal of Speech and Hearing Disorders, 17*, 269–278.

Itard, E. M. (1802). *The savage of Aveyron.* London.

Ivey, S., Center W., & Tanner, N. (1968). Effect of cultural deprivation on language development. *Southern Speech Journal, 34*, 28–36.

Jackson, J. A. (1944). A survey of psychological, social, and environmental differences between advanced and retarded readers. *Journal of Genetic Psychology, 65*, 113–131.

Jensen, A. R. (1969). How much can we boost IQ and scholastic achievement? *Harvard Educational Review, 39*, 1–123.

John V. (1963). The intellectual development of slum children: Some preliminary findings. *American Journal of Orthopsychiatry, 33*, 813–822.

John, V., & Goldstein, L. (1964). The social context of language acquisition. *Merrill-Palmer Quarterly, 10*, 265–275.

John, V. P., & Horner, V. M. (1970). *Bilingualism and the Spanish speaking child.* In F. Williams (Ed.), *Language and poverty: Perspectives on a theme* (pp. 140–152). Chicago: Markham.

Katz, I. (1973). Negro performance in interracial situations. In P. Watson (Ed.), *Psychology and race.* Chicago: Aldine.

Keller, H. (1902). *The story of my life.* Garden City, NY: Doubleday.

Kendler, H. H., & Kendler, T. S. (1962). Vertical and horizontal processes in problem solving. *Psychological Review, 69*, 1–16.

Kolers, P. A. (1963). Interlingual word associations. *Journal of Verbal Learning and Verbal Behavior, 2*, 291–300.

Kolers, P. A. (1966a). Interlingual facilitation of short-term memory. *Journal of Verbal Learning and Verbal Behavior, 5*, 314–319.

Kolers, P. A. (1966b). Reading and talking bilingually. *American Journal of Psychology, 79*, 357–376.

Kolers, P. A. (1968). Bilingualism and information processing. *Scientific American, 218*, 78–96.

Labov, W. (1966a). *The social stratification of English in New York City.* Washington, DC: Center for Applied Linguistics.

Labov, W. (1966b). *On the grammaticality of everyday speech.* Paper presented at the annual meeting of the Linguistic Society of America, New York.

Labov, W. (1970). The logic of nonstandard English. In F. Williams (Ed.), *Language and poverty: Perspectives on a theme* (pp. 153–189). Chicago: Markham.

Labov, W. (1972). *Sociolinguistic patterns.* Philadelphia: University of Pennsylvania Press.

Labov, W., Cohen, P., & Robins, C. (1965). *A preliminary study of the structure of English used by Negro and Puerto Rican speakers in New York City* (Final report, U.S. Office of Education Cooperative Research Project No. 3091). Washington, DC: Government Printing Office.

LaCivita, A., Kean, J. M., & Yamamoto, K. (1966). Socioeconomic status of children and acquisition of grammar. *Journal of Educational Research, 60,* 71–74.

Lambert, W. E. (1963). Psychological approaches to the study of language, Part II: On second language learning and bilingualism. *Modern Language Journal, 47,* 114–121.

Lambert, W. E., & Fillenbaum, S. (1959). A pilot study of aphasia among bilinguals. *Canadian Journal of Psychology, 13,* 28–34.

Lambert, W. E., Havelka, J., & Gardner, R. C. (1959). Linguistic manifestations of bilingualism. *American Journal of Psychology, 72,* 77–82.

Lambert, W. E., & Tucker, G. R. (1972). *Bilingual education of children: The St. Lambert experiment.* Rowley, MA: Newbury House.

Langer, S. K. (1957). *Philosophy in a new key.* Cambridge, MA: Harvard University Press.

Lantz, D., & Stefflre, V. (1964). Language and cognition revisited. *Journal of Abnormal and Social Psychology, 69,* 472–481.

Lawton, D. (1963). Social class differences in language development: A study of some samples of written work. *Language and Speech, 6,* 120–143.

Lenneberg, E. (1973). Biological aspects of language. In G. A. Miller (Ed.), *Communication, language and meaning* (pp. 49–60). New York: Basic Books.

Lenneberg, E., & Roberts, J.M. (1956). *The language of experience.* Baltimore: Indiana University Publications in Anthropology and Linguistics, M. 13.

Lerman, P. (1967). Argot, symbolic deviance and subcultural delinquency. *American Sociological Review, 32,* 209–224.

Lewis, M. M. (1963). *Language, thought, and personality in infancy and childhood.* New York: Basic Books.

Lindsey, P. H., & Norman, D. A. (1972). *Human information processing.* New York: Academic Press.

Loban, W. (1966). *Problems in oral English: Kindergarten through grade nine.* Champaign, IL: National Council of Teachers of English.

Luria, A. R. (1966a). Investigation of speech functions: Receptive speech. In A. R. Luria (Ed.), *Higher cortical functions in man* (pp. 373–389). New York: Basic Books.

Luria, A. R. (1966b). Investigation of speech functions: Expressive speech. In A. R. Luria (Ed.), *Higher cortical functions in man* (pp. 390–407). New York: Basic Books.

Luria, A. R., & Yudovich, F. (1959). *Speech and the development of mental processes in the child.* London: Staples.

Lynip, A. W. (1951). The use of magnetic devices in the collection and analysis of the preverbal utterances of an infant. *Genetic Psychology Monographs, 44,* 221–262.

Macnamara, J. (1967). Problems of bilingualism. *Journal of Social Issues, 23*(Whole No. 2).

Mandelbaum, D. G. (Ed.). (1949). *Selected writings of Edward Sapir in language, culture, and personality*. Berkeley: University of California Press.

Mandell, S. (1931). The relation of language to thought. *Quarterly Journal of Speech, 17*, 522–531.

Menyuk, P. (1968). Children's learning and reproduction of grammatical and nongrammatical phonological sequences. *Child Development, 39*, 849–859.

Merleau-Ponty, M. (1945). *Phnoménologie de la perception*. Paris: Gallimard.

Michotte, A. (1954). *La perception de la cauésalité* (2nd ed.). Louvain: Publication Universitaires de Louvain.

Milner, E. (1951). A study of the relationships between reading readiness in grade one school children and patterns of parent-child interaction. *Child Development, 22*, 95–112.

Mowrer, O. H. (1960). *Learning theory and the symbolic processes*. New York: John Wiley.

Noel, D. (1953). A comparative study of the relationship between the quality of the child's language and the quality and types of language used in the home. *Journal of Educational Research, 47*, 161–167.

Ogden, C. K., & Richards, I. A. (1921). *The meaning of meaning*. New York: Harcourt, Brace.

Oléron, P. (1957). *Recherches sur le dévlopment mental des sourds-muets*. Paris: Center National de Recherche Scientifique.

Olim, E. G. (1970). Maternal language styles and cognitive development of children. In F. Williams (Ed.), *Language and poverty: Perspectives on a theme* (pp. 212–228). Chicago: Markham.

Osborn, L. R. (1968). Speech communication and the American Indian high school student. *Speech Teacher, 17*, 38–43.

Osborn, L. R. (1970). Language, poverty, and the North American Indian. In F. Williams (Ed.), *Language and poverty: Perspectives on a theme* (pp. 229–247). Chicago: Markham.

Osgood, C. E. (1960). The cross-cultural generality of visual verbal synthetic tendencies. *Behavioral Science, 5*, 146–149.

Osgood, C. E., & Sebeok, T. A. (1965). *Psycholinguistics*. Bloomington: Indiana University Press.

Palij, M., & Homel, P. (1987). The relationship of bilingualism to cognitive development: Historical, methodological, and theoretical considerations. In P. Homel, M. Palij, & D. Aaronson (Eds.), *Childhood bilingualism: Aspects of linguistic, cognitive, and social development* (pp. 131–148). Hillsdale, NJ: Lawrence Erlbaum.

Peal, E., & Lambert, W. E. (1962). The relation of bilingualism to intelligence. *Psychological Monographs, 76*, 1–23 (No. 546).

Peisach, E. (1965). Children's comprehension of teacher and peer speech. *Child Development, 36*, 467–480.

Piaget, J. (1923). *The language and thought of the child*. Paris: Delachaux & Niestle.

Piaget, J. (1951). *Play, dreams, and imitation in childhood*. New York: Norton.

Piaget, J. (1961). The language and thought of the child. In T. Shipley (Ed.), *Classics in psychology*. New York: Philosophical Library.

Piaget, J. (1962). *Comment on Vygotsky's critical remarks*. Cambridge: MIT Press.

Piaget, J., & Inhelder, B. (1966). *La psychologie de l'enfant*. Paris: Presses University France.

Piecris, R. (1951). Speech and society: A sociological approach to language. *American Sociological Review, 16*, 499–505.

Pinker, S. (1984). *Language learnability and language development.* Cambridge, MA: Harvard University Press.

Plumer, D. (1970). A summary of some environmentalist views and some educational implications. In F. Williams (Ed.), *Language and poverty: Perspectives on a theme* (pp. 229–247). Chicago: Markham.

Preston, M. S., & Lambert, W. E. (1969). Interlingual interference in a bilingual version of the Stroop color-word task. *Journal of Verbal Learning and Verbal Behavior, 8*, 295–301.

Reinecke, J. E. (1988). "Pidgin English" in Hawaii: A local study in the sociology of language. *American Journal of Sociology, 43*, 778–789.

Reitman, W. R. (1965). *Cognition and thought.* New York: John Wiley.

Rheingold, H., Gewirtz, J. L., & Ross, H. W. (1959). Social conditioning of vocalizations in the infant. *Journal of Comparative and Physiological Psychology, 52*, 68–73.

Rodda, M., & Grove, C. (1987). *Language, cognition, and deafness.* Hillsdale, NJ: Lawrence Erlbaum.

Rokeach, M. (1960). *The open and closed mind.* New York: Basic Books.

Rosenthal, R., & Jacobson, L. F. (1968). Teacher expectations for the disadvantaged. *Scientific American, 218*, 19–23.

Roy, J. D. (1987). The linguistic and sociolinguistic position of Black English and the issue of bidialectalism in education. In P. Homel, M. Palij, & D. Aaronson (Eds.), *Childhood bilingualism: Aspects of linguistic, cognitive, and social development.* Hillsdale, NJ: Lawrence Erlbaum.

Ruddell, B., & Graves, B. W. (1968). Socio-ethnic status and the language achievement of first-grade children. *Elementary English, 24*, 635–643.

Russell, B. (1945). *History of western philosophy.* New York: Holt.

Sapir, E. (Ed.). (1921a). *Language: An introduction to the study of speech.* New York: Harcourt, Brace & World.

Sapir, E. (1921b). Language, race and culture. In E. Sapir (Ed.), *Language: An introduction to the study of speech.* New York: Harcourt, Brace & World.

Saporta, S., & Bastian, J. R. (Ed.). (1961). *Psycholinguistics: A book of readings.* New York: Holt, Rinehart & Winston.

Schatzman, L., & Strauss, A. (1955). Social class and modes of communication. *American Journal of Sociology, 60*, 329–338.

Schieffelin, B. B., & Ochs, E. (Eds.). (1986). *Language socialization across cultures.* Cambridge: Cambridge University Press.

Severson, R. A., & Guest, K. E. (1970). Toward the standardized assessment of the language of disadvantaged children. In F. Williams (Ed.), *Language and poverty: Perspectives on a theme* (pp. 309–334). Chicago: Markham.

Sherzer, J., & Darnell, R. (1972). Outline guide for the ethnographic study of speech use. In J. Gumperz & D. Hymes (Eds.), *Directions in sociolinguistics: The ethnography of communication* (pp. 548–554). New York: Holt, Rinehart & Winston.

Shuy, R. W. (1970). The sociolinguists and urban language problems. In F. Williams (Ed.), *Language and poverty: Perspectives on a theme* (pp. 335–350). Chicago: Markham.

Sigel, I., Anderson, L., & Shapiro, H. (1966). Categorization behavior of lower- and middle-class Negro preschool children: Differences in dealing with representation of familiar objects. *Journal of Negro Education, 35,* 218–229.

Sinclair-de-Zwart, H. (1967). *Acquisition du language et dévelopment de la pensée.* Paris: Dunod.

Sinclair-de-Zwart, H. (1969). Developmental psycholinguistics. In D. Elkind & J. H. Flavell (Eds.), *Studies in cognitive development: Essays in honor of Jean Piaget* (pp. 315–336). New York: Oxford University Press.

Skinner, B. F. (1957). *Verbal behavior.* New York: Appleton-Century-Crofts.

Sledd, J. (1965). On not teaching English usage. *English Journal, 54,* 698–703.

Slobin, D. T. (1979). *Psycholinguistics.* Glenview, IL: Scott Foresman.

Stefflre, V., Castillo Vales, V., & Morley, L. (1966). Language and cognition in Yucatan: A cross-cultural replication. *Journal of Personality and Social Psychology, 4,* 112–115.

Steinfatt, T. (1977). *Human communication: An interpersonal introduction.* Indianapolis: Bobbs-Merrill.

Steinfatt, T. (1988). *Language and intercultural differences: Linguistic relativity.* Paper presented at the "Top Three" panel, Intercultural Communication Division, at the annual meeting of the Speech Communication Association, New Orleans.

Stern, C., & Stern, W. (1907). *Die kindersprache.* Leipzig: Barth.

Stewart, W. A. (1964). Foreign language teaching methods in quasi-foreign language situations. In *Non-standard speech and the teaching of English.* Washington, DC: Center for Applied Linguistics.

Stewart, W. A. (1965). Urban Negro speech: Sociolinguistic factors affecting English teaching. In R. W. Shuy (Ed.), *Social dialects and language learning.* Champaign, IL: National Council of Teachers of English.

Stewart, W. A. (1967, Spring). Sociolinguistic factors in the history of American Negro dialects. *Florida Foreign Language Reporter.*

Stewart, W. A. (1968, Spring). Continuity and change in American Negro dialects. *Florida Foreign Language Reporter.*

Stewart, W. A. (1970). Toward a history of American Negro dialect. In F. Williams (Ed.), *Language and poverty: Perspectives on a theme* (pp. 351–379). Chicago: Markham.

Stewart, W. A. (1987). Coping or groping? Psycholinguistic problems in the acquisition of receptive and productive competence across dialects. In P. Homel, M. Palij, & D. Aaronson (Eds.), *Childhood bilingualism: Aspects of linguistic, cognitive, and social development* (pp. 281–298). Hillsdale, NJ: Lawrence Erlbaum.

Templin, M. C. (1957). *Certain language skills in children: Their development and interrelationships* (Institute for Child Welfare Monograph Series, No. 26). Minneapolis: University of Minnesota Press.

Thompson, H. (1966). A survey of factors contributing to success or failure of Indian Students at Northern Arizona University. *Indian Education, 439,* 1–8.

Treisman, A. M. (1965). The effects of redundancy and familiarity on translating and repeating back a foreign and a native language. *British Journal of Psychology, 56,* 369–379.

Triandis, H. (1964). Cultural influences upon cognitive processes. In L. Berkowitz (Ed.), *Advances in experimental social psychology* (Vol. 1). New York: Academic Press.

Turner, J. (1975). Social comparison and social identity: Some prospects for group behavior. *European Journal of Social Psychology, 5*, 5–34.

Vygotsky, L. S. (1962). *Thought and language.* Cambridge: MIT Press.

Wexler, K., & Culicover, P. (1980). *Formal principles of language acquisition.* Cambridge: MIT Press.

Whorf, B. L. (1956). *Language, thought and reality.* Cambridge: MIT Press.

Williams, F. (Ed.). (1970a). *Language and poverty: Perspectives on a theme.* Chicago: Markham.

Williams, F. (1970b). Some preliminaries and prospects. In F. Williams (Ed.), *Language and poverty: Perspectives on a theme* (pp. 1–10). Chicago: Markham.

Williams, F. (1970c). Language, attitude, and social change. In F. Williams (Ed.), *Language and poverty: Perspectives on a theme* (pp. 380–399). Chicago: Markham.

Wilson, H. (1821). *Wonderful characters* (Vol. 2). London.

Wood, B. (1968). Implications of psycholinguistics for elementary speech programs. *Speech Teacher, 17*, 183–192.

Wood, B., & Curry, J. (1969). "Everyday talk" and "school talk" of the city Black child. *Speech Teacher, 18*, 282–296.

Wundt, W. (1900). *Die sprache.* Leipzig: Engelmann.

# II

# LANGUAGE AND CROSS-CULTURAL STYLES

# 4

# Speech and the Communal Function in Four Cultures

GERRY PHILIPSEN • *University of Washington*

*This chapter argues that each culture provides a distinctive way to perform the communal function, that is, to use communication as a means for linking individuals into communities of shared identity. The use of communication in the creation, affirmation, and negotiation of shared identity is discussed through a review of the special role of speech in four cultural communities.*

The long history of communication study is marked by an enduring concern with how symbolic action can serve the needs of individuals and societies. Typically, this concern has been directed to the informative, persuasive, aesthetic, and heuristic functions of communication. Recently, increased attention has been paid to the communal function—that is, to communication as a means for linking individuals into communities of shared identity. Eastman (1985) refers to communal identity as the achievement of "subjective social identity and community membership" (p. 5). She is concerned with how (a) shared attitudes, (b) knowledge and use of culturally specific vocabulary, and (c) competence to speak about context-sensitive topics are efficacious for individuals in such achievements. Philipsen (1987) has defined this as the cultural function of communication, the use of communication in the creation, affirmation, and negotiation of shared identity (p. 249). His emphasis is on the individual's knowledge and use of community-specific discursive forms such as episodic sequences, stories, and aligning actions as sources of insight into and models for situated communal practice. Such approaches have in common a concern with how the individual's understanding and use of linguistic behavior function in the process of identifying the individual with a social group.

Ong (1982) has pointed to the special role of speech, the use of language in social situations, in performing the communal function:

Because in its physical constitution as sound, the spoken word proceeds from the human interior and manifests human beings to one another as conscious interiors, as persons, the spoken word forms human beings into close-knit groups. (p. 74)

Ong's statement is a stimulus for this essay, as a source of inspiration and as a point of contention. It inspires the strategy of inquiring into the cultural function of communication—the examination of how speech, one important medium of communication, joins individuals into communities of shared identity. But so much of what has been learned in the empirical study of speech behavior suggests that *how* speech functions, in lives and societies, *varies* across speech communities (Hymes, 1962, 1972). Thus Ong's statement prompts me to ask: What can be learned about the communal function of speech by studying it in diverse societies?

For the past several years a group of investigators has been studying different cultures and how speaking functions within them. For each of these four cultures the available data include a completed doctoral dissertation plus a book or published papers. Each study involved one or more years of intensive fieldwork in a speech community, with the aim of discovering and describing cultural symbols and meanings, premises, and rules pertaining to speaking. Although the studies were not explicitly or exclusively directed to the communal function, each member of the group has been concerned with the themes developed in Philipsen (1987) and, thus, each study includes some data that are pertinent to the question raised in this essay.

An important feature of each of the projects reviewed here is its use of an ethnography of speaking model (Hymes, 1962). This is a model of description that directs the investigator to study communities of discourse in terms of their distinctive systems of resources and rules pertaining to communicative conduct. Of particular importance is the discovery and description of culturally shaped "ways of speaking" (Hymes, 1974), a term that joins the Whorfian idea of "fashions of speaking" with the commonsense notion of ways of life. It is assumed that the spoken life of various people is so richly varied that knowledge of how spoken life is conceptualized, enacted, and interpreted in a given community is a matter of empirical investigation.

Although the ethnographer of speaking treats a culture as *sui generis* (i.e., as its own thing), assumptions and procedures are used heuristically in the study of a given culture. An assumption guiding the projects summarized here is that cultural premises and rules about speaking are intricately tied up with cultural conceptions of persons, agency, and social relations—that is, rules and beliefs about speech articulate with a larger cultural code defining the nature of persons, whether and how it is that humans can act efficaciously in the world of practice, and what are the possible and appropriate ways in which individuals are linked together in social units. In this sense a code of speaking is a code of personhood and society as well.

## SPEAKING IN PLACE IN TEAMSTERVILLE

The following have been observed as patterns in Teamsterville culture (Philipsen, 1972, 1975, 1976, 1986):

(1) the expression of a belief that neighborhood speech practices—and therefore the speaker's speech—are substandard in relation to the mainstream speech of American society, accompanied by an aggressive persistence in the use of the neighborhood practices and the aggressive negative sanctioning of neighborhood residents who deviate from neighborhood practices;

(2) a reluctance on the part of community members to engage in conversation with persons who live outside the four-block space of the speech community and, within the community, a restriction of the spoken part of one's life to meetings of groups of people with whom the interlocutor shares the identity features of age, gender, ethnicity, and location of residence (usually defined in terms of an area of approximately one city block);

(3) the practice of infusing a concern with "place" in every speech episode, such that descriptions of others, attributions of intent to self and others, and decisions about whether and how to interact with others are consistently and systematically expressed in terms of ethnicity, residence, and gender; and

(4) the belief that speech is an efficacious resource for affirming and enacting ties of solidarity and that it is, for ordinary community members, inefficacious in economic and political assertions, such as in making a living and in disciplining children.

These beliefs and practices can be summarized in terms of the idea of "place" as a fundamental theme and motive in Teamsterville spoken life. Teamstervillers perceive the world as being shaped by a finely developed sense of place. They see boundaries, social and physical, where some others do not, and this vision serves a major unifying perception in their worldview. The centrality of place in the cultural outlook is reflected in a strong concern for locating people in social-physical space, in a view of places as locales whose boundaries rightly enclose and shelter some people and deny entry to others, and in a pervasive concern that oneself and others know and stay in their proper place both hierarchically and socially.

How, in such a social world, is the cultural function performed? Taken from the perspective of the individual speaker, the following can be specified. The use of the neighborhood style of speaking is one obvious practical act that can be performed by individuals to instantiate "subjective social identity and community membership" (Eastman, 1985, p. 5). Each time a speaker speaks in the neighborhood style, that speaker performs an act of identification; she or he identifies with the social group by using a way of speaking that historically has defined that group. It is historical in that the practice is handed down from generation to generation and in that there are written reports, widely publicized, about the neighborhood speech style. These widely publicized reports make at least a superficial knowledge of Teamsterville speech ways a part of the larger common culture of Chicago.

The use of the neighborhood speech style is an act of identification in two mutually reinforcing ways. First, it is an act by which the speaker "gives off" to others the impression that the speaker is a member, is "from around here" and "belongs around here." That is, as directed to one's interlocutors the use of neighborhood speech makes an identity claim. Second, it is an act by which speakers themselves hear their own speech as similar to the speech of a particular group of others. Thus, the use of neighborhood speech is an act in which one experiences oneself as a member. Taking both ways together, such acts of speech are powerful acts of what I call "membering"—a word that captures something that the verbs *enact, announce, affirm, establish,* and the like do not quite express alone.

A second principle governing membering through language use in Teamsterville is that the person must spend a great deal of time in sociable interaction among a group of people with whom the person has a matched social identity—matched in terms of age, gender, ethnicity, and residence. The purpose of such groups is "to hang together in times of fun and trouble" for the sake of pure association. It is in the company of such a group that the member feels most alive, most "a person," as some outsiders might say.

In Teamsterville culture the model person is a *persona*, that is, a person with a specified set of social attributes, who is acting out his or her prescribed role among a specified *dramatis personae*. The model person has a place and is in place. Speech activity through which the speaker signals that he or she is in the proper place is efficacious in expressing to others and in affirming to the speaker the identification of the speaker with the group. The key principles of action by which such membering is accomplished are (a) the use of the local, nonstandard dialect and (b) being copresent with others of one's own cohorts.

## EXPRESSING ONESELF IN NACIREMA CULTURE

Shortly after completing the Teamsterville fieldwork, I initiated a long-term study of mainstream American culture. *American culture* here refers to the system of symbols and premises that has been reported in such well-known studies as those of Varenne (1977) and Yankelovich (1982). Using Horace Miner's well-known term, I refer to this as Nacirema culture (*Nacirema* is *American* spelled backward).

One of the core themes that stimulated our group's studies of Nacirema culture is the idea of the deep structure of a Nacirema communal event. It was my intent to formulate the underlying principles of speaking operative in a speech event in which Nacirema interlocutors would experience a sense of "subjective social identity and community membership" (Eastman, 1985, p. 5). These principles can be expressed as follows: (a) Every individual in the event should be given a period of time to say to the group whatever it is that is of concern to the individual, and (b) it is the responsibility of all individuals to be attentive to what each other individual expressed during his or her turn to talk.

In an unpublished study conducted in 1975, Mary Jo Rudd and I investigated rules for speaking in middle-class families in a community in Southern California. We observed and listened intently to tape recordings of Nacirema conversation at family "dinner time," a speech event in which the participants relentlessly insisted that all family members be allowed a turn at talk—because each person "has something to contribute." We found that the people we observed believed strongly that one's place in the family, defined by a role, such as "father," should not be a basis for interrupting or curtailing the speech of others because each person's utterance is believed to be uniquely valuable. For these Nacirema individuals, speech is a way to express one's psychological uniqueness, to acknowledge the uniqueness of others, and to bridge the gap between one's own and another's uniqueness; it is a means by which family members, for example, can manifest their equality and demonstrate that they pay little heed to differences in status—practices and beliefs that would puzzle and offend a proper Teamsterviller.

In Seattle, Washington, five years later, Tamar Katriel and I listened to many Nacirema tell their life stories—stories in which great moral weight was placed upon interpersonal "relationships." Each party was not only free, but also felt a sense of pressure, to express and celebrate her or his uniqueness and to explore and understand the other's distinctive individuality. This was manifested most sharply in what we came to call the "communication ritual," a structured sequence of communicative acts in which intimate partners take turns disclosing difficulties experienced with self and relationship. In the ideal version of the ritual, both interlocutors disclose and listen intently to the disclosures of the other. If both parties are close (disclosive), supportive (of the other's "real self"), and flexible (willing to change their view of self or other in the face of interpersonal "feedback"), then the ideal is further realized.

"Dinner time" and the "communication ritual" are speech events whose rule structure and associated beliefs illustrate what I had proposed as the deep structure of a Nacirema speech event in which individuals experienced a sense of social identification through the use of language. Of course, each of these is an intimate, not a communal, event, but this intimate ideal is being pressed as the ideal for other, more communal, relationships; that is, it is being transferred to, or imposed upon, the public domain (see Sennett, 1978). The transference of this deep structure from the intimate to the public domain is revealed in an application of the structure to a prominent Nacirema public scene, the television talk show *Donahue*, hosted by Phil Donahue.

Katriel and Philipsen (1981) introduced the idea that *Donahue* is a public ritual that expresses and affirms core North American concepts and values pertaining to personhood, society, and communication. It is a widely-viewed, and widely-understood, enactment of an episodic sequence that is meaningful to bearers of Nacirema culture.

It displays an episodic sequence by which interlocutors can experience a sense of subjective identity and community membership, a sense that can be vicariously experienced by those viewers who are code bearers.

Carbaugh (1984, 1987) has presented a detailed analysis and interpretation of the culture displayed on *Donahue*. One part of that culture is a system of communication rules, invoked on the show, which he articulates as follows:

- *Rule 1:* In the conversations of *Donahue*, (a) the presentation of "self" is the preferred communication activity, and (b) statements of personal opinions count as proper "self" presentations.
- *Rule 2:* Interlocutors must grant speakers the moral "right" to present "self" through opinions.
- *Rule 3:* The presentation of "self" through opinions should be "respected," that is, tolerated as a rightful expression.
- *Rule 4:* Asserting standards that are explicitly transindividual, or societal, is dispreferred since such assertions are heard (a) to constrain the preferred presentations of "self" unduly, (b) to infringe upon the "rights" of others, and (c) to violate the code of proper respect.

These rules for self-presentation on *Donahue* reflect important features of the culture displayed on that show. One is an emphasis on the existential and moral standing of the "self" as a distinctive, autonomous, and powerful but delicate entity. A second is the importance placed on attentiveness to the distinctiveness of others. A third is the insistence that "society" not be allowed to constrain "self," as reflected in Rule 4, which proscribes the use of transindividual standards for inhibiting or evaluating individual expression. To speculate on how Carbaugh's findings apply to the present concern, I propose that when a Nacirema participates in a speech event in which she or he hears self and others following these rules, that is a point at which membering is experienced.

The *Donahue* rule structure, like the rule structure of family dinner time and of the communication ritual, is a particular expression of the more general, underlying deep structure, posited above, for Nacirema speech events in which the communal function is performed. One contribution of Carbaugh's study is to show this culture at work in a public speech event that is widely experienced as intelligible and consequential in American society.

In Nacirema culture, the model person is a unique *self* whose uniqueness is expressed and affirmed in and through "communication" (close, supportive, flexible speech) with others. "Communication," as a culturally defined way of speaking, constitutes a dialogic relationship in which the self not only is expressed but is actively engaged in the other's experience of the speaker and of a distinctive other. The ideal social relationship is one constituted by dialogic commitments rather than one defined by a set of transpersonal, historically determined expectations. To experience a sense of shared identity, from the standpoint of this code, requires speech events in which these central values and beliefs about persons, social relationships, and communication are articulated and affirmed. Such events are those in which the individuals experience themselves and others expressing their distinctive selves, and in which, they experience themselves and others aggressively attending to the distinctiveness of others' selves.

## ISRAELI DUGRI SPEECH

In her ethnographic study of Israeli ways of speaking, Katriel (1983, 1986) has systematically described and interpreted the cultural meanings of *dugri* speech, translated from the Hebrew as straight or direct talk. She specifies its cultural meanings in terms of five dimensions—as sincere, assertive, natural, solidary, and matter-of-fact speech. It involves speech acts in which one person confronts another in such a way as to display images of honesty, in the sense of being true to one's feelings; of assertiveness, in the sense of strength or determination to express a view that is unpalatable to the hearer; of naturalness, in the sense of spontaneous, simple, unadorned speech; of solidarity, in the sense of suspending roles and rules in the creation of egalitarian, undifferentiated, individuating relations; and matter-of-factness or antistyle, in the sense of a preference for deeds over words.

Dugri is a way of speaking intimately bound up with the subculture of the Sabras, native-born Israelis of Jewish heritage, mainly of European descent. "To speak dugri," as one of Katriel's informants put it, "is to act like a Sabra." The Sabra represents the construction, in Israel, of a new Jew who had "come to the Land of Israel to build and be both personally and communally rebuilt in it" (Katriel, 1986,

p. 17). Sabras, the children of pioneers settling in a new Jewish state, developed a unique culture that features a rejection of the genteel European culture from which they were descended and, in particular, of the European Jews' way of relating to the larger European society, a way characterized by defensiveness, restrictiveness, and passivity as an adaptive mechanism.

It is in the spirit of the Sabra cultural agenda that the dugri way of speaking can be understood as communal speech. That agenda consists of the building, in Israel, of a new Jewish identity as well as a new Jewish society that can stand strong in opposition to external forces of various kinds, including externally imposed standards of evaluation and conduct. The new Jew would be productive in labor and would strive to create a just and egalitarian society. Dugri speech, which consists of one person speaking to another in such a way as to suspend the usual requirements of politeness and decorum associated with their role relationship, enacts this cultural agenda symbolically. Its sincerity, in speaking from the heart, reveals the speaker in his or her fundamental humanness; its assertiveness enacts a commitment to shake off the stance of passivity; its naturalness flaunts convention and artifice; its solidariness thematizes the ideal of building a society; and its matter-of-factness underlines the desire to take people, things, and conditions as they are.

Where it is enacted, talking dugri is a powerful way for Sabras to experience a subjective sense of shared identity and community membership. It is in such moments that speaker and listener can project and reaffirm their identity as Sabras.

Images of personhood, society, and communication are expressed in the cultural meanings of dugri speech. Society is elevated in dugri to a position of paramount importance, a position that necessarily, even happily, is superior to the individual person. The individual is stripped of any pretension to preciousness and fragility, as in the Nacirema code, but is, like the Nacirema person, characterized in terms of equality with and differentiation from others. But the Sabra person is not, like the Nacirema person, defended or protected from the restraining forces of society—rather, the Sabra's rationale for living is, to a great degree, his or her potential for serving and, in and through his or her social life, constituting the new Israeli society. Dugri speech symbolizes how individuals can, ideally, be linked together in social ties: The speaker, in flaunting the conventions associated with the old society, in suspending the conventional procedures for treating individuals with the respect for which the old code qualified them by virtue of their achieved or ascribed status, "disassociates himself from a given structural relationship or social paradigm, while at the same time asserting a deeper affiliation with a more basic and encompassing one" (Katriel, 1986, p. 66).

## COMMUNAL SPEECH IN AN APPALACHIAN COMMUNITY

The affirmation and construction of communal ties is an important function of speech in the Appalachian community of Bond, Kentucky, studied by George B. Ray (1983, 1987). On the basis of ethnographic participant observation for a period of two years, Ray described in detail the structure of the community's prominent speech situations and speech events, with an eye to interpreting the means and meanings of speech to residents of Bond. The practice of "huddling," the speech situations of "porch talk" and "supper," and the community ideals of egalitarianism and respect all contribute to a cultural pattern of speaking that has specific implications for the communal function of speech.

One of the most striking features of the community's social life is the expressed desire "to experience life with others" (Ray, 1983, p. 167). To experience life with others, for a member of the Bond speech community, requires people (a) to be together in the same scene and (b) to signal to others that one is "all right." The signaling of one's own and the experiencing of others' being "all right" is effected through many tactics and realized in many different speech events.

"Huddling" in Bond suggests a key to understanding communal speech there. Huddling means that people get together to talk in small public or private gatherings. Huddling groups consist of interlocutors who are well known to each other, such as close friends or family, but are not necessarily segregated as to age or gender. The basic rules of huddling are that no one should speak too much, no one should do anything to upset others, one should appear reserved and modest, and one should not exaggerate. Perhaps the fundamental rule of huddling is that each participant give her- or himself up to the experience of simply "passing the time" with others, with no instrumental agenda or purpose. The ideal of huddling is realized to the extent that each participant makes of the event no more and no less than phatic communion.

The enactment of huddling and of "passing the time" is illustrated in several different speech situations, including "porch talk" and family "supper." In the former, there is an implicit episodic sequence of four steps: (a) Participants inquire about each other's overall condition ("You all right today?"), (b) there is an extended period of general conversation about topics of local interest (neighbors, weather, crops), (c) leave-taking is negotiated, and (d) leaving is consummated. The sequence provides for unlimited time to be together and is begun with an inquiry into the well-being of each participant, thus satisfying the key criteria for a huddling event in Chestnut Flat.

Family supper is an event in which the family is together. It is not necessary that serious discussion takes place. Although there is not, in Bond, evidence for the Nacirema concern that every person takes a turn at talk, there is a concern, particularly on the part of parents, that everyone be together so that the parents can reassure themselves that everyone is "all right." This is manifested in (a) presence at the meal time, (b) the general physical appearance of the child, and (c) whether or not the child eats the usual portion of food. As one of Ray's (1983) adult informants said about going to the parents' home to have supper with them:

> I think when we go there [home] you don't have to say a lot. If you see each other, you know if they are well, if they are sick or have a cold. Mom always said, "You look so thin. Have you been sick?" It doesn't take long. Just to look at you and make sure you are all right. It doesn't matter if you stay long or not. It's just the effect to be there and see them. (p. 171)

The Bond code of persons emphasizes the essential equality of persons as well as the importance of "respect" for the feelings and well-being of others. Particular, known individuals are vitally important to social life because they are the personnel for one of the community's fundamentally important social processes, huddling, and thus important communication processes are devoted primarily to discovering and verifying that one's present, and potentially future, interlocutors are "all right." In moments of sociation in which one experiences life with others, for its own sake, without the intrusion of other mental, emotional, or linguistic tasks, the residents of Bond enact a fundamentally communal sequence of actions. Thus it is in such moments that one experiences a subjective sense of social identity and community membership. For the individual in Bond, then, the strategy for performing the communal function consists of the following injunctions: (a) Spend time in the presence of other known interlocutors; (b) during such time spent together, devote oneself primarily to the "task" of being together without imposing any purpose that would compete with the phatic one; (c) engage in those acts that would signal attentiveness to the well-being of others and that would signal one's own well-being; and (d) modulate one's own linguistic action (safe topics, no exaggeration, appear reserved) so as to avoid engaging in any activity that would disturb the equanimity of the interlocutors, and thus of the occasion.

## CONCLUSION

This survey of ways of speaking in four cultures has revealed four culturally different ways of using speech so as to experience a subjective sense of social identity and community membership. These ways of speaking differ in terms of what they implicate about cultural views of persons, society, and speech, and these views are linked to culture-specific episodic sequences for performing the communal function of speech.

Teamsterville culture defines the person as a social persona, in terms of an achieved or ascribed social identity. Society in this culture is the arrangement of persons in hierarchical and socially segmented relationships. Speech that reveals and reinforces the speaker's place in the social structure is efficacious, in Teamsterville culture, for performing the communal function.

In Nacirema culture the differentiated, unique self is of intrinsic value. Selves can be joined together in appropriate social relations by using speech that unites essentially disparate selves in interpersonal relationships. Bearers of this culture can experience themselves as social beings in those moments in which interlocutors achieve a sense of reciprocal disclosure of self and attentiveness to the disclosures of others.

Israeli Sabra culture emphasizes the importance of individual acts that reject the inherited culture of class relations and domination and that affirm the equality of persons in a newly created society. The self in such a culture is viewed as strong enough to create a strong society, in concert with other selves, and as something that is strong enough to be suppressed, ignored, or checked in the service of the new society. Society is sufficiently important and sufficiently delicate that it requires selves who will, through their assertive, self-effacing actions, act so as to strengthen the society against any actual or potential threats. A bearer of this culture experiences a subjective sense of social identity precisely in those moments of symbolic affirmation of the social over the personal good.

In Bond the individual self is most fully alive in the company of others who are attentive to the person's well-being. Social experiences are most satisfying that bring interlocutors together for the experience of being in the company of fellows who wish one well. The individual is most likely to experience him- or herself as socially linked with others in those moments in which self and others have given up themselves to a period of extended copresence, without the intrusion of an instrumental agenda and with framing acts of attentiveness to the well-being of individuals present and the equanimity of the group.

These studies suggest that each of the four cultures reviewed here includes culture-specific episodic sequences for experiencing a subjective sense of social identity and community membership. This finding is consistent with the thesis advanced by Philipsen (1987) that each culture provides a distinctive way to perform the communal function. The implication of this is that although Ong's (1982) thesis that speech unites humans into groups is supported by the data reviewed here, Ong's thesis is seriously qualified in the light of cross-cultural data that suggest that *how* speech performs the communal function is subject to considerable cultural variation.

# REFERENCES

Carbaugh, D. (1984). *On persons, speech, and culture: Codes of "self," "society," and "communication" on Donahue*. Unpublished doctoral dissertation, University of Washington.

Carbaugh, D. (1987). Communication rules in Donahue discourse. *Research on Language and Social Interaction, 21*, 31–61.

Eastman, C. (1985). Establishing social identity through language use. *Journal of Language and Social Psychology, 4*, 1–20.

Hymes, D. (1962). The ethnography of speaking. In T. Gladwin & W. Sturtevant

(Eds.), *Anthropology and human behavior* (pp. 13–53). Washington, DC: Anthropological Society of Washington.

Hymes, D. (1972). Models of the interaction of language and social life. In J. Gumperz & D. Hymes (Eds.), *Directions in sociolinguistics: The ethnography of communication* (pp. 35–71). New York: Holt, Rinehart & Winston.

Hymes, D. (1974). Ways of speaking. In R. Bauman & J. Sherzer (Eds.), *Explorations in the ethnography of speaking* (pp. 433–451). Cambridge: Cambridge University Press.

Katriel, T. (1983). *Towards a conceptualization of ways of speaking: The case of Israeli "Dugri" speech*. Unpublished doctoral dissertation, University of Washington.

Katriel, T. (1986). *Talking straight: Dugri speech in Israeli Sabra culture*. Cambridge: Cambridge University Press.

Katriel, T., & Philipsen G. (1981). What we need is communication: "Communication" as a cultural category in some American speech. *Communication Monographs, 48*, 301–317.

Ong, W. (1982). *Orality and literacy: The technologizing of the word*. London: Methuen.

Philipsen, G. (1972). *Communication in Teamsterville: A sociolinguistic study of speech behavior in an urban neighborhood*. Unpublished doctoral dissertation, Northwestern University.

Philipsen, G. (1975). Speaking "like a man" in Teamsterville: Culture patterns of role enactment in an urban neighborhood. *Quarterly Journal of Speech, 61*, 13–22.

Philipsen, G. (1976). Places for speaking in Teamsterville. *Quarterly Journal of Speech, 62*, 15–25.

Philipsen, G. (1986). Mayor Daley's council speech: A cultural analysis. *Quarterly Journal of Speech, 72*, 247–260.

Philipsen, G. (1987). The prospect for cultural communication. In D. Kincaid (Ed.), *Communication theory: Eastern and Western perspectives* (pp. 245–254). New York: Academic Press.

Ray, G. (1983). *An ethnography of speaking in an Appalachian community*. Unpublished doctoral dissertation, University of Washington.

Ray, G. (1987). An ethnography of nonverbal communication in an Appalachian community. *Research on Language and Social Interaction, 21*, 171–188.

Sennett, R. (1978). *The fall of public man*. New York: Random House.

Varenne, H. (1977). *Americans together: Structured diversity in a midwestern town*. New York: Teachers College Press.

Yankelovich, D. (1982). *New rules: Searching for self-fulfillment in a world turned upside down*. New York: Random House.

# 5

## Fifty Terms for Talk
### A Cross-Cultural Study

DONAL CARBAUGH ● University of Massachusetts, Amherst

*This chapter examines cultural terms for talk in different cultural communities and conducts a cross-cultural analysis of their levels of application and message functions. The findings suggest that indigenous labels for speaking (a) identify speech at three distinctive levels, as acts, events, and styles, and (b) are used to convey multiple levels of meanings. A structural framework that organizes the levels and meanings is proposed, with a special application to intercultural communication.*

In the past 25 years, a large fund of ethnographic studies (more than 200) about speaking has developed (Philipsen & Carbaugh, 1986). Several critics have commented on the lack of comparative studies among them (Bloch, 1976; Leach, 1976; Watson-Gegeo, 1976). These published studies and the ethnographic perspective that guides them provide a rich empirical base for such comparative study, especially since comparative study was one of the fundamental impulses that gave birth to the ethnography of communication. As Hymes put it in 1962, "Why undertake such [ethnographic] work? . . . so that systematic descriptions can give rise to a comparative study . . . a 'comparative speaking' beside comparative religion, comparative law, and the like" (p. 102). While there are few comparative studies of speaking that have heeded Hymes's early call (but see Braithwaite, 1981; Keenan, 1976; Rosaldo, 1982), there is now an ample empirical base upon which to conduct cross-cultural studies.

My purpose in this chapter is to analyze comparatively the phenomenon of cultural terms for talk as they occur in various systems of communication. The basic data of the study are ethnographic interpre-

AUTHOR'S NOTE: *An earlier version of this chapter was presented at the seminar on the Ethnography of Communication, Speech Communication Association, Chicago, 1986.*

tations of the words and the meanings that people from various cultural fields use to conceive of and evaluate speech. My most general goal is to discover the levels of enactments and the types of meanings that these words about speech suggest. I will pursue that goal through a cross-cultural comparative study.

The type of study conducted here follows others who have attempted to identify cultural variation across speech communities in order to develop conceptual frameworks for understanding specific features of communication performance. For example, Irvine (1979) examined how political meetings were conducted among Wolof (Senegal), Mursi (Ethiopia), and Ilongot (Philippines) in order to develop an "analytical framework of formality" in communicative events; Lein and Brenneis (1978) compared children's discourse of White Americans, Black Americans, and rural, Hindi-speaking Fiji resulting in a theory of "argument" that embraces cultural variability; Philips (1976) compared how Anglos and Native Americans sustained interaction in order to examine how talk is regulated; and Keenan (1976) used Malagasy and English speech patterns as a comparative test of Grice's maxims. These studies demonstrate how cultural resources of speaking, and ethnographic reports about them, can be pressed into the service of communication theory. Similarly, the present report compares various cultural resources in speaking, terms for talk, and proposes an analytic framework about such terms that has cross-cultural utility. Such comparative research is necessary both to test the generality of the specific local patterns of any one society and to develop theoretical frameworks that are sensitive to cultural variation. A consequence of such inquiry is a renewed perspective on various analytical models that may themselves be skewed by features of "Western cultures." As much has been suggested by Rosaldo's (1982) use of Searle's speech act theory, Keenan's (1976) use of Grice's "universal maxims," or Katriel's (1986) appropriation of Goffman's theory of face. The charge of the present study is somewhat different from these. Comparative study is used more to construct a cross-cultural theory of terms for talk, and less to critique extant theory, although lines of inquiry related to the latter are discussed.

Comparative research serves other important purposes, especially concerning intercultural communication. As is highlighted in the studies above, and will become clearer below, cultural conceptions of talk vary widely such that for some, like the Kuna, the Waiwai, the Yanomamo, the Yucatec, the Trio, some Black Americans, and the

Antiguans, events of coparticipation and simultaneous verbal performance are culturally identified and valued, while for others, as for
some North Americans, cultural terms identify and value verbal
genres guided by the basic rule: one speaker at a time. For some, like
the Fiji and the Ilongot, when social relations are strained, cultural
talk is preferred that treats strained relations very indirectly, while for
others, especially some North Americans, strained relations create
moments for "supportive communication" and "sharing" where "the
relationship" is discussed explicitly. For some, such as the Ilongot and
Israeli Sabra, cultural "talk" highlights a sense of the actor as a member in broad social and cultural groups. For others, like the Anglo-
American and Paliyan, cultural "talk" motivates a model for the actor
*as an individual*, over and against the broader social system.

Each of these cases provides important implications for understanding intercultural communication, particularly as it unveils deep moral
systems that guide what constitutes proper "talk" itself. In practice, it
is important for persons to understand that cultural models motivate
such speech performances, especially when miscommunication occurs, as when some persons violate others' expectations, for example,
by talking (or keeping silent) while others talk, by speaking indirectly
(or directly) about strained relations, or by invoking broad social
models (or personal ones) for communication conduct. Cultural
terms for talk and related cultural performances lead some persons in
one direction and others in another. What is suggested, then, as a
matter for both practice and theory, is an understanding of initial
moments of intercultural contact, less as the "reduction of uncertainty" and "anxiety" (Gudykunst, 1988), and more as an invocation
of various and deeply coded patterns for talking. A productive path
for developing a theory of intercultural communication is thus a sustained and intensive look at cultural terms for talk, to develop a
sensitivity to cultural variation in the bases for "talk" itself, especially
where these reveal deep differences, for what is coherent as talk and
what is proper to say.

After describing the criteria used for selecting the cases, I will (a)
introduce the main ethnographic cases used in the study, then sketch
the method used for the analysis, (b) present four levels of cultural
terms that reflect distinctive speech performances, (c) interpret the
general types of messages that are highly salient when people label
their speech, and (d) summarize the structural framework that organizes these cultural terms for talk, with special attention to intercul-

tural communication theory and practice. The most general goal is to explore several cultural practices through indigenous terms for talk in search of the basic principles that hold, generally, within and across the cases.

## ETHNOGRAPHIC CASES

### *Criteria for Selection*

Several ethnographic field studies were chosen to ground the report because each met three basic criteria: (a) Each case is a published ethnographic account of native conceptions about speaking, conducted explicitly within the ethnography of communication program of research (Hymes, 1972; Philipsen & Carbaugh, 1986); (b) each account includes some systematic description and interpretation of indigenous terms used to conceive of and evaluate speech; and (c) each account includes description of actional sequences and contexts to which the cultural terms refer. Thus the study is based upon published reports that use a general theoretical lens, focus it upon a general class of phenomena, including interpretations of both cultural terms about talk and the cultural performances so labeled. Thus the study explores not only the ideational domains of words about speech outside their actional contexts, but also their meanings and functions with reference to specific sociocultural scenes.

### *The Cases and Method*

The main data for the study consist of seven ethnographic cases (which represent eleven different societies). The first and perhaps exemplary case is of speech activity among Afro-American peasants of St. Vincent, British West Indies (Abrahams & Bauman, 1971). The second case is more recent and thorough, exploring the ways of speaking among the San Blas Kuna of Panama (Sherzer, 1983). The third case is itself a comparative study of "ceremonial dialogues" in six South American societies (Urban, 1986). The fourth is of the speech acts and oratory of the Ilongot of the northern Philippines (Rosaldo, 1973, 1982). The fifth explores the various verbal performances of the Hindi-speaking Indians of Bhatgao, Fiji (Brenneis, 1978, 1984). The sixth is a set of cases that describe an American system of speech through the words and phrases that label it

(Carbaugh, 1988; Katriel & Philipsen, 1981; Michaels, 1981). The last provides an extensive cultural study of "talking straight" among the Israeli Sabra (Katriel, 1986). Other cases are interspersed throughout this report, but these seven form the primary corpus for the present study.

I reviewed the above cases, recording cultural terms that identify an indigenous pattern of speech as well as the type of speech to which the terms referred. Following this procedure yielded ethnographic interpretations of 50 cultural terms for talk.[1] I asked: What cultural features are used to describe these 50 instances? Then, what analytic framework will account for this cultural variation? I constructed my response through a multi-implicational space (see Campbell, 1975) that mapped a kind of cultural-case by instance-of-term-for-talk by features-of-the-talk interaction for each datum—for example, Fiji, song challenge, an event of competitive battle, sung, between different religious groups, parties alternate turns, purpose is to demean and insult, and so on. I attempted to identify all key features for each instance.[2] I then constructed an analytic scheme, guided by the specialized Hymesian vocabulary, that could embrace the cultural diversity reported in the features, and that subsequently provided the organization for this report (around levels of enactments and types of messages). Following this procedure, I discovered a tremendous variation in cultural terms for talk, which were variously described by ethnographers, enacted by participants, and conceptualized at several distinctive levels, sometimes simultaneously. My task was to propose a heuristic framework that should be of use in future, similar investigations. I will begin by describing a complex interplay of cultural terms for talk as they apply to distinctive theoretical levels, then move on to discuss the salient types of messages within and across these levels.

## LEVELS OF CULTURAL TERMS FOR TALK

As I began reading about cultural terms for talk, seeking to order such cultural variety, I noticed that not all terms were operating on the same level. Some terms referred to things individuals do with words, others to moments of simultaneous speech and/or coparticipation, and still others to general cultural standards that were used to evaluate various moments of individual and/or collective verbal enactment. I was thus led to ask: On what levels are these terms operating?

What kinds of communication performances are being identified through cultural terms? Are these terms identified by ethnographers and laypersons alike?

There are at least three distinctive levels of use that characterize cultural terms for talk: terms that describe acts, terms that describe events, and terms that describe styles. The first two distinguish verbal performances fundamentally along a monologic-dialogic dimension. The last refers to a broader ordering of talk, itself consisting of a set of acts and events. All levels have been used in at least some cultural systems of communication, thus each occurs variously in studies of cultural terms for talk. While these three levels are of central concern to this report, there is a fourth functional level that is more peripherally related. I will discuss it after defining and illustrating the other three.

## The Act Level

Several cultural terms point to *individual performances of communication*.[3] For example, among the St. Vincentians, when a person's words are annoying, loud, aggressive, and self-assertive, they may be labeled "getting on rude" (Abrahams & Bauman, 1971, p. 765). This native label is one of "a folk taxonomy of speech acts" deemed indecorous, bad, or rude (p. 765). In this community, these types of acts motivate much talk about talk, resulting in a refined lexicon about verbal acts of individuals that are disapproved, less pleasing stylistically, and unruly. Conversely, those acts warranting approval are stylistically pleasing and decorous and are expressed through a much less refined semantic field. Thus there is a more refined lexicon for discussing unfavorable acts than there is for discussing the favorable. The St. Vincentians identify speech behavior as consisting of individual acts distinguished along "three sets of oppositions" (approved or sensible versus disapproved or nonsensible, elevated, controlled style versus a broken, less controlled style, and decorous versus indecorous) (Abrahams & Bauman, 1971, p. 765). Thus we are led to see and hear what a St. Vincent individual is doing when labeling speech; he or she is identifying individual speech acts made intelligible through "oppositions" within a native semantic field.

Others have analyzed words about words similarly. For instance, Sherzer (1983, p. 98) describes the Kuna's *chief's speak* (*summakke*) as a formal speech-making conducted by a chief when there are no other chiefs available for a ritual dialogue or when no (dialogic) chants are available on the topic of concern. Because this performance, identified by the Kuna as chief's speak, involves a monologue by only one speaker, it is an act. Brenneis (1978) describes how the Fiji term *parbachan* identifies that part of religious meetings when an individual gives a religious yet political speech. Bauman (1972) describes how the La Have Islanders identify "news" and "yarns" as artful acts where an individual discusses current events or "the supernatural," respectively. Recently, Wierzbicka (1985) had explored various native terms for acts of speech, and proposes a semantic metalanguage for their cross-cultural study. These reports discuss instances of speech conduct that are identified by natives, with each labeling monologic acts that an individual has done. On this level, cultural terms for speech refer to acts of speech that are talked about and performed by one person.

In each of these instances, a cultural term is being used to identify the verbal performance of an individual, be it a tuneful weep or religious speech. At this level, what an individual is doing with words is identified and culturally coded.

### The Event Level

A second level goes beyond individual acts, indicating a type of speech performance that requires two or more speakers. On this level, persons are labeling enactments that are episodes, events, or *coenactments of communication*.[4] Through this labeling, indigenous terms are used to identify interactive and dialogic accomplishments. For example, Sherzer (1983) has described the Kuna *chanting* as follows:

> Chanting begins in the form of a ritualized dialogue between two "chiefs," in the presence of and for the benefit of the audience. The two "chiefs" straddle their hammocks in what the Kuna call the *nai* (hanging position), their feet barely touching the ground. For the entire duration of the chanting their arms are fixed at their sides; they stare into space and do not change their facial expressions. The "chief" designated to chant begins in a soft voice. After each verse . . . the second "chief," the *apinsuet* (responding chief), replies with a chanted *teki* (thus, it is so, indeed) . . . or *eye* (yes). (pp. 73–74)

Urban (1986) has described similar "ceremonial dialogues" in six South American societies. Other examples include contrapuntal conversations in Antigua (Reisman, 1975), interactive narratives in Yucatec, Maya (Burns, 1980), or a ritualized form of "communication" among some Americans (Katriel & Philipsen, 1981). Interlocutors identify each as a cocreation among multiple persons without which the event would lose force and integrity as a culturally identifiable form. These cultural terms identify forms of communication requiring coparticipation, sometimes in front of an audience. In each case, multiple speakers are necessary if the event is to be enacted efficaciously. These few examples help demonstrate a second level of cultural categories about speech, that is, cultural terms about coenactments of communication.[5]

### The Style Level

*Style* here refers to a way of organizing native labels for alternative ways of speaking and the rules for selecting them (Ervin-Tripp, 1972).[6] Style becomes important in the study of cultural terms because it provides a sense of spoken enactment (act or event) as a selection of one rather than others. So, for example, the St. Vincentians use two phrases, *talking sense* and *talking nonsense*, to identify two prominent ways of speaking, with specific acts of "decorous and deferential language" instantiating the former while "being hesitant or indecorous . . . or being totally out of control" gives voice to the latter (Abrahams & Bauman, 1971, pp. 763–764). Similar dynamics appear among Fiji Indians, where *sweet talk* often employs a mode of indirectness in religious and political speeches (acts of *parbachan*) and *jungle talk* employs more direct, combative events such as those in *song challenges* (Brenneis, 1978). Among the Ilongot, acts and events deemed *crooked* are distinguished generally from those deemed *straight* (Rosaldo, 1973). Among the Cibecue Apache, three cultural terms distinguish three general styles of speaking, each made up of identifiable acts and events—*ordinary talk, prayer,* and *stories* (Basso, 1984). And among the Malagasy, a simple everyday style consisting of acts and events is distinguished from acts and events more ceremonial, for example, *kibary* and *rasaka* (Keenan, 1975; compare Sherzer, 1983, pp. 185–222).

These terms identify speech at a different level, as general ways of speaking, each consisting of a set of acts and perhaps events and scenes, thus labeling determinate varieties of communication. Below I will sketch some of the specific messages about communication that are signaled variously through these varieties—message of mode, structure, tone, and force of agency. The major point here is simply that persons use terms for talk to identify a third level of communication, *native labels about ways of speaking*, for example, the act of *talking trupidness* is an instance of the style of *talking nonsense* (Abrahams & Bauman, 1971). These are elements of style (a general organization of verbal means and selections therefrom), itself including but raising distinctive concerns from those of acts (an organization of individual acts, and outcomes) and events (an organization of coenactments). The levels need to be understood as such.

### The Functional Level

A fourth level, the functional shaping of speech, is frequently discussed in these studies, but is somewhat peripheral to the present concerns since it addresses an indirect outcome of cultural terms for talk, rather than a native organization of its means. Several ethnographers have identified social outcomes of acts, events, and styles that participants have labeled. For example, Urban (1986) describes native labels about "ceremonial dialogues" throughout South America. His finding is that speech so labeled serves a metacommunicative function, that is, the labeling identified for participants a "model for" conduct between those of "maximal social distance;" it educates participants to a kind of "dialogue" that can manage conflict. Thus Urban's analysis moves from native labels about speech, through the ceremonial performance of cyclical events, to what the events accomplish for participants. It is the last element of the performance that highlights a metacommunicative function (i.e., the identification and enactment of the event provides a model for its performance). Urban (1986) thus demonstrates how indigenous labels for speech identify powerful symbolic events in speech, in this case ceremonial forms, that communicate *indirectly* about speech as a model for social interaction. Similarly, any verbal and/or symbolic conduct could be interpreted to some degree as, to use Geertz's (1973) phrase, "saying something," with messages speaking at one level directly about acts, events, and/or styles, and at another more indirectly about common values, rules of conduct, and/or judgments of legitimacy.

The functional claim that cultural terms for talk accomplish various sociocultural ends, indirectly and reflexively, must be distinguished from the claim about explicit cultural terms for communicative acts, events, and styles. The former responds to the question, What are the culturally identified verbal actions *doing*? The latter responds to a very particular kind of doing through the more fundamental question, What verbal actions are identified, and what does the act of identification indicate? Focusing upon cultural categories about speech acts, events, and styles makes the indigenous shaping of communication itself the topic of explicit concern. Identifying such social and cultural shapes is, of course, contingent upon the particular forms given speaking by natives. In short, the former question yields claims about the more indirect outcomes *of* speech, outcomes that are sometimes culturally identified; the latter, an organization *in* speech of its native means. That there are apologies and how they are used are related but distinctive concerns.

The distinction I am drawing here between what might be called direct lexical shaping and indirect functional shaping of speech can be further sharpened with two examples. First, consider someone's saying, "I've got to be honest with you." As a disclaimer, it explicitly labels *in* speech a subsequent act as an "honest" one, invoking a set of expectations about the kind of verbal performance(s) to follow (Carbaugh, 1988). Now consider the account, "At least she was honest!" It accomplishes a more indirect outcome *of* speech, identifying a previous act as such so as to praise its speaker, to promote another's face. Where a functional analysis of these messages holds some promise, especially with regard to cultural messages about the message, of special concern here are natives' explicit references to acts, events, and styles of communication. Rather than asking how the cultural category of "honest" speech is being used, I am asking, What is the category of speech deemed "honest"? Both the functions of speech and categories in speech (about speech) are similar in their social and interactive shaping of communication, but both differ in the degree to which the reference to communication is made relatively *directly in speech*, as with cultural categories about speech, or is *indirectly of speech*, as with the metacommunication of ceremonial dialogues or the interactive forces of "preindexes" (see Beach & Dunning, 1982). The main focus of this report is on the shaping of speech directly as it is labeled by natives, rather than its indirect shaping as the result of its social performance.[7]

In sum, ethnographic studies of cultural terms for talk identify verbal performances at four levels: (a) the level of act, cultural labels about individual acts of communication; (b) the level of event, cultural labels about coenactments of communication; (c) the level of style, cultural labels about general ways of speaking and selections therefrom; and (d) the functional shaping of speech, the various outcomes of identified speech (e.g., its social uses or value).

By distinguishing these levels, we can understand better both (a) native terms used directly to identify communication, as performances of acts, events, and/or styles, and (b) how such means of speech are used more indirectly by natives (e.g., as in providing models for social conduct).

## SALIENT MESSAGES IN CULTURAL TERMS FOR TALK

As I examined cultural terms for talk, I noticed several cultural features were recurring across at least some of the cases. Thus I asked, What features of communication are being discussed with cultural terms for talk? In the end, I discovered that the cultural terms were being used by natives not only to refer to aspects of their talk itself, but further to refer to social relations and persons. As persons' cultural communication is talked about there are various types of messages conveyed. In what follows, I have tried to distill the general types of messages that get codified as natives label their communicative acts, events, and styles. Of main concern are the natural types of messages codified in indigenous terms like *tuydek, getting on rude, chanting, being honest,* and *sweet talk.*

The messages discussed here are of three general types: messages about communication itself, messages about sociality, and messages about personhood. These messages may be conveyed more literally, as are those about communication, or relatively metaphorically, as are those about sociality and personhood. As cultural terms for talk are used, persons may convey various messages simultaneously. Cultural terms for talk are multivocal, polysemic, and coherent. The most *salient* messages codified in cultural categories about speech are (a) messages about communication itself, (b) messages about sociality, social relations, and institutions, and (c) messages about personhood. The first message is getting done more directly (talk about talk is referring literally to aspects of the talk itself); the second and third messages may be getting done more indirectly (talk about talk is referring to present social relations and models of personhood).[8]

The general interrelation of the three message types is carefully analyzed by Rosaldo (1982), who argues that for laypersons and analysts alike, ways of conceiving language are intimately linked to models of human agency and personhood. As much is also concluded by Sherzer (1983, p. 210). How can we classify the salient messages in cultural terms for talk? What are speakers telling each other as they use these terms?

### Messages About Communication

It is no surprise that as speakers talk about their talk they talk about communication. One might ask, however, what aspects of communication gets talked about when cultural terms for talk are used. There are four messages, each of which is highly salient, but nonessential, when talk is identified culturally.[9]

One type of message concerns the *mode*, or the prevailing manner for the enactment. As persons identify and define streams of speech, they attend to its manner as direct or indirect. Toward the direct end of the continuum are the Israeli style of *dugri* (Katriel, 1986), the Fiji style of *straight speech* (Brenneis, 1978), and an American act and event of *being honest* (Carbaugh, 1988). Toward the more indirect end are the Kaluli style of *hard talk* (Feld & Schieffelin, 1981) and the Fiji style of *sweet speech* (Brenneis, 1978). Katriel (1986) has suggested that this mode may be further interpreted through the aspects of literalness, simplicity, assertiveness, and immediacy. What these studies and ways of speaking suggest is this: A mode of directness/indirectness is present in communication, codified in native terms, and forms one salient dimension along which native terms for talk are distinguished.

Identifying the mode of cultural terms for talk can be of value within, as well as across, cases. For example, Fijians identify *parbachan* as an act of sweet talk that is ostensibly a religious speech, but by using "coy reference" and indefinite pronouns the speaker indirectly broadcasts wrongdoings of particular others in order to provoke interest and attract third parties as mediators (Brenneis, 1978). The allusive mode displays standards to persons for communal membership and protects the speaker from retribution, since "he does not make direct accusations" (Brenneis, 1978, p. 165). This mode of *parbachan* contrasts sharply with the Fiji *song challenges*, in which social groups confront each other directly, through threats and insults, in order to do competitive battle. Through familiar forms of address (such as nicknames) and singular second-person pronouns, others are demeaned and insulted. In mode, the direct song challenge is like the American *being honest*, in which intents and purposes are spoken unencumberedly, or the Israeli dugri, in which literalness and sincerity are overriding concerns. Conversely, the indirect parbachan is more like the Ilongot *crooked language*, which is "rich in art and wit" (Rosaldo, 1973, p. 193). Thus the mode can serve within cases to distinguish one cultural moment from another, as well as across cases, to compare and contrast cultural modes of expressions.

A second message in cultural terms for talk concerns *the relative degree of structuring of the code*. Is the cultural talk that is lexicalized subject to extra rules and conventions? At the less structured end we have a more flexible and elaborate ordering of acts, such as "conversation" in "everyday Kuna," which involves "more informal, casual, and spontaneous verbal interactions" (Sherzer, 1983, p. 42). Similarly, the cultural terms *griping* among the Israelis (Katriel, 1985), *sharing* among Americans (Carbaugh, 1988), or *chat* among the Wolof (Irvine, 1979) refer to speech behavior that is more flexibly structured. The rules for these routines enable fluid exchanges among many participants. At the other end are more fixed kinds of talk, where participation is more restricted—in who should speak, how they should gesture and posture, what should be said, and how—such as the ceremonial dialogues in South America (Urban, 1986), the traditional Ilongot "meeting" (Rosaldo, 1973, pp. 204–205), and the "discussions" and "meetings" of the Wolof (Irvine, 1979).

In American English, virtually any person can be said to "share," so long as he or she has "feelings" or "thoughts" to express, and can do so in a way that supports those present and speaks to a purpose common to those present. Thus these few rules for the routine enable many kinds of contributions from anyone who happens to be present. The term thus refers to a more flexible communication event in which anyone may participate, in almost any way (Carbaugh, 1988). Perhaps the best demonstration of the fixed and restricted structuring of speech is the *Kantule language* of the Kuna (Sherzer, 1983). This type of speaking is especially difficult for the uninitiated to understand and is a central part of a girl's puberty rites. The pattern of speaking takes years to learn through an apprenticeship and involves a specialized vocabulary and parallel structures of grammar and meaning. The performance of Kantule language is usually shouted and accompanied by the playing of a special flute. The performance itself occurs well into a multiday festival. According to Sherzer (1983), this way of speaking is

> the most immutable of all Kuna ritual discourse. It is repeated identically, including every single phoneme and morpheme, each time it is performed. The extremely realistic *ikar* [way of speaking, verbal text] precisely reflects the set of events in which it plays a central, organizing, and directive role. It describes in minute detail every aspect of the puberty rites and associated activities and festivities, from the preparation of the participants to the cutting of the young girl's hair to the eating of a special meal and drinking of the *inna* [a fermented drink which is made and consumed during the festival]. (pp. 144–145)

Thus as persons invoke cultural terms for talk, a salient message is the degree of structuring of the code. To what degree is this kind of talk restricted to classes of participants? To what degree is it conducted on special occasions, in particular places? To what degree is it conducted for very specific purposes? To what degree does it use a specialized vocabulary, grammatical structure, or semantic domain(s)? These are the kinds of questions sometimes responded to when persons use their cultural terms for talk. These specific aspects of messages—or, more precisely, these messages in cultural terms about the structuring of kinds of speaking—could be summarized along dimensions as relatively *fixed or flexible* (Sherzer, 1983), and as relatively *elaborated or restricted* (Bernstein, 1972). In either case, native terms for talk tend to codify messages about the degree of structuring of speech, indicating whether a kind of talk is more fixed and restricted or more flexible and elaborate.

A third message in cultural terms for talk refers to the *tone*, the emotional pitch, feeling, or key, appropriate to the act, event, or style. Take, for example, the St. Vincent case. Two general styles of communication are talked about, *talking sweet* and *talking broad* (Abrahams & Bauman, 1971). When speech is identified as sweet or ruly, part of what is referred to, especially in "tea meetings," is a climate of *control* over the verbal performance, so that acts occur in appropriate sequence and one's message content is proper. When speech is identified as broad or unruly, as some "pit boys" rancor during "tea meetings," it is identified as *less controlled*, thus less aligned with the traditional climate of the meetings. A second example of differing tones is the distinction drawn in American communication between "giving a lecture" and "giving a talk" (Wierzbicka, 1985). Both sets of labels draw attention to kinds of speaking that may be very similar in mode and structure but differ in tone, with the former phrase marking a *more formal* kind of talk and the latter a *less formal*. One might also overlay another dimension of tone onto these, highlighting the former as more *serious* and the latter as more *playful*.

Aspects of structuring of communication codes and the emotional pitch of social settings have been discussed as elements of formality in communicative events (Irvine, 1979). I separate them here as degrees of structuring, from fixed to flexible, or restricted to elaborate, and tone, from formal to informal and perhaps serious to playful, in order to classify distinctions speakers have made between highly structured formal events (e.g., "ceremonial dialogues") and highly structured informal events (e.g., "verbal duels"; see Garner, 1983), less structured formal events (e.g., the "tea meeting"; Abrahams & Bauman, 1971) and less structured informal events (e.g., "sharing" and contrapuntal "conversations"; Reisman, 1975).

The last message I will discuss is the *efficaciousness of communication as an action* (see Philipsen, 1986). The question addressed here is this: Is this culturally identified act, event, or style of speech a more or less substantial form of action? Some Americans identify talk as "chitchat" or insubstantial, and "communication" (Katriel & Philipsen, 1981) and "being honest" as more substantial. The first identifies accomplishments that are heard to be relatively unimportant, such as passing time, while the last two are heard as culturally valued models of being, for example, "an individual" and "self," or bonding, in "relationship." Similar to "communication" in efficaciousness, if different in sociocultural accomplishment, is the Burundi *ubgenge* (Albert, 1972). This term for talk identifies a valued, necessary, and substantial way to speak in order to manipulate a hierarchical social order if one is to receive requisite goods and services. Conversely, in at least one Black American community, *talking shit* is considered relatively insubstantial as an action (Bell, 1983), as is *telling story*, which "lacks veracity" among St. Vincentians (Abrahams & Bauman, 1971), or *griping* among Israelis (Katriel, 1985). In these cases, as in the American chitchat, the forms of speaking are identified so as to mark relatively insubstantial moments of social action.

In at least two cases, talk is the subject of sets of proverbs or myths, where the efficaciousness of speaking becomes a central theme. Seitel

(1974) describes how specific Haya "proverbs for speech"—a genre of spoken texts that the Haya identify as talk about itself—help the Haya identify which acts of speech are substantial and which are not. Urban (1984) describes a similar dynamic of a Shokleng myth, identified as a "speech about speech," where the key theme is the efficaciousness of speech as an action. Thus as speech is identified by indigenous terms *and tropes*, one possible message conveyed is its relative status as a social action, marking some sayings as more substantial and/or efficacious than others.

### Messages About Sociality

As persons use cultural terms for talk, they may also be talking indirectly about their society, their relations among each other, and the institutions in which they find themselves and through which they speak (see Briggs, 1984; Rosaldo, 1982). Take, for example, the St. Vincentian act of *making commess* (Abrahams & Bauman, 1971, p. 767). When acts are identified as *making commess*, a message is conveyed that says something like: the person is talking about him- or herself and his or her own problems and is not of any harm to you or I or our social life. This act contrasts with *making melee,* one type of making commess. When a person's acts are identified as making melee, the message is that he or she is making a kind of speech about others and their relations (what one might call gossip); that kind of speech act stirs up trouble and causes harm. It is no longer a personal identity at stake, but public reputations. As St. Vincentians so label their talk, they assess their *social relations* as stable to disrupted and their *social institutions*, where different norms carve out some identities for management over others, be it the speaker's dignity or others' honor.[10]

Consider another example, the song challenges of the Fiji. Identifying an event as such identifies a social scene where relations between religious groups are strained, a kind of contest is staged, and the institution of religion is heard as able to embrace such ritualized conflict. According to Donald Brenneis (1978, p. 162), the phrase *song challenge* identifies an event in which participants "attack and shame their opponents." Prodded by an audience, each group tries to make the opposing group "so mad they cry":

> The performers are groups of co-religionists, with a lead singer and a chorus. . . . The parties alternate turns, beginning with moderate songs

about their own religion and escalating to increasingly abusive and personal attacks upon members of other groups. . . . The event ends when one group feels it cannot restrain itself from physical violence much longer and sends for outsiders to end the competition. (p. 162)

Clearly, to use the term *song challenge* to identify a kind of talk is to convey messages about the mode, tone, and so on of the communication, but it says more than that. It identifies a verbal scene where relations are strained, in conflict; participants are engaged in competitive battle. Further, such battle is linked intimately to religious institutions. Thus to use this cultural term for talk is to speak not only about communication, but also about social relations and institutions.

Regarding social relations, the messages may be characterized from *solidarity* (symmetrical we-ness), as in dugri and ceremonial dialogue, to *power* (asymmetrical ability to exercise formal controls), as in song challenges. Relational messages may be conveyed from *closeness*, as in "communication" (Katriel & Philipsen, 1981), to *distancing and polarizing*, as in the stratification of speakers through the La Have "argument" (Bauman, 1972). About institutions, terms for talk may imply a general assessment from goodness to badness. Suggested here is an implicit meaning that may radiate from cultural categories about talk and comment upon institutions. For example, as North Americans discuss and praise "communication" (Katriel & Philipsen, 1981), "being honest," and "sharing" (Carbaugh, 1988), they endorse those institutions that support such enactments. Families, self-help groups, and family-type businesses are valued because they express a caring institutional life, they support "sharing" and "close communication" better than, say, political parties or large corporations. Similarly, Kuna chants, arguings, and agreeings, especially grounded in the "gathering house," speak intimately of Kuna political institutions and authority (Sherzer, 1983, pp. 72–109).

Note how all of these cases, from St. Vincent to the Fiji to the American to the Kuna, are alike in their use of terms for talk to discuss social relations and institutions. But they vary in fundamentally important ways—whether relations are evaluated along dimensions of solidarity to intimacy, competitive to cooperative, close to distant, powerful to powerless. Messages about institutions vary likewise, be they more formally structured as in religion or politics or less formally structured as in community and self-help groups.

My general point here builds on the work of Sapir (1931) and the above ethnographic cases, all of which suggest that cultural terms for communicative routines provide one possible point of access into sociality, its relations, and its institutions (see Briggs, 1984). As persons conceive of and evaluate their talk, they may be commenting upon social relations and institutions, the constituents of society. As talk is culturally identified and labeled, institutions, as well as social relations, are subjects in the commentary.

### Messages About Personhood

As Rosaldo (1982) discusses Ilongot speech acts, she unveils the intimate links between the cultural shaping of languages and the types of persons who speak them. It is noteworthy that a Western ear, tuned to American English, is more ready to hear the phrases *nature of language* and *types of persons* and perhaps less ready for natures of languages and type of individuals. I am simply pointing to a ready cultural premise of "main essence" underlying studies of languages and the premise of "infinitive variety" underlying studies of persons. These intuitions should tell us something about the way English tends to construe language and persons, especially as we examine the links among language use, its native shaping, and personhood (see Briggs, 1984, p. 7).

Consider the Ilongot case. Rosaldo (1982, pp. 224–227) informs us that the Ilongot have an exemplary kind of act she calls a directive, including the cultural terms *tuydek* (commands), *bege* (requests), and *tengteng* (order, warning). According to Rosaldo, the Ilongot directive is a kind of act that is animated not so much by intentions of individual Ilongot speakers, but by exigencies of cooperativeness in social situations. The motives and meanings invoked through such acts are not as much intentional or individual as they are relational and communal. What Rosaldo suggests is an intimate link between the nature of speech performance and the senses of the persons who do them. In this case, directives are part and parcel of a sociocentric personhood, motivated by social concerns for cooperative movement, hierarchy, and bonding (see Shweder & Bourne, 1984). To be an Ilongot person is to speak less as an individual who makes private information public by negotiating with independent others, and more as an appendage within a socially organic membrane. So, when Ilongot identify their talk as tuydek and so on, they do not so much identify what individuals are doing with their words, but what a social conglomerate predicates.

Where motives in Ilongot are more relational, meanings more public, and persons more sociocentric, through others exemplary acts, such as "propositions," one might enact intentional motives, more private meanings, and more egocentric models of personhood. Rosaldo's (1982) study forces us to examine the intimate link between the ways speech is identified and used by natives, as in tuydek versus propositions, and the type of personhood enacted, sociocentric organic versus egocentric contractual.

The link between analytic frameworks about communication phenomena and cultural premises for communication and personhood is a complex one that I can do no more than sketch here. With regard to cultural terms for talk, the issues fall on at least three levels:

(1) *The cultural level:* What common premises about personhood are expressed as patterns of speaking are identified? Rosaldo (1982) suggests that premises of "psychology" and "individuality" run through the language of speech act theory, which thus results in a deep culture skewing, rendering sociocentric patterns of speaking, such as the Ilongot, as more egocentric than they rightly are.

(2) *The social level:* Within speech communities, are there types of persons associated with cultural terms for talk? Easy examples are the phrases *men's speech* and *women's speech* or *Black speech* and *White speech*, each suggesting acts, events, and styles of speaking that are distinct to each group, with each set, in turn, expressing messages about persons who are members of that social group.

(3) *The content level:* Some cultural terms for talk identify a kind of talk in which messages about persons are the main topics of discussion, for example, gossip and making commess among the St. Vincentians.

Talk, so identified, makes messages about personhood, preferred and dispreferred qualities, toward and untoward conduct, it's basic theme. All three levels suggest an intimate link between cultural terms for talk and models of personhood. They constitute cultural premises for being a person that are expressed through such terms for talk.

Elsewhere I have sketched four dimensions of personhood that may come to the fore as persons label their speech (Carbaugh, 1988). The first concerns the *loci of motives*, be they more relational, as with the Ilongot or Balinese (Geertz, 1973), or more intentional, as in North American "communication" or among the Paliyan (Gardner, 1966). The second concerns the *bases of sociation*, be they more organically enmeshed, as evidenced in the Ilongot directive, the Balinese, or the Navajo (Witherspoon, 1977), or more contractually interdependent, as among the American and Paliyan. The third concern is for *styles of personhood*, be they more impersonal and positional, as in the Fiji song challenges, or more intimate and personal, as in American sharing (suggested by Hymes, 1972, following Mead). The fourth concern, hierarchically above the other three, may suggest *overall types of personhood*, enacted through cultural categories of speech, with the former poles creating a sociocentric organic model, and the latter a more egocentric contractual model (Shweder & Bourne, 1984).

When people label their speech, they invoke conceptions about personhood. We need to listen for these messages, especially as persons use them to construct their senses of communication acts, events, and styles. Listening this way will help bring common senses of personhood from the past into the present communication scene, so, in the performance, we may hear cultural messages about personhood and society as well as those about communication.

## STRUCTURE OF CULTURAL TERMS FOR TALK: A LOOK AT INTERCULTURAL COMMUNICATION

As a result of the above comparative study of particular cases, we may conclude that the variation in cultural terms for talk can be explained within an analytical framework that has intercultural utility. First, cultural terms for talk identify speech on several levels, as acts, events, or styles, and more peripherally as accomplishing several functions. Ethnographers have studied words that label speech on these various levels, and sometimes these levels have been discussed simultaneously. One way to develop our theory of these communication phenomena is to distinguish these levels, the qualities of each, and the relations among them.

A second observation is: three levels of messages are communicated prominently through indigenous terms for speech. That is, as persons label their speech, they are talking not only about communication (about its modes, degree of structuring, tone, efficaciousness), but also about sociality (social relations and institutions), and models of personhood (loci of motives, bases of sociation, styles, and types). Put another way, persons use cultural terms for talk as a way to speak directly and literally about words and as a way to talk more metaphorically about interpersonal relations, social institutions, and models for being a person.

This analytic framework suggests two basic questions for studies of cultural terms for talk: (a) What level(s) of performance does a given cultural term for talk identify? (b) What messages are conveyed in its use? Any given term for talk may refer to performances at one or more levels, by conveying messages of primarily one or several types. Thus the framework suggests a set of concepts that point to distinctive, but sometimes overlapping, levels, and to several aspects of messages, all of which are salient, but none of which is essential in any given case.

The framework has utility in several ways. First, the framework has a descriptive utility. It sensitizes one to important phenomena in speech, cultural terms for talk, providing a class of phenomena for study and a way to describe its levels and messages. Thus the framework has utility for developing cultural descriptions. Second, the framework has comparative utility. It can be used for further cross-cultural studies, testing its adequacy across more cases, revising when necessary, perhaps by refining what is meant by each aspect of messages and by adding additional dimensions such as the functional accomplishments of terms for talk. Third, the framework has theoretical utility. It gives perspective to a communication phenomenon by providing, in principle at least, a system of concepts the interrelations among which account for cultural variation. Finally, the framework has a practical utility, especially when applied to intercultural communication, for it sensitizes speakers to the radical and/or subtle differences that may underlie cultural conceptions (and enactments) of talk and suggests ways of unraveling such deep—or more surface—perplexities.

Intercultural communication undoubtedly involves persons who come together and act in ways they consider most appropriate. By now, it is of no surprise that some individuals consider a direct mode of communication of value with strangers, as would a Sabra who is speaking dugri or a North American wanting to "really communicate." This mode conflicts rather obviously with the more indirect and valued "crooked language" of the Ilongot or the communication acts of silence identified by western Apaches as proper for "meeting strangers" (Basso, 1970). The fact of such differences is one major finding of this report. Persons, as culture bearers, identify and use highly particular and highly valued forms of communication. Part of the task of students of intercultural communication is to recognize that fact and build theories accordingly. As a practical matter, upon each moment of such recognition, various bases for social action could be laid bare, made more available for critical reflection and discussion, with the possibility for coordinated—if not cooperative—action enhanced.

Turning for a moment to two research programs in intercultural communication, I can demonstrate the kind of complementary insight gained by a comparative ethnography of speaking. Barnlund and his associates have recently been comparing the role of speech acts (compliments and apologies) in Japanese and American contexts (Barnlund & Araki, 1985; Barnlund & Nagano, 1987). This is an important program of study, for it helps to explore the link between cultural premises and patterns of speaking. Such investigation could be grounded better, however, if it asked first: What is the nature of the verbal performances that are identified by Japanese or North Americans, as—for example—an apology? Is such a pattern salient in the society? If so, is it an act? Is it an event? What messages are associated with the form? What is its place in the local cultural system? Do Japanese invoke a sociocentric personhood when apologizing, thus marking "the social relations and scene" for interactional concern? Do Americans invoke a more egocentric personhood, thus marking speaker's face for interactional concern? The nature of the spoken pattern within a social and cultural life, the level of performance identified, and its cultural messages are critical information for conducting such cross-cultural studies.

A second program of research explores reports about moments of intercultural contact, and explains them with psychological (e.g., cognitive complexity, uncertainty, anxiety), social (e.g., expectations, similarity), communication (e.g., network, competence) and cultural (e.g., high- and low-context, masculine and feminine, individual and collective) variables (Gudykunst, 1983, 1985, 1988). This program has yielded many research reports by exploring interrelations among these variables and has continued its effort to identify a basic set of axioms that explain moments of intergroup and intercultural communication. It is important, however, to identify what is missing from these studies, such as analyses of *actual enactments* of talk during moments of intercultural and intergroup contacts and description of *cultural patterns of communication* that are used during such contacts.

Looking back to this program after examining the 11 societies and 50 terms for talk of concern to the present essay raises some questions, especially with regard to "the cultural variables." What do such variables tell us about actual communication performances, their cultural patterning, or moments of intercultural contact? Surely there is a need for discussion of these issues, with responses assessed in terms of both intercultural practices and communication theory. Discussing the links among the present study and these two prominent programs of research not only helps to demonstrate how a comparative ethnography can complement and contribute to already established programs of intercultural communication theory and research, but also suggests a general way to approach conduct in intercultural practices.

## NOTES

1. The following analysis claims to include all of the major cultural terms for talk that were reported in each consulted work. A total of 11 societies were studied, with 6 reported in the Urban study (including the Kuna), yielding (rather incidentally) 50 cultural terms for talk and 211 cultural features. The 11 societies and 50 terms providing the central corpus of study are as follows: for the St. Vincentians (a total of 17), *talking sense, talking nonsense, talking sweet, talking broad, acting behave, getting on rude, calling name, calling out name, giving fatigue, making commess, talking nigger business, making commess* (a second type), *making melee, making vexation, getting on ignorant, telling story,* and *talking trupidness*; for the Kuna (a total of 10), Kuna language (*Tule Kaya* or *Kaya*), everyday Kuna, lullabies (*koe pippi*), *tuneful weeping, chief language* (or *gathering house language*), *chanting* (*namakke*), interisland ritual speech, chief's speak (*summakke*), *stick doll language,* and Kantule language; for the South American societies (a total of 8), the Waiwai *yes-saying,* the Trio *nokato, sipsipman,* and *tesmiken,* the Yanomamo ritualized conversation (*yaimu*), the Jivaroan Shuar and Achuar ceremonial *greeting* and *war dialogue,* and the Shokleng origin-myth telling (*waneklen*); for the Ilongot (a total of 7), commands (*tuydek*), requests (*bege*), orders (*tengteng*), *straight speech, nawnaw* (persuasion through fabrication), *crooked language,* and *purug oratory*; for the Fiji (a total of 4), song challenge, political speech (*parbachan*), *jungle talk,* and *sweet talk*; for American English (a total of 3), *being honest, sharing,* and *communication*; and for the Israeli Sabra (a total of 1), *dugri* (talking straight).

2. Following Hymes (1972), a cultural feature was identified as a basic component that, combined with others, provided the constituent parts of an indigenously named way of speaking. But, as is shown below, the cultural features analyzed for this study produced an elaboration of the basic Hymesian vocabulary. The elaboration consists mainly of my discussing the Hymesian component of "participant" as personhood and its identifiable parts, and further as social relations, adding institutions as a kind of

"scene," separating "key" into mode and tone, and discussing "norms" and their force as efficaciousness.

3. A total of 21 terms refer to the act level: the Israeli *dugri* (Katriel, 1986); the American *being honest* (Carbaugh, 1988); the Fiji *parbachan* (Brenneis, 1978); the Ilongot *tuydek, bege, tengteng,* and *purug oratory* (Rosaldo, 1982, 1973); the Kuna *lullabies, tuneful weeping,* and *chief's speech* (Sherzer, 1983); the St. Vincentian *calling name, calling out name, giving fatigue, making commess, talking nigger business, making commess* (again), *making melee, making vexation, getting on ignorant, telling story,* and *talking trupidness* [(Abrahams & Bauman, 1971). The act level consists of 38% of the total sample (n — 55), the 5 additional instances being the result of 3 terms (*being honest, dugri,* and *purug* oratory) that refer to performances at more than one level.] "Note that I use the term *act* to refer simply to things one person can do with words; I do not here intend to invoke the more special sense of "speech act" developed by John Searle."

4. A total of 18 cultural terms for episodes or events were recorded, constituting 33% of the sample (n — 55): the Israeli *dugri* (Katriel, 1986); the American *being honest, sharing,* and *communication* (Carbaugh, 1988; Katriel & Philipsen, 1981); the Fiji *song challenge* (Brenneis, 1978); the Ilongot *purung oratory* (Rosaldo, 1973); the Waiwai *yes-saying;* the Trio *nokato, sipsipman,* and *tesmiken;* the Yanomamo *ritualized conversation;* the Jivaroan Shuar and Achuar of Eastern Ecuador *greeting* and *war dialogue;* and the Shokleng *origin-myth telling* (all in Urban, 1986); the Kuna *chanting, ritual island gathering, stick doll language,* and Kantule language (Sherzer, 1983).

5. The distinction drawn here between act and event raises a question about those verbal performances that require, on the one hand, two persons speaking at the same time, such as the Mayan story-telling (Burns, 1980) and the Antiguan "contrapuntal conversation" (Reisman, 1975), and those that require sequencing of nonsimultaneous acts among participants such as the communication ritual (Katriel & Philipsen, 1981) and song challenges (Brenneis, 1978). The present framework suggests that both are events because both require coparticipation, albeit coparticipation that differs in structure, tone, social relation, and model of person. The latter are suggested by interpreting the types of messages, suggested below, in each cultural term for talk.

6. A total of 16 cultural terms for styles of speaking were recorded (29%, n — 55): the Israeli dugri (Katriel, 1986); the Fiji jungle talk and sweet talk (Brenneis, 1978); the Ilongot crooked speech, straight speech, and nawnaw (Rosaldo, 1973); the Kuna language, everyday Kuna, and chief language (Sherzer, 1983); and the St. Vincentian's distinctive but nonexclusive talking sense, talking nonsense, talking sweet, talking broad, acting behave, and getting on rude (Abrahams & Bauman, 1971).

7. The distinction I am drawing could be further developed by reference to identifiable means for speech, and ends of speech, both of which may be reported and labeled by participants. Thus "really communicating" identifies for some Americans a means for speaking, but it also identifies culturally identifiable ends—either in itself, "communication," and/or of "self" awareness, and/or a close "relationship" (Katriel & Philipsen, 1981). Since participants sometimes identify means as ends, and ends as means, cultural terms for speech are used polysemically to identify speaking and its outcomes. For analysts, the distinction between the two must be clearer so as to identify when cultural terms are used to identify an available means of communication, such as "communication" as a means of sociation, and when they identify other sociocultural

accomplishments, such as "communication" as a type of sociation. One possible path for investigating the distinction is offered below through interpretations of salient messages.

8. A total of 211 cultural features were recorded. The present analysis accounts for 197 (or 93.4%) of these, distributed across the message types as follows: messages about communication (a total of 83), mode (13), degree of structuring (29), tone (31), and efficaciousness (10); messages about sociality (a total of 34), social relations (25), and institutions (9); and messages about personhood (a total of 80), loci of motives (23), bases of sociation (13), styles (22), and types (22). The 14 cultural features that were omitted cluster loosely into aspects of context such as public-private or audience size (4), nonverbal factors such as posturing and gesturing (7), and elements of pacing (3). Upon completing the analysis, it seems even these could be reinterpreted with the aspects of context serving as messages about tone/social relations, and the nonverbal factors and elements of pacing included as messages about structuring. However, these features were excluded from the present analysis. Limitations of space prohibit presentation of a grand table displaying which cultural features, of which terms, fall under which message type. A complete listing may be requested from the author.

9. The phrase *highly salient but nonessential* applies to each aspect of the analytic framework presented here, and suggests the necessity of testing each through an application to cultural practices. Thus at each moment a cultural term for talk is used, a theoretically and empirically grounded way of listening is suggested: Is the cultural term saying something about communication (its mode, degree of structuring, tone, or efficaciousness)? Is it saying something about sociality (social relations and institutions)? Is it saying something about personhood (loci of motives, bases of sociation, styles or types of personhood)? Any particular cultural term for talk may exploit some messages more than others, and they may rule in some messages while explicitly ruling out others (e.g., "straight talk" may indicate more about the mode of speaking than its technical structuring; see below). But any moment where cultural terms for talk are used, in principle at least, some aspects of the framework are ignited. The ultimate utility of the framework of course depends upon its future application to various cultural practices and making modifications that such application may require. Ultimately, the theory would enable the analyst to particularize from the general framework, pinpointing distinctive features in cultural terms for talk, thus addressing criteria of cultural adequacy, and to generalize from the particular case, demonstrating what is of general interest about the case, thus addressing criteria of cross-cultural adequacy through comparative study.

10. The term *social relations* refers here simply to the relations among participants. *Social institutions* refers to a system of norms (Schneider, 1976).

# REFERENCES

Abrahams, R., & Bauman, R. (1971). Sense and nonsense in St. Vincent: Speech behavior and decorum in a Caribbean community. *American Anthropologist, 73*, 762–772.

Albert, E. (1972). Culture patterning of speech behavior in Burundi. In J. Gumperz & D. Hymes (Eds.), *Directions in sociolinguistics: The ethnography of communication.* New York: Holt, Rinehart & Winston.

Barnlund, D., & Araki, S. (1985). Intercultural encounters: The management of compliments by Japanese and Americans. *Journal of Cross-Cultural Psychology, 16,* 9–26.

Barnlund, D., & Nagano, M. (1987). *Apologies: Japanese and American style.* Paper presented at the annual meeting of the Speech Communication, Boston.

Basso, K. (1970). To "give up on words": Silence in the Western Apache culture. *Southwestern Journal of Anthropology, 26,* 213–230.

Basso, K. (1984). "Stalking with stories": Names, places, and moral narratives among Western Apache. In E. Bruner (Ed.), *Text, play, and story: The construction and reconstruction of self and society* (Proceedings of the American Ethnological Society). Washington, DC: American Ethnological Society.

Bauman, R. (1972). The La Have island general store. *Journal of American Folklore, 85,* 330–343.

Beach, W., & Dunning, D. (1982). Pre-indexing and conversational organization. *Quarterly Journal of Speech, 68,* 170–185.

Bell, M. (1983). *The world from Brown's Lounge: An ethnography of Black middle-class play.* Champaign: University of Illinois Press.

Bernstein, B. (1972). A sociolinguistic approach to socialization; with some reference to educability. In J. Gumperz & D. Hymes (Eds.), *Directions in sociolinguistics: The ethnography of communication.* New York: Holt, Rinehart & Winston.

Bloch, M. (1976). [Review of R. Bauman & J. Sherzer (Eds.), *Explorations in the ethnography of speaking*]. *Language in Society, 5,* 229–234.

Braithwaite, C. (1981). *Cultural uses and interpretations of silence.* Unpublished master's thesis, University of Washington.

Brenneis, D. (1978). The matter of talk: Political performances in Bhatgaon. *Language in Society, 7,* 159–170.

Brenneis, D. (1984). Grog and gossip in Bhatgaon: Style and substance in Fiji Indian conversation. *American Ethnologist, 11,* 487–506.

Briggs, C. (1984). Learning how to ask: Native metacommunicative competence and the incompetence of fieldworkers. *Language in Society, 13,* 1–28.

Burns, A. F. (1980). Interactive features in Yucatec Mayan narratives. *Language in Society, 9,* 307–319.

Campbell, D. (1975). "Degrees of freedom" and the case study. *Comparative Political Studies, 8,* 178–193.

Carbaugh, D. (1987). Communication rules in Donahue discourse. *Research on Language and Social Interaction, 21,* 31–62.

Carbaugh, D. (1988). *Talking American: Cultural discourses on Donahue.* Norwood, NJ: Ablex.

Chick, K. (1985). The interactional accomplishment of discrimination in South Africa. *Language in Society, 14,* 299–326.

Ervin-Tripp, S. (1972). On sociolinguistic rules: Alternation and co-occurrence. In J. Gumperz & D. Hymes (Eds.), *Directions in sociolinguistics: The ethnography of communication.* New York: Holt, Rinehart & Winston.

Feld, S., & Schieffelin, B. (1981). Hard talk: A functional basis for Kaluli discourse. In

D. Tannen (Ed.), *Georgetown University Round Table on Languages and Linguistics 1981*. Washington, DC: Georgetown University Press.

Gardner, P. (1966). Symmetric respect and memorate knowledge: The structure and ecology of individualistic culture. *Southwestern Journal of Anthropology, 22*, 339–415.

Garner, T. (1983). Playing the dozens: Folklore as strategies for living. *Quarterly Journal of Speech, 69*, 47–57.

Geertz, C. (1973). *The interpretation of cultures*. New York: Basic Books.

Gossen, G. (1974). *Chamulas in the world of the sun: Time and speech in a Maya oral tradition*. Cambridge, MA: Harvard University Press.

Gudykunst, W. B. (1983). Uncertainty reduction and predictability of behavior in low- and high-context cultures. *Communication Quarterly, 31*, 49–55.

Gudykunst, W. B. (1985). A model of uncertainty reduction in intercultural encounters. *Journal of Language and Social Psychology, 4*, 79–98.

Gudykunst, W. B. (1988). Uncertainty and anxiety. In Y. Y. Kim & W. B. Gudykunst (Eds.), *Theories in intercultural communication*. Newbury Park, CA: Sage.

Hymes, D. (1962). The ethnography of speaking. In T. Gladwin & W. Sturtevant (Eds.), *Anthropology and human behavior* (pp. 13–53). Washington, DC: Anthropological Society of Washington.

Hymes, D. (1972). The interaction of language and social life. In J. Gumperz & D. Hymes (Eds.), *Directions in sociolinguistics: The ethnography of communication*. New York: Holt, Rinehart & Winston.

Irvine, J. (1979). Formality and informality in communicative events. *American Anthropologist, 81*, 773–783.

Katriel, T. (1985). "Griping" as a verbal ritual in some Israeli discourse. In M. Dascal (Ed.), *Dialogue: An interdisciplinary approach*. Amsterdam: J. Benjamins.

Katriel, T. (1986). *Talking straight: "Dugri" speech in Israeli Sabra culture*. Cambridge: Cambridge University Press.

Katriel, T., & Philipsen, G. (1981). What we need is "communication": "Communication" as a cultural category in some American speech. *Communication Monographs, 48*, 302–317.

Keenan, E. (1975). A sliding sense of obligatoriness: The poly-structure of Malagasy oratory. *Language in Society, 2*, 225–243.

Keenan, E. (1976). The universality of conversational postulates. *Language in Society, 5*, 67–80.

Leach, E. R. (1976). Social geography and linguistic performance. [Review of Bauman & Sherzer, *Explorations in the ethnography of speaking*]. *Semiotica, 16*, 87–97.

Lein, L., & Brenneis, D. (1978). Children's disputes in three speach (sic) communities. *Language in Society, 7*, 299–323.

Michaels, S. (1981). "Sharing time": Children's narrative styles and differential access to literacy. *Language in Society, 10*, 423–442.

Philips, S. U. (1976). Some sources of cultural variability in the regulation of talk. *Language in Society, 5*, 81–95.

Philipsen, G. (1986). *The ethnography of communication: From an assumptive to an empirical foundation*. Paper presented at the meeting of the American Anthropological Association, Philadelphia.

Philipsen, G., & Carbaugh, D. (1986). A bibliography of fieldwork in the ethnography of communication. *Language in Society, 15*, 387–398.

Reisman, K. (1975). Contrapuntal conversations in an Antiguan village. In R. Bauman & J. Sherzer (Eds.), *Explorations in the ethnography of speaking*. Cambridge: Cambridge University Press.

Rosaldo, M. (1973). I have nothing to hide: The language of Ilongot oratory. *Language in Society, 2*, 193–223.

Rosaldo, M. (1982). The things we do with words: Ilongot speech acts and speech acts theory in philosophy. *Language in Society, 11*, 203–237.

Sanches, M. (1975). Introduction to metacommunicative acts and events. In M. Sanches & B. Blount (Eds.), *Sociocultural dimensions of language use*. New York: Academic Press.

Sapir, E. (1931). Communication. *Encyclopedia of the Social Sciences, 4*, 78–81.

Schneider, D. (1976). Notes toward a theory of culture. In K. Basso & H. A. Selby (Eds.), *Meaning in anthropology*. Albuquerque: University of New Mexico Press.

Seitel, P. (1974). Haya metaphors for speech. *Language in Society, 3*, 51–67.

Sherzer, J. (1983). *Kuna ways of speaking: An ethnographic perspective*. Austin: University of Texas Press.

Shweder, R., & Bourne, E. (1984). Does the concept of the person vary cross-culturally? In R. Shweder & R. Levine (Eds.), *Culture theory: Essays on mind, self, and emotion*. Cambridge: Cambridge University Press.

Urban, G. (1984). Speech about speech in speech about action. *Journal of American Folklore, 97*, 310–328.

Urban, G. (1986). Ceremonial dialogues in South America. *American Anthropologist, 88*, 371–386.

Watson-Gegeo, K. (1976). [Review of R. Bauman & J. Sherzer (Eds.), Explorations in the ethnography of speaking]. *Language, 52*, 745–748.

Watzlawick, P., Beavin, J., & Jackson, D. (1967). *Pragmatics of human communication*. New York: Norton.

Wierzbicka, A. (1985). A semantic metalanguage for a cross-cultural comparison of speech acts and genres. *Language in Society, 14*, 491–514.

Witherspoon, G. (1977). *Language and art in the Navajo universe*. Ann Arbor: University of Michigan Press.

# 6

# Life Demands *Musayara:* Communication and Culture Among Arabs in Israel

YOUSUF GRIEFAT • TAMAR KATRIEL • *University of Haifa*

*This chapter analyzes the folk-linguistic term musayara as it is used in the discourse of Arabs in Israel. The interactional ethos encapsulated in the notion of musayara is examined with reference to its cultural-historical underpinnings. An understanding of the interactional ethos of musayara compared to the* dugri *ethos of native Israeli Jews (Katriel, 1986) is argued to provide some insights into the potential for miscommunication in intercultural encounters between Arabs and Jews in Israel.*

## INTRODUCTION

The Arabic folk-linguistic term *musayara* (which refers to "going with" or "accompanying" one's partner in conversation) is associated with an other-oriented, "humoring," "conciliatory" attitude, with individuals' effort to maintain harmony in social relations. The term and its derivatives (e.g., *musayir*, a person disposed to doing musayara) carry many potent overtones for cultural members.[1] Our Israeli Arab respondents' talk was sprinkled with a variety of semiformulaic expressions that underscored the centrality of this cultural orientation in their lives, for example: "Musayara is in the blood of every Arab person"; "You drink it with your mother's milk,"; "It's in the air, you breathe it in."

The traditional notion of musayara can be traced to its historical roots in both religious Islamic doctrine and the high degree of interdependence that characterized the social relations of early Arab communities. Indeed, the art of comporting oneself with social delicacy was praised by pre-Islamic poets, who were keenly aware of the role of such stylized conduct in the maintenance of harmonious social relations within the close-knit tribal group. This cultural orientation received explicit religious legitimation with the advent of Islam, as expressed in the elaborate literary tradition of *adab* (the ways of politeness, etiquette) that flourished from the beginning of the eighth century and was influenced by the cultures of newly Islamicized nations.[2]

In everyday discourse, the notion of musayara is typically invoked in passing judgment on social actors or social conduct. A person may be praised for being musayir or criticized for consistently failing to conform to the social/interactional norms associated with the musayara code. Such a person may be referred to by the term *jilda*—the rough, impenetrable husk of a tree.

It appears, then, that the notion of musayara encapsulates much that is distinctive to Arabic speechways and interpersonal conduct, and that "doing musayara" is a major communicative vehicle for the maintenance of social relations and the cultivation of traditional patterns. We propose, therefore, that musayara be considered as an articulation of a cultural "ethos"—the moral and aesthetic patternings distinctive to a cultural group (Bateson, 1958; Geertz, 1973). A leaning toward "modernization" may be associated with a repudiation of the musayara ethos. So, while for many cultural members acting with musayara is an expression of interpersonal sophistication, of maturity and self-control, those who reject the injunction to do musayara (typically some of the members of the younger generation) consider it an expression of self-effacement and lack of assertiveness—attitudes that should not be promoted in modern times, and that are self-defeating in political struggles (see Sharabi, 1975).

A vivid and touching example of generational differences in attitudes toward doing musayara was given to us by one of our respondents, a highly educated professional. He vividly recalled an exchange he had had with his elderly father during which they discussed some marital difficulties the son was experiencing at that time. The father interceded, saying to the son, "Sayerna, she is your wife, after all" (act with musayara toward her—i.e., compromise, don't bring the conflict to a head, try to smooth things over, she is your wife). To this the son replied in a way that shocked his father to such an extent that he subsequently reminded him of the exchange again and again in later years. The son's reply was: "Precisely because she is my wife I won't act with musayara toward her."

Reflecting on the interchange, the son said that our probings into the cultural meanings and uses of musayara made him realize that he had applied to the situation a Western cultural logic according to which interpersonal difficulties, especially those experienced with "significant others," need to be addressed explicitly and elaborated upon by the parties involved. It is through such mutual confrontation that interpersonal bonds can be revitalized and reaffirmed (see Katriel & Philipsen, 1981). The son said he had felt he would not be taking his wife seriously if he allowed issues to be "pushed under the rug." His father, he explained, expected him to come forth with a show of magnanimity, and interpreted his unwillingness to act with musayara on that occasion as a rejection not only of his wife, but also of the binding force of social relations and the family as a locus of order in communal life.

Underlying these very different valuations, however, there is a basic understanding of the intricate working of musayara as a culturally "named" interactional pattern. It is this overall pattern and the "cultural logic" underlying it that hold our attention in this chapter.

## DATA ANALYSIS AND INTERPRETATION

Our analysis draws in a cumulative fashion on data derived from a number of complementary sources, gathered between 1982 and 1986:

(1) an ethnography of speaking conducted by the first author in a Bedouin settlement in the Galilee, employing both participant observation and interviewing methods, which took folk-linguistic notions, musayara among them, as its focus (Griefat, 1986);

(2) sociolinguistic interviews with bilingual Arabs from both rural and urban backgrounds (which took place either one on one or in small groups) were conducted in Hebrew, and recorded respondents' efforts to explicate the notion of musayara to a cultural outsider;[3] and

(3) insights derived from both Arab and Jewish students' field exercises and discussions, which involved conceptions of and attitudes toward each other's communication styles (these exercises focused on, but were not limited to, the folk notions of doing musayara and speaking *dugri*, as the latter term is employed in both spoken Hebrew and spoken Arabic; Katriel, 1986).

### The Musayara Interactional Code

Generally speaking, behavior designed to enhance commonalities rather than differences, cooperation rather than conflict, and mutuality rather than self-assertion would be interpreted as involving musayara. In Brown and Levinson's (1987) terms, doing musayara involves an array of politeness strategies designed to signal concern with one's interlocutor's "positive" face wants, that is, indications of support for the other's image of him- or herself. Expressions of musayara imply a wide range of prescriptions and proscriptions. Thus there is great emphasis on displays of involvement and participation, such as being accessible in the sense of being prepared to give of one's time and attention whenever this is required. Thus some of our younger respondents said they were accused by their elders of failing to act with musayara when they terminated an unplanned social visit to attend to a previous commitment. They said the pace of modern life and the many demands placed on them, especially when their work took them outside the community proper, make it impossible for them to abide by the rules of musayara and be as constantly available to conversation and visiting as people who were living a slow-paced traditional life could be.

Verbal acts of musayara can be marked by a sense of *conversational restraint* on the one hand or *conversational effusiveness* on the other:

(1) Conversational restraint is displayed through strict adherence to procedural rules of deference, the avoidance of interruptions and topic shifts, and the effort made to avoid topics of potential discord or any remarks that could be interpreted as confrontational. Restraint also is exercised in the use of one's voice and speaking rights—loudness and hurried pace are shunned, and interruptions are avoided.

(2) Conversational effusiveness involves a variety of interactional tactics that function to dramatize and to intensify interpersonal bonds. These interactional tactics include the effusive use of many "layers" of greetings, the use of multiple, accentuated deferential or affectionate forms of address, accented displays of attentiveness, and the open sharing of personal resources, in both time and effort.

The example of the use of special forms of address in doing musayara will illustrate the larger pattern of conversational effusiveness. For an address form to be "heard" as involving musayara it has to be contextually interpreted as going beyond the norm. Thus doing musayara involves more than just basic rules of social interaction that tell you, for example, that you have to address your uncle as "my uncle." This form would be a minimal one, indicating that one is appropriately respectful, but no more. But addressing one's uncle as "my father" would signal the intention of showing special, particularized bonding, in the spirit of musayara.

Similarly, addressing someone who had not gone on the pilgrimage to Mecca as "Haj" rather than, say, "Abu X' (that is, going beyond the rules of propriety) signals particular respect. This pattern of "fictional address" (see Antoun, 1968) involves (as one of our respondents put it) a widely accepted "norm of going beyond the norm," which is typical of musayara of the effusive variety in all its manifestations. Another example of musayara in the domain of address terms involves a strategy of "fictional symmetry" in the exchange of kin or role terms, for example, as when a grandfather affectionately addresses his grandson as "my grandfather" (the term that would apply to himself) rather than "my grandson" (the appropriate kin designation).[4]

Whether the spirit of musayara is manifested in interactional restraint or interactional effusiveness, it is made possible based on the assumption that participants share an interactional "base" from which they depart in one direction or another in making their metacommunicative statement about the relationship at hand. As we discuss below, these expressive possibilities are socially distributed in particular ways (see Albert, 1972; Friedrich, 1972; Hymes, 1974; Keenan, 1974).

### The Musayara Dimensions

The social dimensions of status and degree of familiarity have emerged as decisive for the understanding of the ways in which acts of musayara are socially distributed in intracommunal encounters. We can distinguish among four broad types of social contexts, and attendant functions, for doing musayara. The first has to do with social rules pertaining to structural inequality, to the hierarchy of social relations in the community, and is associated with what we call the *musayara of respect*. The second involves situational inequality and is a reversal of the first, since it is extended from the higher to the lower in status in moments of exigence. We have, accordingly, dubbed it the *musayara of magnanimity*. The third involves relations of either equality or inequality and is associated with the pursuit of self-interest. We refer to it—after the usage of one of our informants, who spoke of it as "the small politics of everyday life that we do all the time"—as *political musayara*. The fourth type of musayara is specifically associated with conflict situations, and will be referred to as the *musayara of conciliation*. Let us consider each one in some detail.

The *musayara of respect* is typically extended to persons higher in status—to the older from the younger, to men from women, to a Haj or to a sheikh from a simple villager. In all these cases the status inequality is due to the relative positions individuals occupy in the hierarchy of social relations. The musayara of respect is also typically employed between status equals who are unfamiliar with each other and is gradually "dropped" if their relationship becomes that of close friends.

The ability to do musayara requires the virtue of self-control, a virtue both children and women are said to lack, as well as an ability to use language indirectly and artfully. So, whereas women and children are expected to act with musayara toward grown men, who are considered their status superiors, they are not considered sophisticated enough to be able to utilize the resources of language and etiquette in an elaborate way. Their *musayara of respect* usually takes the form of tactics of evasion, of nonresponse, or of interactional restraint, and it tends to be slighted by the men.

The *musayara of magnanimity* is typically extended in contexts in which the *musayara of respect* would not ordinarily be appropriate. Thus, although a child or a woman would not ordinarily expect to be treated with musayara by grown men, an exigency, such as an illness, would justify treating them with musayara. Some spoke of it as "the musayara of the sick" and some generalized it to "the musayara of the weak" that can be displayed in times of exigency. For example, a teacher may refrain from punishing a student who has misbehaved, saying that he will do musayara one more time. Similarly, some respondents mentioned the "musayara of the stranger," the magnanimity to the one who is out of his or her cultural waters, so to speak, and needs help, especially in allowing his or her interactional gaffes to slip by.

*Political musayara* involves relations of inequality defined not in social but in situational terms. Being in need of someone may put one temporarily in a position of relative disadvantage in relation to a person who otherwise would be considered one's status equal, or even one's inferior. Thus people testified that they have gone out of their way to act with musayara toward those whose good will they wished to secure for specific reasons. For example, a man said that for several years he took care to do musayara to a woman he would ordinarily try to evade because he was interested in her daughter as a possible match for his son. He said when he chatted with her from time to time he always greeted her profusely, using multiple forms of address as a sign of respect.

Finally, *musayara of conciliation* is invoked in the context of conflict between status equals, who are familiar with each other and would ordinarily not invoke the mode of musayara in their interactions. Partners in a confrontal exchange may be enjoined by friends to do musayara toward each other as gestures of appeasement and not to allow the conflict to escalate. As long as one's "point of honor" is not felt to be compromised (see Bourdieu, 1966), the injunction to do musayara may serve effectively to restore harmony in social relations. When a participant's "honor" (i.e., public self-image) is jeopardized (e.g., when a man's manliness is put to the test through direct offense or indirect insinuation against his wife, mother, or sister), then the plea to do musayara and smooth over a conflictual situation is likely to be ignored. In other words, a situation of highly escalated conflict, or a fight, is one in which the cultural injunction to do musayara is suspended.

Another type of context in which doing musayara is consensually suspended is one in which the accuracy of factual information is very important and no embellishment of facts can be tolerated. An example of such a context that appeared in our data involved a man's attempt to secure reliable information regarding the person and family of a possible bridegroom for his daughter. Intent on learning all he could in this crucial interchange, he asked his interlocutor to cut the musayara and speak the dugri, the truth. In contexts where crucial information is sought, the slipperiness and ambiguity attending the exercise of musayara cannot be tolerated.

The above classifications are no more than an attempt to systematize some of the contexts and functions associated with doing musayara. Given cases are, of course, ambiguous or multivocal in various ways and to various degrees. Take, for example, the very common case of a merchant being said to act with musayara toward a customer by offering a reduction on the price of the merchandise he or she is interested in. Here the musayara of magnanimity and political musayara become interlaced: In offering a reduction, the merchant is both taking account of the customer's situation and at the same time establishing business credit, so to speak, with the customer and, possibly, his or her larger group.

### The Musayara Strategies

Employing a distinction proposed by Beeman (1986) in his study of Iranian communicative style, we might say that in the aforementioned types of interactional contexts the ethos of musayara provides a pattern for the resolution of two distinct problems faced by interactants: the problem of *appropriateness* and the problem of *effectiveness*. Beeman (1986) posits two basic categories of core interaction conventions in a society, each of which is relevant to the notion of doing musayara in one of the aforementioned categories of social context:

> *Prescriptive conventions* are operations in communicative behavior that reinforce a state of affairs that will be perceived by individuals in interaction as normal or expected. By conforming to these prescriptive interaction conventions, individuals meet criteria of *appropriateness* in their dealings with others. *Strategic departures* are operations in communicative behavior that violate expectations in systematic interpretable ways in order to accomplish specialized communicative tasks such as persuading, expressing emotion, joking, threatening, or insulting. By skillfully adjusting their speech between prescriptive conventions and strategic departures, participants in interaction are able to excel in *effectiveness* in communications. (p. 7)

Acts of musayara can thus be intended and interpreted either as tokens of respect that serve to uphold a hierarchical social order or as strategic moves that depend on participants' assessment of the social relations between them, and that dramatize a conciliatory, concessive orientation. At the same time, it is important to note that doing musayara does not imply a complete subordination of one's self-interests to those of one's interlocutor. Indeed, conduct that is perceived as overly self-ingratiating is not acceptable. For example, an elderly man was heard to scold his son for lending out work tools indiscriminately, for being unable to refuse a request: "If you had been a girl, you would have been kidnapped," he quipped, expressing his displeasure in metaphorical terms.

Respondents also pointed out that one could go overboard in trying to humor others. When this is overdone, the overly ingratiating conduct of the person is natively referred to as *masax jux* (literally, "wiping the dust off the elegant, silken clothes of the ruler" as a show of concern). The mention of this term never failed to amuse our respondents. One person laughingly told an anecdote that to him exemplified behavior falling under the category of masax jux in the political domain, the context in which it is most frequently mentioned. He recounted that before the elections, one of the candidates for a local political office used to go back and forth by the bus station in his shiny car and offer rides to the people who were waiting for a bus. When the elections were over, his shiny car was no longer seen anywhere near the bus station. Acts falling under the category of masax jux violate the sense of subtlety and indirection associated with acts of musayara. Thus one can fail to fulfill the expectations associated with doing musayara on more than one ground: by not being considerate enough or, on the other hand, by being self-effacing. Doing musayara appropriately thus requires competency and cultivation and cannot be equated simply with nonassertive behavior.

The interactional subtlety characterized by exchanges described as involving musayara is exemplified by the following encounter observed by the first author, in which hints and metaphors were used to convey critical messages indirectly but clearly enough to be understood by those present. The exchange took place as part of the *diwan*, the semiformal gathering of grown males in the home of one of them. Conversation concerned the issue of girls' high school education, which required commuting to a nearby city. One of the participants said that it went against the tradition, and that it might jeopardize the family's honor. He spoke in general terms, invoking the notion of tradition as a widely accepted source of authority. Nevertheless, everybody knew that his words were directed to a particular participant whose daughter was going to high school. The addressee at whom the hint was directed responded with comparable artfulness: "What shall I tell you, friends, not all the lambs are taken to the slaughter." The Bedouin, the speaker implied, does not slaughter a lamb casually, but, rather, chooses a fat lamb or a thin lamb, all according to the status of the visitor he expects. Through the use of this metaphor, the speaker expressed the view that not all girls are alike, not all of them will do things that jeopardize the family's honor, even if they are given the chance to do so. Both speakers used strategies of indirection that require verbal agility, both managed to convey their messages in ways that were clear but did not openly commit them to a particular position or give cause to open confrontation. Thus the nature of the message remained ambiguous, debatable, and open to various interpretations. Other devices used to this end, and with similar effect, are traditional sayings, proverbs, stories, and passages of poetry.

Our final example illustrates a Bedouin elder's use of musayara in addressing a Jewish dignitary who came on an official visit to a settlement and was aware of the inhabitants' widespread discontent with the kinds and level of employment they were given. Using metaphorical, ornate language, the Bedouin said: "The government is our father and our mother. We feel this when we come to complain about the situation and ask for assistance. Instead of a tent we now have a modern house that you have filled up for us with clocks that tick away the whole day long. We need sources of employment so that we can pay all the bills that go with all these clocks." In this indirect and deceptively naive, but highly respectful, way, the village elder pointed out to the government representative that providing modern conditions of living for the local population is a job half done; they also need means of supporting this modern way of life presented to them as "progress" by the dominant Jewish population.

None of the indirection and rhetorical flair heard in the elder's address could be found in the speech of a younger member of that same community who bluntly said in a televised discussion: "The situation is such that the Bedouin settlement has turned into a kind of work-camp since there is no industry or agriculture that could provide employment within the settlement." Some young people explicitly denounce the elders' reliance on musayara and the use of personal ties in their dealings with the Jewish authorities. As one young person said: "In the state one has to stand up for one's rights forcefully, and keep close watch over the way our interests are being handled in government offices." Indeed, whereas the value of acting in the spirit of musayara in internal communal relations is by no means uniformly upheld, a bitter point of disagreement relates to the role of musayara in contacts with cultural outsiders, especially in the realm of politics. In these contexts musayara most frequently takes the form of the interactional restraint associated with the position of the less powerful.

In conclusion, let us briefly summarize the interactional semantics of doing musayara as they figured in the foregoing discussion:

(1) *Acts of musayara are other-directed social gestures* designed to maintain harmony in communal relations by upholding the social order, by mobilizing individuals' good will in conflict situations, by enhancing the

recognition of individual circumstances, and by promoting interpersonal affect.

(2) *Acts of musayara have a concessive flavor.* In doing musayara one is understood to "give up" something in the form of tangible or intangible "goods," such as money, time, effort, momentary social positioning (lowering oneself by elevating the other), or the expression of one's beliefs and opinions. A mere verbal gesture of flattery to a passing woman would not be called musayara, but rather *mudjamala*, since there is no sense that anything of the "self" has been "given up." Notably, however, the concession typically relates to minor issues that do not affect one's honor, and is, moreover, understood to serve one's larger interest in the maintenance of the social order or, specifically, to serve one's longer-range "political" goals.

(3) The cultural injunction to do musayara involves a generalized norm that says that *one should go beyond widely accepted interactional norms.* This may take the form of either interactional restraint or effusiveness, as we have described them, depending on who the participants are and what their relationship to each other is. When doing musayara is a matter of speech, there are also language-related criteria of form that have to apply for a speaker's words to qualify as an expression of musayara.

## CROSS-CULTURAL STYLES

### Communication Tension

In its broad outlines, the ethos of musayara echoes cultural communication patterns found in other traditional societies (e.g., see Albert, 1972; Beeman, 1986; Keenan, 1974; Rosaldo, 1973; Beeman, 1986). What seems particularly striking about the folk notion of musayara is that it embodies a keen consciousness of the tension between individual pragmatic and expressive concerns on the one hand and the demands of communal life on the other. This tension is fundamental to human societies and thus becomes expressively elaborated in what Philipsen (1987) has called the forms of cultural communication: ritual, narrative, and social drama. In the case of musayara this tension becomes a widely acknowledged and symbolically potent cultural focus, and is given form as well as name in a culturally shared communicative style that is at the same time socially regulated and given to individual inflection.

Rosen (1984) refers to a similar overall pattern of essential indeterminacy in the interpersonal bargaining that constitutes Moroccan social life, which he likens to the archetypal Moorish form, the *arabesque*, describing it as follows: "Simple in concept, yet elaborate in design, its draped arcades, hedged round by divine oration, describe a model of regularity and certitude, and, at the same time, a template for contingency and contrariety" (p. 192). It seems to us that the interactional "dance" subsumed under the folk notion of musayara is another, differently colored, manifestation of this pattern.

The high praises for doing musayara heard from tradition-oriented members of the community, be they elderly men or young fundamentalists, are not, however, sung by all. As noted earlier, many members of the younger generation emphasize its restrictiveness, which is acutely felt and resented by those who desire to have more of a say in critical life decisions, such as vocational aspirations or choice of marriage partner. When these young people openly contest the particular cultural arrangements embodied in and symbolized by the value of doing musayara, it is clearly a broader cultural and social configuration that they are rejecting. However, as some of our respondents pointed out, the grip of the musayara ethos on most community members is still such as to help smooth over discords everywhere: "The young does musayara to the old, and the old does musayara to the young," as one respondent put it. In short, the ethos of musayara is instrumental in helping the community mend social ruptures even as they relate to breaches associated with the code itself. In the following section, we will compare the interactional ethos of musayara with the dugri ethos of native Israeli Jews.

## *Intercultural Encounters*

Our experience as participants in the intercommunal dialogue of Arabs and Jews in Israel, our many discussions with both Arabs and Jews relating to interracial tensions, and our reading of the journalistic coverage of the intercultural scene (ongoing coverage as well as focused accounts such as that found in Shipler, 1986) and of scholarly treatments of it (e.g., Caplan, 1980) suggest that, over and above conflicts of interests and general belligerency, intercultural encounters between Arabs and Jews are all too often deflected due to conflicting cultural communication styles. Juxtaposing our study of the ethos of musayara and a previous study of the Sabra (native-born,

Jewish) ethos of "straight talk," natively known as dugri speech, may provide some insights into why Arabs and Jews "rub each other the wrong way" even, at times, in encounters in which good will seems to prevail. We would like to propose that communication between members of the two cultures is often impeded by unmatching assumptions and conflicting evaluations of various aspects of the communication process itself. Some of these can be traced to the dimension of "directness/indirectness" or, in Brown and Levinson's (1987) terminology, to "politeness strategies" as they have been given distinctive cultural patterning in speaking dugri and in doing musayara.

Just as the folk-linguistic notion of musayara encapsulates values and meanings that are central to the Arab speech communities in which it is used, so the folk-linguistic notion of dugri speech (or *dugrijut*, in its nominalized form) embodies a focal cultural orientation associated with the Sabra culture of modern Israel. Thus speaking dugri in Israeli Sabra culture involves the choice of a "direct" strategy in performing an act that poses a threat to one's interlocutor's "positive" face (Brown & Levinson, 1987). In "saying it dugri," one first of all speaks one's mind (as opposed to keeping one's thoughts to oneself, or being silent on the issue); moreover, one does so in explicit, forceful, and unembellished terms (rather than "softening" one's remarks through the use of some form of indirection). It is a style that is highly confrontational in tone and intent.

Sabra dugri speech manifests the attitude of "antistyle," an attitude predicated on the cultural disjunction between the categories of words (*diburim*) and deeds (*ma'asim*), and is associated with a pragmatic orientation. Notably, this attitude itself becomes stylized and ritualized. Dugri speech is thus a symbolic expression sociohistorically anchored in a set of cultural meanings and values: the notion of sincerity as it has evolved in modern Western ideologies; the value of assertiveness and an activist orientation, which is conceptualized as counteracting the traditional passivity attributed to Diaspora Jews; an aesthetic of simplicity and a high value placed on solidarity.

If we are right in claiming that for members of mainstream Israeli culture, the general flavor of interactional life is colored by the meanings and values associated with the dugri ethos, and that for Israeli Arabs the meanings and values associated with the ethos of musayara demarcate the central parameters of social interaction, then it would seem that the incompatibility of cultural styles between Arabs and

Jews on the dimension of directness indeed contributes to misunderstandings of all sorts.

In what follows we will briefly delineate the major points of conflict in terms of cultural premises related to communication that seem to us to underlie some of the difficulties in intercultural encounters between Arabs and Jews in Israel.

First, the Sabra dugri speaker's assertiveness involves a focus on the speaker's own face, a concern with behaving interactionally in such a way as to project the image of a "proper" member of the Sabra culture, one who is enjoined (and not afraid) to speak his or her mind in a straightforward way. The assertive dugri mode thus implies concern for the speaker's face rather than for the addressee's face and is diametrically opposed in orientation to the other-oriented mode associated with doing musayara, which involves giving rather than claiming face. The coming together of these two orientations in an intercultural encounter can be problematic indeed.

Second, dugri speech is motivated by a high value placed on the idea of sincerity in its Western interpretation (see Trilling, 1971). This notion is predicated on the expectation of correspondence between avowal and feeling, between one's inner world and one's behavioral display. As Keddie (1963) has pointed out, the mode of sincerity is a Western modern notion that is not part of traditional Islamic cultures, so, for example, "Middle Eastern intellectuals are quite aware that there may be a difference between a man's public utterances and private beliefs." Keddie further suggests that "the frequency of a distinction between what is said and what is believed . . . seems also to arise from the influence of centuries-long traditions of esoterism, double meanings, and precautionary simulation" (p. 28). This accepted disjunction between one's inner self and one's public image allows participants to maintain a high degree of ambiguity in social communication, and to embellish the facts in pursuit of one's goals and in the service of rhetorical flourish. As a result, Arab communication is perceived by many Jews to involve a high degree of "fabulation" (to use Caplan's, 1980, term), and to inspire little trust.

Third, dugri speech involves a momentary suspension of the requirements of the immediate social situation and social relations and the invocation of more encompassing relations of solidarity grounded in cultural membership. Doing musayara, on the other hand, involves a set of cultural injunctions that are highly sensitive to various aspects of the social situation, such as participants' ages, genders, and degree of familiarity (see Rosen, 1984, for a discussion of the Moroccan person as "homo contextus").

Fourth, speaking dugri is associated with an attitude of spontaneity, with the elevation of "naturalness." Doing musayara, on the other hand, is associated with the capacity for self-control, which is associated with a high positive value placed on cultivation—the "culture" rather than the "nature" end of the continuum. The sense of virtue accompanying the Sabra's employment of straight talk is obviously not easily communicated to an Arab interlocutor.

Fifth, the dugri ethos gives expression to an aesthetic of simplicity, to an attitude of antistyle, which is predicated on the cultural contrast between deeds and (mere) words. The ethos of musayara is associated with the high cultural value placed on the Arabic language (see Ferguson, 1968), with a delight in its stylistic possibilities, which Patai (1983) has called rhetoricity. For Arabs, the Sabra style smacks of unfathomable literal-mindedness.

Sixth, the directness associated with the dugri interactional code implies a preference for nonmediated, face-to-face communication. People say they prefer the dugri approach to one that involves "speaking behind the back." In saying it "straight to the face" one both displays trustfulness and inspires a sense of trust. Straight talk is thus seen as counteracting the use of gossip to circulate unfavorable information. Speaking dugri is also often contrasted with "diplomacy." For Arabs, on the other hand, passing on social information via an indirect channel is often a preferred strategy, as it reduces the risk to participants' "face." For them, straight or dugri talk in the style of the quintessential Sabra is not an expression of trust but rather is often experienced as offensive, even abusive. Mediation is, indeed, an important communicative vehicle in contexts of interpersonal conflict and negotiation. As one of our respondents described it, each party does musayara to the mediator who comes to the litigants' home and tries to bring about conciliation. These divergent cultural attitudes toward the communicative encounter may well color the ways in which exchanges between Arabs and Jews may become deflected even in the wholehearted pursuit of a cultural and political *modus vivendi*.

## CONCLUSION

The Israeli Jew, for whom dugri speech and the mode of directness define an idiom of cultural self-definition, and the Israeli Arab, for whom "life demands musayara," both have a great deal of cultural learning to do before they can speak "person to person," either in interpersonal encounters or in the context of political negotiations. To be a person, as Geertz (1976) reminds us, is to be a person-in-a-culture. What it means to be a person-in-a-culture can be gleaned, at least in part, through a study of the assumptions and displays of personhood that give shape to cultural communication styles. However broadly sketched and tentative such a study must ultimately remain, however partial the attempt to convey a sense of self to a cultural other, we believe such exploration is a necessary step toward better intercultural understanding and mutual acceptance.

## NOTES

1. Our study relates specifically to Arabs in Israel (respondents included both Moslem and Christian Arabs, as well as Druze). Our reading of the literature, however, suggests that the social norms associated with doing musayara might be associated with a larger "speech field," in Hymes's (1974) terms, cutting across dialectal and regional differences within the Middle East (see Assadi, 1980; Beeman, 1986; Gilsenan, 1967; Keddie, 1963; Koch, 1983; Patai, 1983; Rosen, 1984; Sharabi, 1975).

2. Griefat (1986) provides a more detailed discussion of the historical/cultural underpinnings of musayara.

3. We are grateful to the many Arab and Jewish students who participated in ethnography of communication courses at the School of Education at the University of Haifa during the years 1982–1986 for many helpful examples, comments, and queries, as well as to the many other individuals who were willing to share their perceptions and stories with us. We owe a particular debt of gratitude to the late Dr. Sami Mar'i, whose wise counsel and constant encouragement made it possible for us to pursue this project.

4. This strategy is mentioned by Khuri (1968) in relation to patterns of bargaining in the marketplace.

## REFERENCES

Albert, E. (1972). Culture patterning of speech behavior in Burundi. In J. Gumperz & D. Hymes (Eds.), *Directions in sociolinguistics*. New York: Holt, Rinehart & Winston.

Antoun, R. (1968). On the significance of names in an Arab village. *Ethnology, 7*, 158–170.

Assadi, R. (1980). Deference: Persian style. *Anthropological Linguistics, 22,* 221–224.
Bateson, G. (1958). *Naven.* Stanford, CA: Stanford University Press.
Beeman, W. (1986). *Language, status and power in Iran.* Bloomington: Indiana University Press.
Bourdieu, P. (1966). The sentiment of honor in Kabyle society. In J. G. Peristiany (Ed.), *Honor and shame: The values of Mediterranean society.* Chicago: University of Chicago Press.
Brown, P., & Levinson, S. (1987). *Politeness.* Cambridge: Cambridge University Press.
Caplan, G. (1980). *Arab and Jew in Jerusalem: Explorations in community mental health.* Cambridge, MA: Harvard University Press.
Ferguson, A, (1968). Myths about Arabic. In J. Fishman (Ed.), *Readings in the sociology of language.* The Hague: Mouton.
Friedrich, P. (1972). Social context and semantic feature: Russian pronominal usage. In J. Gumperz & D. Hymes (Eds.), *Directions in sociolinguistics: The ethnography of communication.* New York: Holt, Rinehart & Winston.
Geertz, C. (1973). *The interpretation of cultures.* New York: Basic Books.
Geertz, C. (1976). From the native's point of view: On the nature of anthropological understanding. In K. E. Basso & H. S. Selby (Eds), *Meaning in anthropology.* Albuquerque: University of New Mexico Press.
Gilsenan, M. (1967). Lying, honor and contradiction. In B. Kapferer (Ed.), *Transaction and meaning: Directions in the anthropology of exchange and symbolic behavior.* Philadelphia: Institute for the Study of Human Issues.
Griefat, Y. (1986). *Musayara as a communicative pattern in Bedouin culture.* Unpublished master's thesis, School of Education, University of Haifa, Israel. (in Hebrew)
Hymes, D. (1974). *Foundations in sociolinguistics.* Philadelphia: University of Pennsylvania Press.
Katriel, T. (1986). *Talking straight: "Dugri" speech in Israeli Sabra culture.* Cambridge: Cambridge University Press.
Katriel, T., & Philipsen, G. (1981). "What we need is communication": "Communication" as a cultural category in American speech. *Communication Monographs, 48,* 301–317.
Keddie, N. R. (1963). Symbol and sincerity in Islam. *Studia Islamica, 19,* 27–63.
Keenan, E. (1974). Norm-makers, norm-breakers: Uses of speech by men and women in a Malagasy community. In R. Bauman & J. Sherzer (Eds.), *Explorations in the ethnography of speaking.* New York: Cambridge University Press.
Koch, B. (1983). Presentation as proof: The language of Arabic rhetoric. *Anthropological Linguistics, 25,* 47–70.
Khuri, F. (1968). The etiquette of bargaining in the Middle East. *American Anthropologist, 70,* 698–706.
Patai, R. (1983). *The Arab mind.* New York: Charles Scribner.
Philipsen, G. (1987). Prospects for cultural communication. In L. Kincaid (Ed.), *Communication theory from Eastern and Western perspectives.* New York: Academic Press.
Rosaldo, M. (1973). I have nothing to hide: The language of Ilongot oratory. *Language in Society, 2,* 193–223.

Rosen, L. (1984). *Bargaining for reality: The construction of social relations in a Muslim community*. Chicago: University of Chicago Press.

Sharabi, H. (1975). *Introduction to the study of Arabic society*. Jerusalem: Salah Addein. (in Arabic)

Shipler, D. (1986). *Arab and Jew: Wounded spirits in a promised land*. New York: Times Book.

Trilling, L. (1971). *Sincerity and authenticity*. Cambridge: Cambridge University Press.

# 7

# Linguistic Strategies and Cultural Styles for Persuasive Discourse

BARBARA JOHNSTONE ● *Texas A&M University*

*This chapter describes the ways in which culture, language, and rhetorical situation come together to shape persuasive strategies used in the European West and the Arab and Iranian East. It is an attempt to find a way of combining a view of rhetoric that sees persuasive style as a facet of culture, and hence to some extent predetermined, with a view that sees speakers as making choices, based in immediate rhetorical situations, among "available means of persuasion."*

Let me begin with three examples of the kinds of communicative problems that this chapter attempts to explain. The first is an essay written by a young Egyptian student for an intermediate-level composition class that was part of an intensive English as a second language (ESL) program. The topic for this assignment was "What was the most frightening experience you ever had?" I have edited out orthographic and syntactic errors, which are not relevant to the present discussion, and have numbered the sentences for later reference:

> (1) The thing that makes me most frightened to think about is death. (2) I don't like it because it takes one of my best friends and when I begin to think if one of my family died, what would happen to me. (3) I love my father, my mother, and my brother and I can't imagine my situation in this case. (4) Really I don't know what I'd do. (5) And really I worry about my father and mother because they are becoming old. (6) And I can't do anything to save them. (7) I am just studying to keep them

AUTHOR'S NOTE: *This is an expanded version of a paper presented at the International Pragmatics Conference, Antwerp, August 1987. A somewhat different version was presented at the Georgetown University Round Table on Languages and Linguistics 1987, Presession on Discourse in Contact and Context. I would like to thank Deborah Tannen, Anne Johnstone, Tim Crusius, and two anonymous reviewers for valuable editorial suggestions.*

happy. (8) And if I knew the way to keep them happy and alive forever, I'd do it and I'd like to give them my life on a gold tray. (9) I feel afraid when I think about this problem. (10) And I don't know how to solve it. (11) I am just praying to God and asking him for a good, long, happy life for my parents.

This is a nice essay, in some ways. The writer expresses his deep and sincere care in forceful and rather poetic language. But there are some obvious oddities, too. The essay doesn't really address the assigned topic, since it is not about an experience, and furthermore, there are some rhetorical strangenesses, such as the writer's unusual use of *really* in sentences 4 and 5, and the fact that four of the eleven sentences in the essay begin with *and* (sentences 5, 6, 8, and 10). There is also a rather large amount of paraphrase for an essay this short, rather than any real development of the writer's thesis: sentences 3, 4, and 10 all say much the same thing, for example ("I don't know what I'd do"), as do sentences 1 and 9 ("The problem of death makes me afraid"). In several respects, then, this is not the sort of essay an American student might be expected to produce in response to an assignment like this.

A second example of miscommunication has to do with service interaction. Several years ago, I met several women who were on the staff of a Washington organization that facilitates educational exchange programs between the United States and various Middle Eastern countries. These women worked as counselors, helping to place Arab students at appropriate American universities and arrange for their transportation, orientation, and housing.

The counselors were all thoughtful, well-educated, and interested in the people they were dealing with; most of them had lived abroad, many had served in the Peace Corps, and some had traveled in the Middle East. Yet they were all frustrated with their job. They felt put upon by their Arab student clients, who, they said, "simply would never take no for an answer." The students would instead phone or write repeatedly to insist on some service that they had already been told was impossible, and then would finally announce to the counselors that they felt hurt and ignored, that the counselors weren't doing their jobs and didn't care about their clients. This was painful for the counselors, who certainly *did* care about their clients and were doing their best to carry out the organization's policies fairly and to communicate clearly. In the end, the counselors decided that the problem was that they were women and their student clients for the most part were men, thus confirming the common but inaccurate North American belief that Arab men don't like women. Gradually they came to dislike the people they were trying to help.

My third introductory example has to do with a more formal speech event, a journalistic interview, in a different Middle Eastern setting— revolutionary Iran.[1] In 1979, Italian journalist Oriana Fallaci was granted an interview with Iran's Ayatollah Khomeini, which was published in the *New York Times Magazine* (Fallaci, 1979). The interview turned into an abusive argument, during which Khomeini accused Fallaci of being a prostitute, Fallaci stripped off her chador, or cloak, in Khomeini's presence, and Khomeini finally ordered Fallaci to leave the room, and from then on refused to see any more Western journalists.

Two sorts of things seem to go wrong in the interview. For one thing, Fallaci often proposes syllogistic arguments to Khomeini, challenging him to reexamine and clarify the logic on which his claims are based. Khomeini, however, rejects these arguments out of hand, simply refusing to respond to them. For example, Fallaci uses the following argument in an attempt to challenge Khomeini's prohibition of alcohol and music: If, according to Khomeini, drinking and singing are sinful, and if the Pope drinks and sings, then the Pope must be a sinner. Khomeini rejects the entire argument, saying, "The rules of your priests do not interest me." Islam, he says, does not allow alcoholic drinks, and "that's all."

The second sort of trouble in the interview also has to do with what appear to be inappropriate responses by Khomeini to Fallaci's questions. Toward the end of the interview, for example, Fallaci attempts (as she does several times during the interview) to get Khomeini to clarify his notion of democracy, by asking him for his definition of the term. Khomeini responds not with a definition, but with a story from the history of Shi'ite Islam, about a dispute between Ali, the seventh-century Imam whom Shi'ite Muslims believe to be the first rightful Muslim leader after Muhammad, and a lowly Jew. In the courtroom where the dispute was to be settled, the judge stood when Ali entered the room, but not when the Jew entered. Ali became angry, pointing out that the contending parties in a lawsuit should be treated the same way, no matter what their social rank. Khomeini ends the story with a rhetorical question: "Can you give me a better example of democracy?" In this and other occasions on which Khomeini responds to a question with a story or an extended analogy, one senses that he may not understand, or may be pretending not to understand, what Fallaci expects his answers to be like. Clearly, something went wrong during the interview; Khomeini and Fallaci seem continually to be talking at cross-purposes.

The three examples of miscommunication I have just presented may seem like disparate places to begin. Yet they all have something in common. All involve cross-cultural differences in styles of persuasion, or in how language is used rhetorically. In what follows, I would like to discuss the connections among rhetoric, culture, and language, particularly as these connections impinge on communication between the European and American West and the Arab and, more broadly, Islamic East. What I will try to do is to suggest a way of describing and thinking about cross-cultural differences in rhetorical language use that takes into account the ways people are constrained by the languages they speak and the communicative patterns of the cultures to which they belong, and the ways people use language and rhetoric creatively in particular communicative situations.

To do this, I will first introduce what I think is an important distinction between *persuasive strategies*, by which I mean, broadly speaking, the various means of persuasion available to any speaker, and *persuasive style*, or a speaker's general tendency, resulting in part from cultural and historical factors, to adopt one particular persuasive strategy in *any* situation. I will then describe and exemplify three different persuasive strategies, which I will call *quasilogic*, *presentation*, and *analogy*. I will discuss the linguistic correlates of each—what sorts of syntactic and lexical choices are most likely to be made in each mode—as well as what I will call the conceptual correlates—what sorts of beliefs about how persuasion works and how decisions are made tend to trigger each mode. Finally, I will talk about how and when each of the three persuasive strategies is likely to become a persuasive style, or the default mode for rhetorical discourse in a culture. This will involve a brief discussion of some cultural and historical facts about the Western, Aristotelian rhetorical tradition, about the theocratic tradition of the Arab world, and about Iranian Shi'ite ideology.

## PERSUASIVE STRATEGIES AND STYLES

Let me now begin to lay out the model of persuasion and the relationships among language, culture, and persuasion with which I would like to work. First, I would like to elaborate on the distinction I have made between *persuasive strategies* and *persuasive styles*. Persuasive strategies are the range of options from which a speaker selects in deciding on an appropriate tactic or combination of tactics for persuasion in a given situation. Clearly, we do not use the same tactics in every situation that calls for rhetorical discourse. All of us have access to a range of communicative strategies, verbal and nonverbal, among which we choose in situations where persuasion is necessary. Sometimes we use logic; sometimes we tell stories; sometimes we employ displays of emotion, threats, or bribes; sometimes we simply repeat what we want until our interlocutors give in. It is these tactics—the broad range of possible choices for how to persuade that is part of a speaker's communicative competence—that I refer to as *persuasive strategies*. Speech communities, and subgroups within them, may differ to some extent in the range of strategies available to their members. Keenan (1974) points out, for example, that Malagasy women may use direct requests for action, while Malagasy men are constrained to use more indirect, formalized strategies for persuasion. But no speaker is ever limited to a single strategy for persuasion in all situations, and it is likely that some strategies, based as they are in basic human ways of thinking, are universal. (Narrative may be one such strategy; see Bruner, 1986.)

To the extent that rhetorical situations—ones in which persuasion is necessary—are familiar, deciding on the most appropriate strategy does not pose a problem.[2] There are, however, situations in which a speaker may not know how best to proceed because he or she is faced with an unfamiliar rhetorical task, or with an interlocutor whose responses he or she is unable to predict. Such situations include, but are not limited to, the ones that occur in cross-cultural contexts. A person's initial, reflexive choice of persuasive strategy in situations like these, the strategy or set of strategies he or she assumes to be the best and the most universally applicable, is what I refer to as *persuasive style*. Persuasive styles are culturally predisposed. North Americans and other Westerners, I will claim, are most likely to use a persuasive strategy based on syllogistic, demonstrative logic; their persuasive style is what I will call *quasilogical*. In other cultural settings, other persuasive styles are likely. Note that I am not claiming that North Americans always try to persuade by appearing to be logical. I am simply claiming that for North Americans quasilogic is the most easily available and most obvious default choice for cases in which no other strategy immediately suggests itself.

Consider, for example, the following situation.[3] A young North American woman spending a study year in Greece went to the post office to pick up a parcel mailed from home. The package was addressed to the woman, in care of the Greek friend with whom she was staying. The North American was told by the postal clerk that the package could not be released to her, because it was addressed not to her, but to her Greek friend. The friend was unfortunately out of town, and the woman needed the parcel right away.

The North American woman began by explaining to the postal clerk that the package was in fact hers, using as logical evidence for this claim the fact that it had her name on it. She displayed her passport to assure the clerk of her identity. This, however, did not work; the man was adamant in his refusal to give her the parcel because, he said, it was not addressed to her. The woman then tried several variations of her logical argument, all to no avail. The clerk finally announced that it was time for his break and slammed down the parcel pickup window, leaving the North American woman to storm out of the post office in utter frustration.

Sitting in a cafe, the woman thought over the situation and decided on a new persuasive strategy, one that she suspected might be more suitable in the Greek context of the interaction. She returned to the post office, but this time, instead of waiting in front of the parcel pickup window, she opened a door marked "private" and walked confidently into the room behind the window, where the packages awaiting pickup were arranged on shelves. She had seen where her package was stored, and she went directly to it, picked it up, and announced to the postal clerk who was now on duty that it was hers and that she was taking it. When the new clerk began to object, she repeated, in her most forceful voice, that the parcel was hers and that she would now take it home. She then walked out with her package.

It is not important for our immediate purposes to understand in detail exactly why this change of tactic worked. While we see in this scenario further evidence about persuasive strategies, about the range of choices a person has in any rhetorical situation, the scenario also illustrates something about persuasive styles. The North American woman's first line of attack was to use a persuasive strategy based on logic, a strategy in which claims are made and evidence adduced to support these claims. ("This package is mine because it has my name on it; I am who I claim to be because I have a passport with my photo and that name in it.") She used this strategy unreflectively, assuming that it would work; it was only after further thought that she decided on a change of strategy.

I have now made clear the distinction between persuasive strategies and persuasive styles. I would like next to discuss three persuasive strategies in more detail, and then to examine the historical and cultural facts that have predisposed each of the three to become the persuasive style of at least one cultural group.

### Three Persuasive Strategies: Linguistic Correlates

The three persuasive strategies I would like to discuss are what I call *quasilogic*, *presentation*, and *analogy*.[4] Figure 7.1 presents in schematic form the material to be covered in this section.

The term *quasilogical* is borrowed from Belgian philosopher of rhetoric, Chaim Perelman (see Perelman & Olbrechts-Tyteca, 1958/1969). Quasilogical argumentation is informal, nondemonstrative reasoning that takes its effectiveness from its similarity to formal, demonstrative logic. By making use of the structure and the vocabulary of formal logic, persuaders in the quasilogical mode create the rhetorical impression that their arguments are logically incontrovertible. The goal of quasilogical persuasion is to *convince*, to make it seem impossible for an audience using its powers of rationality not to accept the arguer's conclusion.

One of Perelman's examples of quasilogical argumentation in-

|  | Quasilogic | Presentation | Analogy |
|---|---|---|---|
| distinguishing model | model from formal logic; convincing | model from poetry; moving | model from narrative; teaching |
| linguistic correlates | use of "logical connectives": <u>thus</u>, <u>hence</u>, <u>therefore</u> . . . | "rhetorical deixis": <u>here</u>, <u>now</u>, <u>this</u> | formulaic language: "You know what they say"; "That reminds me" |
|  |  | visual metaphors: <u>behold</u>, <u>look</u>, <u>see</u> | "the words of the ancestors"; proverbs |
|  | subordination; integration | coordination/ parataxis/ parallelism; involvement | chronology; timeless past ("once upon a time"); involvement |

Figure 7.1: Three persuasive strategies.

volves the informal use of the mathematical notion of *transitivity*. Formally speaking, *transitivity* is a property of certain relationships, such as equality or numerical superiority, that makes it possible to infer that because the relationship holds between $a$ and $b$ and between $b$ and $c$, it therefore holds between $a$ and $c$: If $a$, for example, equals $b$, and $b$ equals $c$, then $a$ equals $c$. Informal, or quasilogical, uses of transitivity treat relationships that are not in fact transitive as if they were. One such nontransitive relationship is friendship; a quasilogical argument that could be built with this relationship might be this: If John is a friend of mine, and I am a friend of Sue's, then John and Sue ought to get along well.

Note that the linguistic form of this argument is exactly the same as that of the formally transitive, demonstrative argument about $a$, $b$, and $c$. Quasilogical arguments borrow their strength not only from their propositional similarity to formal reasoning, but also from their linguistic similarity: They are characterized by their use of what writers' handbooks call "logical connectives" like *thus*, *hence*, and *therefore*, as well as by their use of hypotactic, subordinate structures, such as the conditional clauses needed to relate premises to conclusions. Quasilogical persuasive discourse is highly *integrated*, to borrow a term from Wallace Chafe (1982): Clauses are explicitly related to each other as superordinate claims and subordinate sources of support for these claims.

In order to make it as clear as possible that each individual has access to a range of persuasive strategies, I have chosen examples of all three strategies I am discussing from the work of one person, Martin Luther King, Jr. I need hardly point out that King is universally respected as a master of rhetorical discourse; his speeches and his writing, as well as his nonverbal strategies, have clearly been persuasive in causing important social change. While King was especially adept at making appropriate and effective choices among the rhetorical strategies available to him, his situated choices are in principle no different from the choices any speaker makes in attempting to adapt to audience and other contextual factors.

The following paragraph from King's "Letter from a Birmingham Jail" (Washington, 1986, pp. 293–294) exemplifies quasilogical persuasive discourse. The paragraph is constructed on the model of a series of syllogisms, with the universal quantifiers *all* and *any* marking major premises and *so* marking conclusions.

Now what is the difference between [just and unjust laws]? How does one determine when a law is just or unjust? A just law is a man-made code that squares with the moral law or the law of God. An unjust law is a code that is out of harmony with the moral law. To put it in the terms of Saint Thomas Aquinas, an unjust law is a human law that is not rooted in eternal and natural law. Any law that uplifts human personality is just. Any law that degrades human personality is unjust. All segregation statutes are unjust because segregation distorts the soul and damages the personality. It gives the segregator a false sense of superiority, and the segregated a false sense of inferiority. To use the words of Martin Buber, the great Jewish philosopher, segregation substitutes an "I-it" relationship for the "I-thou" relationship, and ends up relegating persons to the status of things. So segregation is not only politically, economically and sociologically unsound, but it is morally wrong and sinful. Paul Tillich has said that sin is separation. Isn't segregation an existential expression of man's tragic separation, an expression of his awful estrangement, his terrible sinfulness? So I can urge men to disobey segregation ordinances because they are morally wrong. (From "Letter from a Birmingham Jail," in *Why We Can't Wait* by Martin Luther King, Jr. Copyright © 1963, 1964 by Martin Luther King, Jr. Reprinted by permission of Harper & Row, Publishers, Inc.)

King begins here by arguing that segregation laws are unjust, because they are "out of harmony with the moral law," and any such law is, according to Aquinas and others, unjust. He then uses a similar argument to show that segregation laws are sinful: Sin is separation, according to Tillich, and segregation is "an existential expression of man's tragic separation"; therefore, segregation ordinances are morally wrong and should be disobeyed. Note that the first of these two arguments is really an argument from authority, and hence not demonstrative. The second argument has the form A = B (sin is separation), C = B (segregation is an expression of separation), therefore C = A (segregation is morally wrong). This would constitute formally valid proof only if "is" in the major premise and "is an expression of" in the minor premise meant what = does; in fact, they do not. The rhetorical force of King's arguments comes not from their formal validity but from the ways they make use of the structures of formal arguments.

In contrast to quasilogical persuasion, with its underlying metaphor of persuasion as a process of rational convincing, *presentational* persuasion could be said to be based on the assumption that being persuaded is being moved, being swept along by a rhythmic flow of words and sounds, in the way people are swept along by poetry. The goal of presentational persuasion is to make one's claim maximally present in the audience's consciousness, by repeating it, paraphrasing it, and calling aesthetic attention to it.

The language of presentational persuasion is characterized by its rhythmic, paratactic flow. Rather than having to jump from level to subordinate level, readers or hearers are swept along by parallel clauses, connected in coordinate series. Visual metaphors also help to make the persuader's claim present, as if the claim were actually in the audience's line of vision; hearers are told to "look," "see," or, in languages in which a comparable word exists, "behold." Presentational discourse also makes use of what Lakoff (1974) has called "rhetorical deixis," the use of terms like *here, now*, and *this*, from the spatial and temporal realms, in reference to ideas. In contrast to the dense, "integrated" style of quasilogical discourse, which calls on the audience's rational (or, as Bruner, 1986, pp. 12–13, would say, "paradigmatic") minds, presentational discourse creates "involvement" (Chafe, 1982; Tannen, 1987) in the way good poetry does.[5]

An example of presentational discourse is from King's "I Have a Dream" speech (Washington, 1986, pp. 217–218). In connection with the visual nature of presentational persuasion, it is interesting to note Coretta Scott King's comment on the effect of this speech: "At that moment it seemed as if the Kingdom of God *appeared*" (Washington, 1986, p. 217; italics added).

> We have also come to this hallowed spot to remind America of the fierce urgency of now. This is no time to engage in the luxury of cooling off or to take the tranquilizing drug of gradualism. Now is the time to make real the promises of democracy; now is the time to rise from the dark and desolate valley of segregation to the sunlit path of racial justice; now is the time to lift our nation from the quicksands of racial injustice to the solid rock of brotherhood; now is the time to make justice a reality for all God's children. It would be fatal for the nation to overlook the urgency of the moment. This sweltering summer of the Negro's legitimate discontent will not pass until there is an invigorating autumn of freedom and equality.

King makes use here of all the features of presentation I have just listed: long patterns of syntactic parallelism in the clauses beginning with "now is the time"; poetic alliteration and imagery as, for example, "the dark and desolate valley of segregation"; and repeated appeals to here and now. The first selection discussed at the beginning of this chapter, the Arab student's essay, is also essentially presentational, hence its inappropriateness in a setting (an American narrative theme assignment) that calls for chronological order and quasilogical development.

A third persuasive strategy is analogy. Analogical persuasion works by calling to mind, explicitly or implicitly, traditional wisdom, often in the form of parable- or fablelike stories. Anyone who has ever countered an overcritical friend by saying, "People in glass houses shouldn't throw stones," or used a "When I was your age" story to talk a greedy child out of something, has made use of analogical persuasion. Analogical rhetoric persuades by teaching, reminding its audience of time-tested values by the indirect mode of storytelling. Analogical arguers persuade by having their audiences make lateral, abductive leaps between past events and current issues.

The language of analogical persuasion is the language of folktales, with their formulaic openings and closings, and the timeless and placeless quality signaled by expressions like "once upon a time, in a land far away." As do all narratives, stories used as analogies involve chronology and the linguistic markings of chronology, as well as what Labov (1972) and others refer to as "evaluation," or the various linguistic devices that underscore the pointfulness of stories.

Below are two examples of persuasive analogy from Martin Luther King's "Letter from a Birmingham Jail" (Washington, 1986, pp. 290, 294). The first is part of King's answer to the implied question "Why are you in Birmingham?"; the answer takes the form of references to Christian precedent.

> Beyond this, I am in Birmingham because injustice is here. Just as the eighth century prophets left their little villages and carried their "thus saith the Lord" far beyond the boundaries of their hometowns; and just as the Apostle Paul left his little village of Tarsus and carried the gospel of Jesus Christ to practically every hamlet and city of the Graeco-Roman world, I too am compelled to carry the gospel of freedom beyond my particular hometown. Like Paul, I must constantly respond to the Macedonian call for aid.

In the following excerpt, King defends civil disobedience with reference to biblical examples.

Of course, there is nothing new about this kind of civil disobedience. It was seen sublimely in the refusal of Shadrach, Meshach and Abednego to obey the laws of Nebuchadnezzar because a higher moral law was involved. It was practiced superbly by the early Christians who were willing to face hungry lions and the excruciating pain of chopping blocks, before submitting to certain unjust laws of the Roman Empire. To a degree academic freedom is a reality today because Socrates practiced civil disobedience. (Both excerpts from "Letter from a Birmingham Jail," in *Why We Can't Wait* by Martin Luther King, Jr. Copyright © 1963, 1964 by Martin Luther King, Jr. Reprinted by permission of Harper & Row, Publishers, Inc.)

King does in these two excerpts precisely what Khomeini does in the second of the two interview selections presented above, the one in which he tells a story from the history of Shi'ite Islam in answer to Fallaci's request for his position on democracy. Khomeini's repeated and insistent use of analogical persuasion and Fallaci's insistence on quasilogical persuasion, as well as the inability or refusal of each to see the other's style in a persuasive light, are at the root of the ultimate failure of their interview (Johnstone, 1986).

### *Conceptual Correlates: Strategies Become Styles*

With each of the three persuasive strategies I have discussed go a set of what I call *conceptual correlates*, an epistemological stance about what sorts of arguments and what sorts of people can be persuasive. By means of a discussion of these conceptual correlates, I would like to begin to relate persuasive strategies to the historical and cultural facts that can predispose one or another persuasive strategy to become the dominant strategy of a cultural group, or that group's persuasive style. Figure 7.2 summarizes this discussion.

Quasilogical persuasion is based on the notion that the key to the persuasiveness of an argument is the ideas that are expressed. If a claim is true, it is true no matter who states it or what sort of language is used. What is important about quasilogical discourse is that its logical structure be orderly. This is the epistemology that underlies the Aristotelian notion that invention and arrangement are prior to mere style, which is simply the dressing up of ideas in clever ways. It is also the epistemology that makes it possible for people like the Arab-student counselors I discussed before to say things like "Those are the rules; I didn't make the rules and I can't bend them." Truth,

|  | Quasilogical | Presentational | Analogical |
|---|---|---|---|
| conceptual correlates | ideas are persuasive | people are persuasive | culture is persuasive |
|  | institutions make decisions | individuals make decisions | history, tradition make decisions |
|  | structure is crucial | words are crucial | aptness is crucial |
| culture/ geography | canonically Western (though not so typical as we suppose) | Eastern (in older and more religious tradition) | |

**Figure 7.2: Three persuasive styles.**

in this view, is not a matter for individual decision. Once established via rational procedures, decisions are no longer negotiable, and they apply in any situation.

Presentational persuasion, on the other hand, is made possible by an epistemological context in which people, not ideas, are responsible for persuasion. What is crucial is the individual's choice of repeated words, phrases, and rhythms with which to move other individuals to belief. Culturally, presentational persuasion is most likely in situations in which truths are imminent, recorded in doctrinal texts or given by God, and not matters for rational decision, and the persuader's task is to make a potentially available truth actually available—or present— in the audience's consciousness. Such cultural settings include those in which religion is central, settings in which truth is brought to light rather than created out of human rationality. One such setting is the traditional Islamic theocracy of the Arab world (Koch, 1983); another is the world of the missionary (see, for example, Harding, 1987). In a presentational world, individuals deal with individuals rather than with ideas or institutions; hence the Arab students' perception that the American counselors who relied on quasilogical arguments for institutional truths were not treating them as people.

Rosaldo (1973) describes an epistemological context much like the one I am describing, among missionized Christian Ilongots, who subscribe to an ideology in which the truth is external and predetermined in a doctrinal text (the Bible), while the traditional Ilongot worldview is egalitarian and nonauthoritarian. Interestingly, however, the linguistic style of Christian Ilongots does not seem to be presentational. It is characterized in Ilongot terms as *straight speech,* and is thought to be direct and explicit, while traditional Ilongot *crooked speech* rhetoric is more elaborate and allusive. Perhaps the direct, unelaborated character of straight speech is partly a response to the Ilongot social context; Christian Ilongots need to set themselves apart from traditional Ilongots, and hence cannot use the same linguistic techniques for persuasion. Straight speech, in other words, may serve presentational ends by different means, since the poetic features of presentational discourse are a marker of traditional style and hence not available to Christianized Ilongots. In any event, Rosaldo's findings serve to underscore the caution that is necessary in generalizing about persuasive styles and strategies that are a function of very specific contexts.

While presentational persuasion is expository (accessible truths are made available by being stated and restated), analogical persuasion is narrative in nature. Analogical persuasion is rooted in the belief that traditional stories—allegories about truth rather than arguments establishing truth or direct statements of truth—are persuasive, and that decisions are best made with reference to historical precedent. What is crucial in a setting like this is the arguer's choice of apt historical examples. Legal argumentation is often analogical, taking its effectiveness from compelling use of precedent. Teachers, too, as well as mothers, shamans, and others whose roles involve being what anthropologists call "culture bearers," use analogy. (See, for example, Ochs, 1973, on the role of proverbs in Malagasy oratory; the papers in Bloch, 1975, also describe situations in which "traditional authority" is at the root of persuasive force.) One figure who personifies this role is the Ayatollah Khomeini; as Beeman (1986, pp. 207–211) points out, the entire rhetoric of the Iranian revolution is based on a return to traditional Shi'ite Islamic values, and Khomeini's role is that of "chief regent" for the Twelfth Imam, the most perfect of men and the one who will judge people's sins at the last judgment. That Khomeini should resort to analogical persuasion seems almost predictable.

## CULTURAL DETERMINISM AND RHETORICAL CRAFT

In conclusion, I would like to make a few comments about a word I have just used—*predictable*. I have suggested that certain historical and cultural settings call forth certain persuasive strategies, turning these strategies into the dominant persuasive styles of people in these settings, and that cross-cultural friction is created as persuasive styles collide. Is it, in fact, predictable that Westerners will resort to quasilogical persuasion, and Easterners to presentational or analogical persuasion? To put the same question in broader terms, Does culture determine language use in rhetorical situations?

My answer to both versions of the question is no. Any persuader has access to a range of persuasive strategies, and his or her choices of persuasive strategies, like his or her choices of words or grammatical structures, are made in the context of the interaction at hand. Culture may predispose certain choices over others, but it does not determine choices. For every example of cross-cultural miscommunication, one could adduce at least one example of cross-cultural communication, at least one case in which interlocutors successfully adapt to each other's cultural styles and personal idiosyncracies. To cite just one example, Martin Luther King's "I Have a Dream" speech was delivered before a mixed audience of Blacks and Whites; White audiences in the 1960s (before the advent of nationally known Black politicians such as Jesse Jackson) were accustomed to the quasilogical style of most White politicians. Yet King's presentational speech was accepted by the Whites in his audience, for whom it was as forceful and persuasive as it was for the Blacks. Persuasion is negotiated in a give and take between speakers and audiences, and rhetoric creates social relations as well as reflecting them (Paine, 1981, pp. 2–5). Cases in which communication fails to occur may be more often noticed than cases in which communication does occur, but I do not think they are more frequent.

What happens, then, in cases like the ones with which this chapter began, in which persuasion is foiled by a clash of styles? Since, as I have pointed out, Westerners do use analogies and poetic discourse persuasively, and since the Muslim world has a long and important tradition of logical inquiry in the Aristotelian tradition, none of the failures of communication in my introductory examples should have had to happen: An American ESL teacher should be able to respond to the poetic force of the Egyptian's essay;[6] Arab students should be able to take American academic counselors at their quasilogical word; Khomeini and Fallaci should be able to interpret what each other did as persuasive in intent. The problems that occurred have their roots not in unbridgeable cultural gaps, but rather in specific rhetorical interactions. What happens in situations like these is somewhat akin to what Bateson (1972) calls "complementary schizmogenesis" (pp. 66–72). Faced with persuasive strategies that seem inappropriate, interlocutors try to repair the situation by becoming more insistent on the strategies they individually think best, and a sort of face-off is created in which setting the strategic tone for the interaction becomes the locus of persuasive force. (If you can force your opponent to play by your rules, rather than your adapting to his or hers, you have a better chance of winning the game.) Thus the interaction changes from one in which persuasion per se is the goal to one in which controlling the means of persuasion is the goal. Problems like this are not simply the result of intercultural difference. At root, I think, they are the result of failures of good will, the will to adapt and understand.

It is for these reasons that I think it is crucial to find ways of talking about rhetoric and culture that do not end in cultural determinism, but that instead treat rhetoric the way Aristotle did, as the craft of finding the best of the available means of persuasion for the rhetorical situation at hand. I have tried to do this by separating persuasive strategies from persuasive styles, and by treating the latter as cultural predispositions rather than as cultural rules. In doing this, I am trying to develop a theoretical framework suitable for thinking about culture and communicative style in a nondeterministic way, in keeping with traditional and recurrent notions about the emergent, situated nature of language and linguistic interaction.

# NOTES

1. See Johnstone (1986) for a detailed analysis of the miscommunication in this interview.

2. The term *rhetorical situation* is used here to refer to a speech situation that calls for persuasive discourse. I use the term somewhat differently than does Bitzer (1968).

3. I am grateful to Susan Heumann for providing this example.

4. It must be stressed that this is by no means an exhaustive list of possible persuasive strategies. Among others might be the persuasive use of emotion (see Bailey, 1983); Quaker "friendly persuasion," in which silence and a special kind of enlightened witnessing ideally give rise to consensus; the strategy of "dynamic opposition" identified by Kochman (1981) as characteristic of American Black style; and a variety of nonverbal strategies, such as sit-ins or other demonstrations.

5. This strategy shares many features with modes of discourse identified with orality (Ong, 1982), and in fact the following example is from a speech. But not all

presentational discourse is spoken, and *oral* is a potentially misleading term when it is used as a descriptor of culture types (see Johnstone, in press).

6. As the American teacher in question, I in fact did find the essay very appealing, and it was one of the things that originally sparked my interest in Arabs' persuasive style. However, essays like this are generally perceived by ESL teachers as repetitive, digressive, and needlessly elaborate (see Kaplan, 1966; Thompson-Panos & Thomas-Ružić, 1983).

# REFERENCES

Bailey, F. G. (1983). *The tactical uses of passion: An essay on power, reason, and reality*. Ithaca, NY: Cornell University Press.

Bateson, G. (1972). *Steps to an ecology of mind*. New York: Ballantine.

Bitzer, L. (1968). The rhetorical situation. *Philosophy and Rhetoric, 1*, 1–14.

Beeman, W. O. (1986). *Language, status, and power in Iran*. Bloomington: Indiana University Press.

Bloch, M. (Ed.). (1975). *Political language and oratory in traditional society*. London: Academic Press.

Bruner, J. (1986). *Actual minds, possible worlds*. Cambridge, MA: Harvard University Press.

Chafe, W. (1982). Integration and involvement in speaking, writing, and oral literature. In D. Tannen (Ed.), *Spoken and written language: Exploring orality and literacy*. Norwood, NJ: Ablex.

Fallaci, O. (1979, October 7). An interview with Khomeini. *New York Times Magazine*, pp. 29–31.

Harding, S. F. (1987). Convicted by the Holy Spirit: The rhetoric of fundamental Baptist conversion. *American Ethnologist, 14*, 167–181.

Johnstone, B. (1986). Arguments with Khomeini: Rhetorical situation and persuasive style in cross-cultural perspective. *Text, 6*, 171–187.

Johnstone, B. (in press). "Orality" and discourse structure in Modern Standard Arabic. In M. Eid (Ed.), *Perspectives on Arabic Linguistics I*. Philadelphia: John Benjamins.

Kaplan, R. (1966). Cultural thought patterns in inter-cultural education. *Language Learning, 16*, 1–20.

Keenan, E. (1974). Norm-makers, norm-breakers: Uses of speech by men and women in a Malagasy community. In R. Bauman & J. Sherzer (Eds.), *Explorations in the ethnography of speaking*. Cambridge: Cambridge University Press.

Koch, B. J. (1983). Presentation as proof: The language of Arabic rhetoric. *Anthropological Linguistics, 23*, 47–60.

Kochman, T. (1981). *Black and white styles in conflict*. Chicago: University of Chicago Press.

Labov, W. (1972). The transformation of experience in narrative syntax. In W. Labov, *Language in the inner city*. Philadelphia: University of Pennsylvania Press.

Lakoff, R. (1974). Remarks on *this* and *that*. In *Proceedings of the Tenth Annual Meeting of the Chicago Linguistics Society*. Chicago: University of Chicago.

Ochs, E. (1973). A sliding sense of obligatoriness: The polystructure of Malagasy oratory. *Language in Society, 2*, 225–243.

Ong, W. (1982). *Orality and literacy*. London: Methuen.

Paine, R. (Ed.). (1981). *Politically speaking: Cross-cultural studies of rhetoric*. Philadelphia: Institute for the Study of Human Issues.

Perelman, C., & Olbrechts-Tyteca, L. (1969). *The new rhetoric: A treatise on argumentation* (J. Wilkenson & P. Weaver, Trans.). Notre Dame, IN: University of Notre Dame Press. (Original work published 1958)

Rosaldo, M. (1973). I have nothing to hide: The language of Ilongot oratory. *Language in Society, 2*, 193–223.

Tannen, D. (1987). Repetition and variation as spontaneous formulaicity in conversation. *Language, 63*, 547–605.

Thompson-Panos, K., & Thomas-Ruzic, M. (1983). The least you should know about Arabic: Implications for the ESL writing instructor. *TESOL Quarterly, 17*, 609–623.

Washington, J. M. (Ed.). (1986). *A testament of hope: The essential writings of Martin Luther King, Jr.* San Francisco: Harper & Row.

# 8

## Telephone Openings and Conversational Universals
### A Study in Three Languages

ROBERT HOPPER  ●

NADA KOLEILAT DOANY  ●  *University of Texas, Austin*

*This chapter advances the claim that structural universals underlie telephone conversational openings in English, French, and Arabic. Specifically, conversational analysis method is used to delineate conversational universals in the three languages. Two tentative conversational universals in telephone openings are proposed at the end of the chapter. Telephone conversation is viewed as a critical activity in this increasingly multilingual, interdependent world.*

Language diversity, according to persistent legend, originated when humans tried to build the Tower of Babel, in order, perhaps, to eavesdrop on heaven. It is curious that no contemporary theory of language proposes a comprehensive and satisfactory explication of the truism that humans speak within thousands of speech communities. We cannot speak to just any human, but only to comembers of speech communities. Speaking with someone is coparticipating in a speech community. Humans who speak and listen in turn to one another usually characterize themselves as speaking a language in common. Many speakers treat the languages they speak as prisons limiting the range of their conversations to coparticipants. Considering cross-linguistic speaking is a bit like wandering in a labyrinth, attempting to recall or recapture some linguistic paradise lost (Steiner, 1975).

That human beings speak thousands of different languages is a truism that, for most us, remains unexplicated. On the surface, all linguistic systems differ from each other in multitudes of details. Some scholars (e.g., Whorf) believe that such code differences make interlanguage communication extremely problematic. However, others argue that in some sense all languages are "put together in similar ways" (e.g., Chomsky, 1957, 1965; Greenberg, 1963). According to this view, all languages are based on universal principles of semantics, syntax, and phonology. Languages exemplify similar basic organizational schemes and differ from one another primarily in peripheral features. An analogy is offered by Clark and Clark (1978):

> Imagine how people would describe three shirts. They would probably stress their differences. Number one is cotton, two is silk, and three is wool. Or number one is plaid, two is polka-dotted, and three is plain. Or number one has short sleeves while two and three have long sleeves. And so on. But note that each comparison presupposes something universal about the three shirts. Each is made from cloth, and what varies is the kind of cloth. Each has a pattern, and what varies is the kind of pattern. Each has sleeves, and what varies is the length of sleeve. (p. 228)

In this chapter we offer universalist descriptions of some practices in telephone speaking. On the basis of these descriptions, we argue that telephone conversations are much the same the whole world over—at least in terms of the problems the speakers face and the sorts of speech objects produced (interactively) during telephone openings. In this task we extend Schegloff's (1968, 1979, 1986, 1987) studies.

The study of telephone talk has focused mainly on conversations in English. To extend and built on these studies, we need to examine telephone speech in other speech communities.

## A CONVERSATIONAL WORLD

The multilingual world we live in is a world of persons in conversation with one another. Because conversations display regularities in the way they unfold, the study of conversational practices across languages may reveal how participants in different "cultures" organize their talk, that is, how they produce and interpret each other's verbal actions across turns. The need for comparative empirical studies is recommended by Schegloff (1986) in these terms:

> Much of the literature in the anthropological and linguistic traditions . . . focuses almost automatically on that which varies between

cultures and speech communities. But underlying that which varies, we can often find themes of interactional organization to which participants are oriented whatever their milieu, and these have no lesser analytic status. Indeed, they may contribute to the sense of significance which analysts attribute to what appears to vary. In any case, "positions" here—whether committed to that which varies or to that which is held in common—should be the product of empirical inquiry, not merely disciplinary commitment.

If there are cultural differences in telephone openings, Schegloff argues, these are important to know and study; and these differences may "evidence the operation of the same underlying organizational concerns."

We attempt description of telephone openings in three languages, focusing on speaking practices common to all three. These practices are described in terms of recurrent problems to which they display orientation. The question becomes, In what terms can the description of universals be forwarded? We select telephone openings as one such environment for the following reasons: First, each instance represents the start of a two-party, audio-only speech event; second, previous scholars have argued that telephone openings display relatively universal sequencing practices; and third, the telephone opening is an important speech event for many people around the world.

To recapitulate, the issue of language universals has been raised by those who claim that structural universals underlie certain speech events, no matter what languages the participants speak.

## THREE INSTANCES

Let us begin with three examples that illustrate similar approaches to telephone openings:

```
(SCHEGLOFF)
  0      ring
  1  R:  Hello::,
  2  C:  H'llo, Clara?
  3  R:  Yeh,
  4  C:  Hi. Bernie.
  5  R:  Hi Bernie.
```

(KELLY)

```
00      ring
01 A:  All
02 C:  Allo Mali:ke
03 A:  Oui?
04 C:  Salut c'est Leslie:
05 A:  Salu:t Leslie::
```

(FAE : translation)

```
00      ring                    رينغ              .
01 A: Hello?                 أ : ألو؟        ١
02 C: Hello Shiri::ne?   ب : ألو  شـيـرين ؟    ٢
03 A: Ye:s,                   أ : إيـ،        ٣
04 C: Nadia                  ب : ناديا       ٤
```

On first hearing the tape recordings from which these transcripts have been prepared, we notice that the participants in the above instances are engaged in the mundane, everyday activity of initiating a telephone conversation. The participants seem to be "going through the motions," or performing routines. Each of these phone beginnings looks and sounds much like the others. Each sequence of talk is accomplished by the parties, turn by brief turn, arranging elements in identical order throughout the three examples: The answerer in each instance responds to the summons (line 01); the first turn of the caller displays recognition of the answerer (line 02), who, in turn, confirms the recognition affirmatively (line 03); the caller then provides a first part of a greeting and self-identifies or simply self-identifies (line 04); this is then followed by a return greeting and, as in cases in the first two examples, an acknowledgment of the caller's name. These instances exemplify the perfunctory, routine character of the beginning of telephone conversations for the different participants. "What seems routine is a methodically achieved outcome" (Schegloff, 1986).

We propose in this chapter to show instances of telephone openings produced as naturally occurring speech events by speakers of English, of French, and of Arabic. Conversation analysis provides our method of research (see Hopper, Koch, & Mandelbaum, 1986; Sacks, Schegloff, & Jefferson, 1974).

## METHOD

Conversation analysis is a method of communication research that regards all social interaction as structured occurrences. Actual singular speech events and sequences are subjected to methodical description. The objects of this description are the sets of formal procedures participants employ in accomplishing conversational interaction (Sacks, 1984, p. 21). Thus conversation analysis asks *how participants themselves produce and interpret each other's actions*. Schegloff and Sacks (1973) have summarized the methodological and analytical assumptions of conversation analysis in these terms:

> We have proceeded under the assumption (an assumption borne out by our research) that in so far as the materials we worked with exhibited orderliness, they did so not only to us, indeed not in the first place for us, but for the co-participants who had produced them. If the materials (records of natural conversation) were orderly, they were so because they had been methodically produced by members of the society for one another and it was a feature of the conversations we treated as data that they produced so as to allow the display by the co-participants to each other of their orderliness, and to allow the participants to display to each other their analysis, appreciation and use of that orderliness. Accordingly, our analysis has thought to explicate the ways in which the materials are produced by members in orderly ways that exhibit their orderliness and have their orderliness appreciated and used, and have that appreciation displayed and treated as the basis for subsequent action. (p. 390)

Conversation is treated then as accomplishment achieved interactively by the participants. This accomplishment is based on what Sacks et al. (1974) label "a local management system," that is, the turn-by-turn system of talk. Sacks et al. have demonstrated that participants accomplish conversational action by constructing their turns at talk in relation to prior and subsequent turns. This is done by participants' monitoring of each other's utterances for possible completion points at which speaker change can possibly occur, and displaying in each turn clues relevant to interpretation of prior turns.

The method employed by conversation analysts relies on repeated listening to tape recordings of naturally occurring conversations. Detailed transcripts of these conversations are used to aid listeners and analysts in their descriptions of the ways in which "utterances accomplish particular actions by virtue of their placement and participation within sequences," that is, how interactants locally and sequentially accomplish conversational action.

In the next segment, we present and unpack Schegloff's (1986) sequential model of telephone openings. The collection of instances cited in English, French, and Arabic in this chapter are from the Conversation Library at the University of Texas at Austin.

## TELEPHONE OPENINGS

The first few seconds of telephone calls recommend themselves to us as objects of study for a number of reasons. Parties to a telephone call begin "from scratch" to construct a situation. Unlike many face-to-face conversations, telephone calls display beginnings at definite moments—when the phone rings and somebody answers it. At moments of opening two parties, blind to each other's identities at the outset, encounter each other and begin to speak and listen to one another. Schegloff conceptualizes telephone openings as "routine achievements" performed by the participants out of structured sets of alternative directions that the talk and the interaction can take. During the opening moments, "a multiplicity of jobs" get done and are managed, turn by turn, by the participants themselves. As Schegloff (1979) comments: "The opening is a place where the type of conversation being opened can be preferred, displayed, accepted, rejected, modified—in short, incipiently constituted by the parties to it."

The model presented by Schegloff exemplifies the notion that talk is structurally organized to resolve recurrent universal problems. One type of utterance organization thought to be universally applicable to telephone openings is the "adjacency pair." Adjacency pairs are sequences of talk of two-utterance length, adjacently positioned, produced by different speakers. They are relatively ordered (i.e., first pair parts are marked as a "first" and second pair parts marked as a "second," with the first pair part preceding the second pair part), and they are discriminatingly related in a way that the first pair part "prescribes" the second pair part in a "conditional relevance" organization:

> By conditional relevance of one item on another we mean: given the
> first, the second is expectable; upon its occurrence it can be seen to be a

second item to the first; upon its nonoccurrence it can be seen to be officially absent—all this provided by the occurrence of the first item. (Schegloff, 1972, p. 364)

Adjacency pairs occur in talk wherever "ordering is required"; they are specifically "fitted" to the solutions of problems at initiation and termination of encounters. Schegloff's sequential model describes how adjacency pair organizations operate at the beginning of telephone calls.

Schegloff (1968) identifies the following adjacency sequences as accomplished by participants at the beginning of North American telephone conversations:

(1) a summons/answer sequence that consists of the telephone ring and the first response uttered by the answerer
(2) an identification/recognition sequence that consists of each party identifying self and displaying recognition of the other
(3) a greeting sequence that consists of an exchange of greeting tokens
(4) a "how are you" sequence—a pair of pairs in which each participant poses an initial inquiry

Each of these entities occupies a position, or "slot," relative to the others. That is, these tasks get accomplished, in most cases, in the order listed—although there are numerous instances in which these accomplishments "overlap" and are prefigured.

Schegloff's sequential model has been challenged by Daniele Godard who compared telephone openings in France and in the United States. Arguing that there are different cultural assumptions toward telephone calls, Godard attempts to demonstrate that the caller in France makes the assumption that his/her call will disturb. Being a "virtual offender," the caller has to compensate for the assumed disturbing behavior by showing that s/he has a good reason for calling, and by transforming the summons to talk into a polite request. This is done, Godard argues, by the caller fulfilling the following sequential tasks:

(1) Checking the number
(2) Naming oneself at the first opportunity
(3) Excusing oneself (optional in case of intimacy)

Godard's data, however, are presented as a general scenarios recalled long after the fact. Therefore, the reporting of details needs to be checked against recordings. Our French language recordings, described in this chapter, do not match Godard's descriptions in some details. In addition, by focusing on the caller's obligations, she has failed to note that openings are interactively carried out by the participants, a move which departs from Schegloff's sequential and interactive model. Whether callers feel the need to check the number they dialed or apologize at the beginning of phone calls, the question remains as to how the tasks performed in the opening "slots" are filled. It is this formulation of telephone openings that we propose as a useful heuristic in at least three languages.

We proceed in the present chapter to describe previous work with our own observations under each of the four headings listed above. We emphasize the first two sequences, the *summons* and the *identification* sequences, because descriptions of these are furthest advanced in past research, and present controversies settle in those data.

### Summons/Answer

Telephone calls begin not with speech or visual prebeginnings, but with a summons noise, such as a ring or a buzz. Usually, the telephone summons has a repetitive character to it, its parts recurring every few seconds until somebody answers or the caller gives up. For a variety of phone calls, as evidenced from our multilingual data, the beginning goes off as follows:

```
(SHELLEY 2)
00          rn::ng
01 Dick: Hello.
(KELLY)
00              rn::ng
01 Ethelle: allo?
(FAE : translation)
```

00      rn::ng   رينغ      •

01 Fadi: allo::    ::ألو : فادي ١

The mechanical ring of the telephone is, like an oral summons in face-to-face interaction, an "attention-getting device." Much like utterances such as "Hey, Joe!" or "Mo:::m!" the telephone ring constitutes the first part of a two-part summons/answer sequence. Nofsinger (1975), in his study on verbal summons, or what he terms "demand tickets," argues that a summons has several functions, one of which is that "it begins a sequence of conditionally relevant units which will obligate its initiator to assume the speaker's role in the conversation. Thus, a necessary characteristic of the demand ticket is that it requires a response which will require a response" (p. 4).

In sum, a summons obligates not only an answer, but also some third turn. Since the third turn may be so constructed as to choose speakers for subsequent turns, a summons-move serves to get an encounter started.

The phone summons requires a response, a second part. Constraints on the second to a summons include "a distribution rule for first utterance," that is, that ordinarily the answerer speaks first (Schegloff, 1968). The first utterance spoken by the one who picks up the phone is a response token such as *hello, yeah,* or a *self-identification/self-formulation.* We examine each of these response tokens below in relation to our findings.

*Hello* is the most common response type to a telephone summons in the United States. By choosing to pick up the phone and utter *hello* as a first turn, the answerer signals a state of interaction. The first utterance, in whichever form it is constructed, provides the caller with a potential "clue" to the identity of the respondent. *Hello,* like *yeah* and self-identification/self-formulation response types, provides a voice sample for recognition by those who might recognize it. In this sequential position *hello* is not primarily a greeting term, but rather a "recipient-designed" answer to the summons (Schegloff, 1968).

If *hello* (in this setting) primarily answers, rather than greets, why is a greetinglike term used so often in this position in American phone calls? *Hello* sometimes occurs as a greeting, especially in face-to-face meetings. In face-to-face talk, *hello*—as greeting—may be the first utterance in an encounter. The telephone-summons-answering *hello* may retain some greetinglike character as a secondary or residual function. The main argument against it accomplishing greeting is that its use in the answer slot is routinely *followed* by other greetings, as will be discussed below.

Like *hello,* the French word *allo* is a response type frequently produced as a first utterance in French and Arabic telephone conversations. (The use of *allo* as a response type in Arabic calls in Lebanon is the result of linguistic borrowing of the term.) The use of *allo* in French and Arabic is, in the majority of cases, restricted to telephone talk and hardly ever occurs in face-to-face encounters. That is, French acquaintances meeting on the street would say something like "bonjour" or "salut," not "allo."

As we mentioned earlier, response types provide a voice sample for recognition by those who might recognize it. Frequently, *hello* and *allo* are produced in a distinctive mode of delivery that provides for speakers to be recognized. Schegloff (1968) calls these forms of response types "signature hello":

(Schegloff)
C:    Hello?
M:    Charlie.
(Kelly)
01    Jean    :    al*lo*:
02    Carole  :    allo Jea:n,
(FAE : translation)

01    Dima    :    al*lo*:                ١   ديما : أُلو

02    Nadia   :    allo Di:*ma*.          ٢   ناديا : أُلو ديما

In all three instances, the second speaking turn includes a display of recognition of the answerer. The recognition in line 02 is evidenced by the terminal pitch used to utter the answerer's name. That the recognition was achieved in the caller's first turn, immediately in adjacent turn to the answerer's hello or allo, displays the caller's recognition of the answerer on the basis of the answerer's hello.

*Hello*, then, has some cross-cultural status as a response to a summons. It is no sacred universal, nor is it the only answer to phone summons in any culture, but *hello* is not just an English greeting term without telephone uses in other languages. There is nothing sacred about the form *hello* or its greetinglike character. The "inventor" of the telephone, Alexander Graham Bell, wished answerer to say "hoy" upon answering, and most any other vocal fragment could accomplish call-opening. There seem to be no principled differences in use or distribution between *hello* and various forms of *yes* that also occur in answers to summons.

*Answering a summons with a self-identification/self-formulation* response type is common in the United States in business and service encounters, such as when answering a phone in a doctor's office, a bank, a department store, or the like. In these "business" calls, recognizability of voices "is not expectable and is not relied on for confirmation of reaching the right recipient" (Schegloff, 1986). Thus self-identification/self-formulation responses (such as "Dr. Snow's office" or "Macy's Customer Service Department") provide ways for confirming or disconfirming whether a caller has reached his or her destination. Evidence of the self-identification/self-formulation response type outside English includes the following:

(Kelly)
00              rin:ng
01  Telephoniste:  B N P (.) bonjou:r

The self-identification type operates as a potent device by which the called directly indicates to the caller whether or not he or she has reached the intended target. The use of self-identification (which may accompany a hello) in the slot immediately after a summons is reserved (in most instances in our collection) to business, professional, and other public encounters.

However, in describing telephone openings in Holland, Houtkoop-Steenstra (1986) observes that in Dutch telephone openings, including domestic, mundane calls, the first turns by the answerer are overwhelmingly done as self-identification:

(Houtkoop-Steenstra, 1986)

| | |
|---|---|
| A. It's Reina de Wind? | A. Met Reina de Wind? |
| C. He*llo:*, it's Bren | B. Ha*llo:*, met Bren |

Whether the answerer responds in a "conventional" way (hello in the United States, allo in France and Lebanon, self-identification in Holland) or not, the "work" performed by the called's first utterance in all languages discussed does not seem to be disturbed. In each case the summons is answered, usually by a person who "belongs" with that phone; that is, the answerer lives in this house or works in this office. A proposal that forwards interaction has been accomplished by means of summons objects. The first function of the first utterance is to accomplish the recognizable responding to, or answering of, the summons. The first utterance's function is to be a second pair part to a summons. The function of the summons is to provide a slot for just such an answer. Openness of a channel of communication is thereby signaled by interaction; incipient interaction is initiated. Additionally, more often than not, vocal "clues" have been given to the caller as to the identity of the person who answered the phone. Evidence shows that the summons/answer opening sequence in English, French, and Arabic calls, obligates a third turn at talk and sets the routine in motion.

### Identification/Recognition

In telephone talk, the parties meeting are visually masked. Therefore, it is often necessary for the participants to identify themselves in speech (Schegloff, 1979): "Whatever a telephone conversation is going to be occupied with, however bureaucratic or intimate, routine or unusual, earthshaking or trivial, it and its parties will have to pass through the identification/recognition sieve as the first thing they do" (p. 27).

The initial sequential locus of the identification/recognition problem in telephone speaking turns out to be the second speaking turn in the phone call, that is, the caller's first speaking turn right after the summons/answer sequence. In fact, as noted above, the summons/answer sequence itself provides information relevant to identification problems.

As mentioned earlier, the opening of a telephone conversation is densely packed, and its organization is somewhat distinctive from face-to-face encounters. In face-to-face meetings, issues of identification and recognition most often occupy prespeech moments, whereas participants in a telephone conversation are constrained to identify themselves in speech through a variety of turn components. Schegloff (1979) identifies nine types of turn components that the caller can use, either as a single utterance or in combination form. Due to limitations of space, we discuss only four of these:

*(1) Answerer's, presumed answerer's, or intended answerer's name or address term, ending with interrogative pitch contour:*

(Schegloff)
```
01   R:   Hello
02   C:   Hello Ida?
03   R:   Yeah
```

(Kelly)

| 01 | Agnes | : | Allo? |
|---|---|---|---|
| 02 | Christine | : | Agne:s? |
| 03 | Agnes | : | oui:? |

(Kelly)

| 01 | Claude | : | Allo:. |
|---|---|---|---|
| 02 | Christine | : | Allo: Madame Grau? |
| 03 | Claude | : | C'est moi. |

(FAE : translation)

| 01 | A | : | Hello? | ١ أ : أ ألو؟ |
|---|---|---|---|---|
| 02 | C | : | Hello Shiri:ne? | ٢ ب : ألو شيرين ؟ |
| 03 | A | : | ye:s, | ٣ أ : إي ، |

In these routine examples, the second speaking turn includes a guess at the name of the call's answerer. The guess nature of turn 02 is shown by the question mark in the transcript, denoting a turn-final upward-intonation, or what Sacks and Schegloff call "try-marking" (Schegloff, 1979, p. 17). Try-marking occurs as a display that the resources for recognition (which include mainly voice recognition from the speaker's first turn) are not adequate for certain recognition, but sufficient for a guess, which is confirmed by the answerer's affirmative utterance in the next turn.

*(2) Answerer's, presumed answerer's, or intended answerer's name or address term in affirmative or terminal pitch:*

(Schegloff)

| C: | Hello? |
|---|---|
| M: | Charlie. |

(Kelly)

| 01 | Jean | : | allo:. |
|---|---|---|---|
| 02 | Carole: | allo Jea:n, | |

The formats mentioned above explicitly display recognition of the answerer by supplying the answerer's name. These second turns, in contrast to the try-marked identifications, show caller's confidence in having offered a correct identification. Also, these turns, like their try-marked cousins, offer vocal information relevant to answerer identification of the caller.

However, in some cases where the answerer does not immediately recognize the caller in such sequences, the called party might address the issue in his or her second turn at talk, as in the following instance:

(Kelly)

| 01 | Paulette: | Allo::? |
|----|-----------|---------|
| 02 | Murielle: | Paulette? |
| 03 | Paulette: | Qui est a l'appareil? |

In some cases, however, the caller might simply issue a greeting without supplying the answerer's name, showing recognition of the answerer from the answerer's first turn. Identification and reciprocal recognition seem to be a most relevant action at first opportunity into the call.

*(3) Greetings:* The gambit for the caller of offering a greeting as a first turn without giving a name produces telephone openings like this:

(Kelly)

| 01 | Marie | : | oui:? |
|----|-------|---|-------|
| 02 | Murielle | : | Bonjou:r |
| 03 | Marie | : | A:h bonjour Murielle |

In this instance, the caller proposes first that the answerer has been identified from the speech sample of the answerer's "oui," and second, that the brief speech sample in the responding "bonjour" has provided sufficient resources for the answerer to recognize the caller as Murielle. Marie's second turn in 03 appears to ratify that expectation, whereby she returns the greeting and identifies the caller by name (Schegloff, 1979). Consider also the following:

(Schegloff)

A: He*llo*::,
B: H*i*:::,
A: Oh: *hi*:; 'ow are you Agne::s,

(FAE : translation)

| 01 | Marwan: | hello? | ١ مروان : ألو؟ |
|----|---------|--------|----------------|
| 02 | Nadine: | hello hi | ٢ نادين : ألو مرحبى |
| 03 | Marwan: | hi | ٣ مروان : مرحبى |

The greeting offered in second turn at talk by the caller displays recognition of the called, according to Schegloff. Such greeting is offered as a first part of an adjacency pair; a second greeting by the called completes the sequence and displays that the answerer has reciprocally recognized the caller.

*(4) Self-identification:*

(Schegloff)
B:   H'llo?
D:   Hi Bonnie. This is Dave.
(Kelly)
01   J-F:   oui?
02   P   :   Allo Jean-Francoi:s? Patrice Calais a l'appareil,

Self-identification most often occurs in combination with other components in the caller's second turn (Schegloff, 1979). In the examples above, however, self-identification occurs in caller's first turn. In the first instance, the caller first offers a greeting and shows recognition of the answerer before self-identifying. In the second instance, the caller displays recognition of the other and then self-identifies; in such cases, the caller quickly moves on to a first topic or reason for the call.

To summarize, identification/recognition sequences can be achieved in a variety of ways. Identification of other by each party is relevant; identification of other is relevant at first opportunity; if recognitional identification is possible, it is preferred. Recognition as an interactional accomplishment has two components: a recognition source and a recognition solution. Preferably, recognition is "effortless." If the recognition work is done wholly in turns to talk, it may occupy turns addressed to it, or it may inform turns occupied with some other sequential work and the recognition solution should occur in the turn after the recognition source, with no gap. Separation of source and solution exhibit trouble or failure to accomplish recognition that warrants repair. Each of the listed components of recognition/identification occurred in each of the three languages studied here, providing some tentative evidence of universals in telephone openings.

In a study of Dutch telephone openings, Houtkoop-Steenstra (1986) reports the following differences between the Dutch and American instances. First, Dutch openings begin with self-identification by the answerer at first speaking turn:

(1)*Answerer and caller both self-identifying:*

(Houtkoop-Steenstra)
[HH:1:2] ((friends))

| A. It's Mies Habots.= | A. Met Mies Habots.= |
| C. =Hi:, i's Anneke de Groot. | C. =Da:g, met Anneke de Groot. |

(2)*Answerer self-identifying, caller providing a voice-sample:*

(Houtkoop-Steenstra)
[PtH:40] ((spouses))

| A. Annelies Kr*au:*wel?= | A. Annelies Kr*au:*wel? |
| C. =*H*I:!= | C. =*D*A:ag!= |
| A. =Hell*o* | A. =Hall*o*! |

Second, Dutch speakers show a preference for caller's self-identification, in contrast to the preference for recognition in the American data. Thus the recognition/identification problem is resolved in two turns.

Houtkoop-Steenstra's argument stresses differences between Dutch and American openings. However, the tasks performed in both the summons/answer and recognition/identification sequences in Dutch conversations retain the characteristics stressed in Schegloff's description of these sequences in English. By self-identifying, the answerer in Holland responds to the summons and offers self-identification to the yet unidentified caller so as to obligate reciprocal identification and show recognition. The first utterance of the answerer is a response type (be it hello, yes, or self-identification); that is, it (a) displays response to a summons, (b) opens a channel of communication, a state of talk, and (c) provides information relevant to answerer's identification. These structural organizations described by Houtkoop-Steenstra fit this description, as do those in our collection. Cultural/language differences in phone openings involve choices among procedural options for doing these jobs. Cross-cultural differences, in this view, show stylistic custom and fashion, rather than functional contrasts.

As mentioned earlier, Godard claims that the caller checks the number before self-identifying. As shown in some of the French examples in our corpus, this is not the case operating here. She may be right but her claims must be submitted to rigorous and systematic listenings to several dozens of openings. In fact, Godard's claim is diametrically opposed to Houtkoop-Steenstra's who claims that the summoned offers first self-identification. This spectrum points out the possibilities that such disparate behaviors are to be expected from one culture to the other. However, the universal thread linking all of these phone calls encompasses three features: 1) the tasks carried out at openings, 2) the ordering of these tasks, and 3) the interactive participatory nature of telephone calls.

### Telephone Greetings

Greetings, Schegloff (1986) writes, "are not separable from the identification work, for it is with a greeting that each party asserts or claims recognition of the other" (p. 129). In many face-to-face conversations greetings are the first spoken messages, but the greetings exchange in telephone talk depends upon the accomplishment of summons/answer and identification/recognition sequences. Furthermore, when a "prototype greeting" such as hello is used in caller's first turn, it is quite often not being used as a greeting. This is evidenced by the caller and answerer doing a subsequent greeting sequence, as in the example below (Schegloff, 1986):

(Schegloff)
| 01 | R: | Hello |
| 02 | C: | Hello Ida? |
| 03 | R: | Yeah |
| 04 | C: | Hi, This is Carla |
| 05 | R: | *H*i Carla. |

In this instance, the use of hello tokens to answer the summons and proceed with identification/recognition does not prevent the participants from saying "hi" in apparent greeting of each other following these earlier actions. Initial hello as an answer to the summons in telephone conversations may accomplish a different function than initial hello in face-to-face speech. Hello tokens in telephone talk may accomplish something like a "pre-greeting" function. An example from our cross-cultural data may elucidate this proposal:

(Schegloff)
| 01 | R: | Hello |
| 02 | C: | Hello Ida? |

(Kelly)
01  Jean:    Allo:.
02  Carole:   Allo Jea:n.
(FAE : translation)

01  A:   allo?                          ١   أ : الو ؟

02       (.)                                ٢    ( . )

02  B:   allo, ha*j*:?                   ٣   ب : الوء حج ؟

In the above French and Arabic examples, the called party answers with "allo." The term *allo* in French is usually restricted to telephone talk, unlike *hello* in English, which can be used in both copresent talk and telephone talk. *Allo* is also used in combination with other greeting components, such as *bonjour*. Ordinarily, there is a constraint on the use of greeting: *one* "per party per occasion, if reciprocal." As shown in the instances below, the caller combines both allo and greeting term, which may suggest that allo is not taken as a greeting but rather as a pregreeting:

(Kelly)
01  Telephoniste:   %Allo.%
02  Genevieve  :   Allo bonjou:r
(FAE : translation)

01  Abu Waleed:   Hello:?             ١   أبو وليد : ألو : ؟

02  Rana       :   Hello good day     ٢   رنا : ألو مرحبى

In these instances, allo is offered by the callers in their first turn in response to the answerer's allo.

### Initial Inquiry: How Are You

The "how are you" sequence is, as Schegloff (1986) notes, an exchange sequence, that is, "after a first such inquiry is answered and the sequence elaborated and/or closed, a reciprocal inquiry by the recipient of the first is relevant, yielding an exchange of 'how-are-you' inquiries and sequences" (p. 130). There exist a variety of alternatives that may occur in the response slot of this initial inquiry. Some responses are utterly routine, such as the following:

```
(Schegloff)
05   R:   Hi Carla.
06   C:   How are you.
07   R:   Okay:.
08   C:   Good.=
09   R:   =How about you.
10   C:   Fine. Don wants to know . . .
(Kelly)
03   Marie    :   A:h bonjour Murielle
04   Murielle:   Comment vas-tu?
05   Marie    :   Ca va:.
```

Sacks (1975) argues that "how-are-you/fine" fills a routine slot leading toward the first topic of the call. How-are-you exchanges are used by participants as state-checks preliminary to further talk. However, if participants use these slots to offer nonroutine, or "marked," responses to inquiry, such responses are oriented to as being unusual and possibly problematic.

Jefferson (1980) describes some subtly marked responses to initial inquiries like "how are you," inquiries that invite a "value-state descriptor":

```
(Jefferson)
Bob  :   [how are you] feeling now.
Jayne:   Oh::? pretty good I gue:ss::
                                   [
Bob  :                            not so hot?
```

Consider also:

```
((Kelly))
03   Murielle:   alors comment vas-tu?
                                 [        ]
04   Claire   :               Bonjou:r
05   Claire   :   o:h ben moi ca va très bien
                                     [        ]
06   Murielle:                     ((fatiguée))
07   Claire   :   un p'tit peu fatiguée
```

The responses to inquiry in the above instances—"Oh, pretty good I guess" and "Oh ben moi ca va tres bien" ("Oh 'ben' me I am doing fine")—display departure from an unmarked or routine response to "how are you" and "comment vas tu." The respondents in both instances begin with a marked version of *oh*; in the English example, Jayne qualifies the value-state descriptor by uttering "pretty good" and continues her further qualification by adding "I guess." In the French example, Claire responds to the inquiry by uttering "oh" and prefacing the value-state descriptor by "ben moi." In both examples, the other participant orients to these features displayed in the called party's response as "premonitors" of some possible problems. The asker of the initial question offers a follow-up question about the respondent's possibly troubled state.

## SUMMARY

The sequential analysis of conversational practices provides us with a method for describing ways in which participants within speech communities produce and organize their talk. In this chapter, we have attempted to show that "routine" telephone openings in English, French, and Arabic accomplish similar ordered tasks. The primary argument in these materials concerns the nature of cross-cultural universals of conversational pragmatics. A universalist position, articulated by Schegloff (1979), is counterposed to various cultural difference positions. Schegloff puts forward a four-part formulation—a sequence of sequences based on evidence of relevance organization in the shapes of interconnected adjacency pairs. It is tempting, but possibly misleading, to construe this ordered set of routines as scripted, set ritual, to construe concrete details of specific instances as claims that all phone openings "sound just alike."

Schegloff's data base is in English, though we claim it has universalist, cross-cultural implications. Certainly we do not claim that every telephone opening sounds just like those in the United States. Rather, there is a certain set of jobs that must get accomplished to do the opening of a state of conversational speaking. There may be certain economics, or structural necessity, that is being displayed in the telephone conversational order in which participants accomplish these tasks. There is a certain appeal in claiming that one must summon-answer to begin any interaction, and that once this business (summoning and answering) is "en train de se faire" the next tasks (mutual identification and displaying of recognition) become specifically relevant.

Identification/recognition work may be the first task facing face-to-face speakers. When no summons is needed, face-to-face meeters may transform themselves into face-to-face speakers by displaying mutual recognition. In face-to-face speaking tasks this may be accomplished visually *before* people begin speaking. On the telephone, this work must happen in speech, and it does not ordinarily begin before the answer to the summons. The first words in face-to-face talk are often greetings, and these become specifically relevant upon mutual displays of recognition.

The claim is not that these three sequence-accomplished tasks occur in temporal phases clinically separable from one another, such that each task must be complete before the next phase begins. Nobody's data suggest that, within any culture. Perhaps that is the only position defeated by cultural difference arguments to date. Of course, cross-cultural studies of telephone openings are in their infancy. Studies based upon tape recordings and detailed transcriptions are still in the minority, shamefully, in cross-cultural studies of the telephone. Studies offering these empirical details from around the globe doubtless illuminate these issues. We strongly urge researchers from various countries to share recordings and transcriptions with one another to promote cross-cultural study of telephone-opening phenomena.

As this research program continues, cultural relativists will err if they construe the concreteness of transcription-and-descriptions by conversational analysts as arguments that there are always four formal adjacency sequences at the opening of phone calls.

Houtkoop-Steenstra's (1986) data show that there are other useful ways to answer the telephone than just to say hello. The apparent Dutch custom of answering with self-identification seems to display efficiency and openness to interaction. Instead of saying hello, Dutch residential answerers self-identify. This practice seems efficient in that it shows specific relevance to an immediate task at hand upon call-beginning, mutual recognition. One might sensibly infer that the telephone is ringing only because somebody wants to speak. The practice of self-identification seems "open" in that it accepts an information deficit in the conversation, and one puts oneself in a potentially vulnerable position by giving away one's name before knowing who is calling. It is tempting based on these data to speculate on the ethos of the Netherlands.

But the key question is: How do the Dutch data fit with Schegloff's (1979) approach? The added information shown when one answers with a self-identification is very nicely placed so that the second part of a summons/answer pair and the same utterance does double duty as the first gambit into displayed mutual recognition. The turns in Houtkoop-Steenstra's data (as in the institutional openings in Schegloff's data and elsewhere) are Janus-shaped. They look backward by seconding-answering the summons, and at the same moment they look forward by a gambit toward recognizability.

Houtkoop-Steenstra appears to take exception to the sequential ordering of an identification phase after summons/answer, because her data show strong components of self-identification in the summons/answer. But in every culture and context imaginable, the summons/answer turn contributes some data toward possible recognition of the answerer.

The following are proposed as formulations of possible cultural universals (extremely tentative ones) from this literature on telephone openings. The picture remains preliminary as to the empirical status or even falsifiability of these descriptions in their present form.

(1) Summons/answer sequences are ordinarily necessary first occurrences in telephone speaking. The term *summons/answer sequence* denotes a strong adjacency-pair bond of conditional relevance between these two acts.

    (1a) Summons objects may be repeated until, but *only until*, an answer is achieved.

(2) Mutual recognition displays are ordinarily the first next business after summoning and answering are under way.

    (2a) Information relevant to recognition is specifically relevant in summons/answers, and highly variable in its explicitness in answer-turns.

    (2b) The variation of explicitness of self-identification is used to mark various sociolinguistic issues. For example, if you live in the Netherlands, or work for Ace Moving Company, these memberships constrain conduct of answering, but not the basic tasks that must be accomplished to begin a state of talk.

# REFERENCES

Chomsky, N. (1957). *Syntactic structures*. The Hague: Mouton.

Chomsky, N. (1965). *Aspects of the theory of syntax*. Cambridge: MIT Press.

Clark, H. H., & Clark, E. V. (1978). Universals, relativity, and language processing. In J. H. Greenberg (Ed.), *Universals of human language*. Stanford, CA: Stanford University Press.

Godard, D. (1977). Same Setting, Different Norms: Phone Call Beginnings in France and the United States. *Language and Society, 6*, 209–219.

Greenberg, J. H. (1963). *Universals of language*. Cambridge: MIT Press.

Hopper, R., Koch, S., & Mandelbaum, J. (1986). Conversation analysis methods. In D. Ellis & W. Donohue (Eds.), *Contemporary issues in language and discourse processes*. Hillsdale, NJ: Lawrence Erlbaum.

Houtkoop-Steenstra, H. (1986, March). *Opening sequences in Dutch telephone conversation*. Revised version of a paper presented at the Talk and Social Structure Conference, University of California, Santa Barbara.

Jefferson, G. (1980). On "trouble-premonitory" responses to inquiry. *Sociological Inquiry, 50*, 153–185.

Nofsinger, R. (1975). The demand ticket: A conversational device for getting the floor. *Speech Monographs, 42*, 1–9.

Sacks, H. (1975). Everyone has to lie. In B. Blount & M. Sanches (Eds.), *Sociocultural dimensions of language use*. New York: Academic Press.

Sacks, H. (1984). Remarks on methodology. In J. M. Atkinson & J. Heritage (Eds.), *Structures of social action*. Cambridge: Cambridge University Press.

Sacks, H., Schegloff, E. A., & Jefferson, G. (1974). A simplest systematics for the organization of turn taking for conversation. *Language, 50*, 696–735.

Schegloff, E. A. (1968). Sequencing in conversational openings. *American Anthropologist, 70*, 1075–1095.

Schegloff, E. A. (1972). Sequencing in conversational openings. In J. J. Gumperz & D. Hymes (Eds.), *Directions in sociolinguistics*. New York: Holt, Rinehart & Winston.

Schegloff, E. A. (1979). Identification and recognition in telephone conversation openings. In G. Psathas (Ed.), *Everyday language: Studies in ethnomethodology*. New York: Irvington.

Schegloff, E. A. (1986). The routine as achievement. In G. Button, P. Drew, & J. Heritage (Eds.), *Human studies*. Dordrecht: Martinus Nijhoff.

Schegloff, E. A. (1987). Between macro and micro: Contexts and other connections. In J. Alexander, B. Giesen, R. Munch, & N. Smelser (Eds.), *The micro-macro link*. Berkeley: University of California Press.

Schegloff, E. A., & Sacks H. (1973). Opening up closings. In J. Baugh & J. Sherzer (Eds.), *Language in use*. Englewood Cliffs, NJ: Prentice-Hall.

Steiner, G. (1975). *After Babel: Aspects of language and translation*. Oxford: Oxford University Press.

# 9

# Power Pronouns and the Language of Intercultural Understanding

STEPHEN P. BANKS • *Arizona State University*

*This chapter proposes a model of language for intercultural communication based on linguistic pragmatics. The model is then illustrated using the case of power pronouns in contemporary English. The canonical forms of pronouns in English and Mandarin Chinese are compared, and interpretations of the pronoun choices are analyzed in terms of their power and solidarity implicatures. An example of recorded and transcribed organizational talk is examined to point out the possible ways intercultural communication can be limited to superficial readings of talk that preclude outgroup speakers of English as a second/ other language from understanding the ideological implications of discourse.*

Language is nearly always accorded a central role in theories of intercultural interaction. For example, language contact research (e.g., Nelde, 1987) inherently focuses on language characteristics and linguistic changes among populations. Similarly, some concept of language inevitably is set forth, explicitly or implicitly, in studies of second language acquisition (SLA) (e.g., Clement, 1986; Garrett, Giles, & Coupland, this volume; Giles & Byrne, 1982). Language also figures prominently in research on ethnolinguistic identity (Edwards, 1985; Giles, 1977, 1979; Giles & Johnson, 1987; Haarmann, 1986), speech/ communication accommodation theory (Gallois, Franklyn-Stokes, Giles, & Coupland, 1988; Giles & Powesland, 1975), and intercultural communication studies (Gudykunst & Kim, 1984; Kim, 1986; Ting-Toomey, 1988).

Despite the clear presence of language as a construct in intercultural research, little attention is paid to the prevalent assumptions about language and the problems that might be presented by those assumptions. This chapter refocuses attention to theorizing about language and intercultural communication in three ways. First, I argue that linguistic pragmatics is an essential but largely neglected aspect of models or theories of intercultural interaction. Second, I propose a model of language for intercultural communication, incorporating pragmatic and other linguistic aspects that bear importantly on understanding intercultural interaction. Finally, I set forth an example of English personal pronoun usage to illustrate problems for linguistic outgroups in achieving full understanding of social relations in work institutions.

## LINGUISTIC PRAGMATICS AND LANGUAGE

Joseph (1987), following the work of Kloss, struggles to differentiate the concepts of dialect and language. He notes that it is difficult to draw boundaries between them "because no two individuals have precisely the same linguistic competence," and because the continual evolution of languages "guarantees that variation will exist within the speech of any community" (p. 3). Not only is there uncertainty about the boundaries at the edges of and within a given language, but there is uncertainty over what might be said to constitute a "speech community" (Romaine, 1982). Moreover, within any group of speakers, the degree of facility in language use is not uniform from member to member, regardless of the members' ethnolinguistic status or identity (Fowler, 1986; Gumperz, 1982; Pateman, 1987). Thus the borders of many constructs involving language and language-using groups appear to be necessarily fuzzy.

This conceptual fuzziness, however, is not confronted in theories of intercultural interaction. In some studies language is presented as an in-place, implicit system that underlies such constructs as speech act or strategy types (e.g., Ting-Toomey, 1988). Most research invokes a concept of language as a monolithic entity, a system that is identifiable and bounded, as in SLA studies of L1 speakers acquiring L2. The weakness of this approach is illustrated by its irrelevance to explaining problems in communication among speakers of varieties of English (Kress, 1985). The justified concern scholars have for negative attitudes toward accented speech (Ryan & Giles, 1982) attests to the importance of accounting for dialect and the performance aspects of varieties within languages. While it is obviously true that languages and varieties are not all linked in a seamless continuum, and it is clearly possible to label conventionally a sample of speech as belonging to, say, L1, the reciprocal assumption—that all speech ascribable to L1 has identical linguistic properties—is clearly not warranted.

Volosinov (1986) argues that language as a system of self-identical linguistic norms is not a real entity, nor is it experienced as a system of norms in the consciousness of speakers. If language is observed "objectively," it would appear to be "the ceaseless generation of language norms" (p. 66).

In addition to conceiving of language as a unitary, bounded system, researchers also view language as a static phenomenon with relatively stable features. This is an odd position to take toward language, considering the overarching goal of scholars to understand what happens in intercultural interaction. A theory or model that accepts language as a preexisting social structure has more in common with Chomskyan linguistics and Saussure's *Langue* than with a communication-oriented view of people using language in interaction. A dynamic view of language focuses on the ways in which specific kinds of interactional work are accomplished by the use of various improvised and conventional codes (Carbaugh, 1985), and it places speakers' and hearers' meanings in the center of the analysis.

Relatedly, language users' competence uniformly has been viewed as either a dichotomous variable—for example, in the ethnolinguistic identity and speech accommodation traditions—or as an aspect of language that is quantifiable by objective measurement, as in much of the SLA and language contact tradition. In the former perspective, speakers are assumed to be either competent or not competent; in the latter, speakers are deemed to be more or less competent, but competence is judged against a norm of performance in the language as a whole, *in the abstract*. A question that begs answering is, Competent for doing what? That is, if competence has to do with capacity for using language, then in order to avoid assuming that all situations make identical demands on language, competence must be evaluated in terms of some particular social circumstance.

What links these deficiencies in conceptualizing language is an absence of the specific work that language is called upon to accomplish. A specification of the work being accomplished can be adduced only by accounting for the context in which interaction takes place. Virtually all research on intercultural encounters has asked of language, How are intercultural variables reflected in language? How would language systematically influence intercultural encounters? I am proposing that research instead ask, What are these people doing with language in this situation, and how does this interaction help us understand intercultural encounters? These latter questions direct us to include linguistic pragmatics in our analyses and theories.

Linguistic pragmatics (Chilton, 1987; Leech, 1983; Levinson, 1983) addresses the integration of the surface forms of language and speech with their range of possible meanings and the concrete outcomes of their performance in actual time and space. Pragmatics explores the ways interactional resources are called on to establish understanding and ongoing interaction among participants. As such, pragmatics is at the intersection of theory and practice, of system and instantiation of the system, of history and living event. The essence of a pragmatics approach to language is evident in Volosinov's (1986) observation that "the meaning of a word is determined entirely by its context. In fact, there are as many meanings of a word as there are contexts" (p. 79).

Chilton (1987) derives from the work of H. Paul Grice two basic aspects of meaning in language and two attendant forms of communication. In the first place, meaning in language has a basic "core" semantic aspect, a relatively stable relationship between symbol and meaning that is grounded in truth-conditional entailments. The second aspect of meaning is wholly context-dependent and is contingent on inferences by the hearer based on both linguistic and nonlinguistic observations. To the degree that the second aspect of meaning is dependent on the first, semantic core, it can be considered an implicative meaning. Both senses of meaning are always present in any instance of language used for communication; hence Volosinov's observation holds, but implicature is added. Contextual meaning is possible because of speakers' assumption of cooperativeness on the part of others in communication (for a full discussion of Grice's cooperative principle, see Levinson, 1983).

Chilton (1987) expands the Gricean approach by demonstrating that while contextual meaning may depend on an assumption of speaker cooperativeness so that functional communication takes place, simultaneously, there is an issue of cooperativeness and noncooperativeness at a more macrosocial level. The latter level encompasses speakers' aims to deceive hearers, distort reality, or accomplish ideological goals in the use of language.

Fundamentally, then, the pragmatic view of language can be distinguished from what might be called the historical linguist's view. The language of speakers in real instances of communication is a set of subjectively experienced, evolving linguistic norms that become what they are by virtue of the work they are called upon to accomplish in a specific social context. The historical linguist has an abstract-objective view of language as a bounded system that preexists its manifestation in speech. Thus, in the pragmatic view, language is a set of opportunities for creating meaning and understanding, and competence represents the degree of access any speaker has through language to meaning and understanding.

## A MODEL OF LANGUAGE FOR INTERCULTURAL COMMUNICATION

The literature of intercultural communication by and large has formulated language in the historical linguist's sense. Following is a model of language that is pragmatics-oriented and accounts for sociocultural differences among interactants. This perspective on language has two "dialectics," or sets of interdependent factors that are manifested as interactional resources and as outcomes of interaction. These are the *competence dialectic* and the *practice dialectic*, and they apply regardless of the cultural milieu of interactants and regardless of whether analysis is directed toward L1, L2, or other language in use.

### *The Competence Dialectic*

Language users behave on the basis of many kinds of knowledge; however, all communicative knowledge can be partitioned into two types—knowledge *of* and knowledge *how to*. The competence dialectic manifests itself in the ongoing tension speakers evidence between generating the core, stable meanings from knowledge of canonical linguistic forms and generating the practical, contextual meanings from knowing how to perform social interaction in the here and now. Thus competence is a pairing of knowing of and knowing how to, a pairing of canonical forms and performance. Canonical forms encompass lexicosemantics, morphology and syntactics, and phonemics; knowledge potentially can range from zero knowledge to expert knowledge. To measure knowledge in terms of native speaker competence is to admit native speaker intuition as a criterion of propriety, an approach that is patently problematic (Coulmas, 1981; Paikeday, 1985). Moreover, native speakers often are unable to articulate their knowledge of canonical linguistic forms. Such knowledge to native

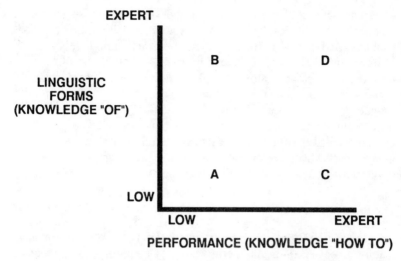

**Figure 9.1: Competence dialectic.**

speakers indeed is intuitive because, as Volosinov (1986) observes, "people do not 'accept' their native language—it is in their native language that they first reach awareness" (p. 81).

In like manner, knowing *how to* conceivably ranges from zero knowledge to expert knowledge (see Figure 9.1). Volosinov identifies two aspects of practice that generate contextual meanings, behavioral performance and ideological performance. While participants attend to behavior in the context of interaction, they concurrently are immersed in a specific ideological context as well, and knowledge of the ideological implications of language uses contributes to the building of contextual meanings. Both are aspects of knowing how to because both are aspects of the moment of interaction; moreover, in this view behavioral and ideological performance shape each other.

The competence dialectic, then, can be envisioned as a two-dimensional grid on which participants can be located in terms of their knowledge of canonical linguistic forms (zero to high) and knowledge how to perform communicative interaction (zero to high). Locating a participant in the low sector of both dimensions, indicated in Figure 9.1 as A, reflects low knowledge of both types. Such would be the case for initial interaction between an English-speaking explorer and a Balinese during their first contact in history. B represents the high knowledge of canonical forms and low performance knowledge characteristic of the accomplished student of a second/other language who has only classroom experience with L2. Area C is problematic because performance can be exactly imitative without a basis in understanding. Properly located in C, then, would be not only the most clever mimics but also "native speakers" of extensive social experience and little discursive knowledge of their mother tongue. Persons located in C generally will be limited in their repertoire of linguistic resources to what they have personally experienced and internalized from their own interaction. Fully competent language users who can generate novel approaches to using language based on their knowledge of linguistic forms are located in D.

### The Practice Dialectic

In the search for meaning in interaction, participants must manage a tension between the cooperativeness in communicative behavior that honors participants' competence and allows them to "make sense" and avoid gibberish and the more encompassing cooperativeness that honors participants' values, ideology, and expectations of ethical behavior (Chilton, 1987). It is possible for these two senses of communication to contradict one another. For example, a politician might honor all the Gricean maxims of quantity, quality, relation, and manner in the sense of logical entailments, thus producing easily comprehensible utterances; yet the politician's speech might simultaneously obscure his or her own ambitions, distort facts, or promote an imbalance of political power. In fact, every instance of successful deception by a speaker is an instance where the first type of communication is positive and the second type is negative.

Thus for miscommunication or nonsense to be avoided, as Grice and others have demonstrated, an assumption of cooperativeness *in the first place* is necessary. To make communication functional in this way is to accomplish what Chilton (1987) calls *simpliciter* communication. To accomplish a transparency of motive and to exhibit one's values, sectional interests, and institutional attachments in the moment of interaction, however, requires not an assumption of cooperativeness but a genuinely cooperative communication. This more encompassing, socially contextualized aspect of communication, which I refer to as *ideological* communication, is strategic insofar as it either conveys or veils the values, motives, sectional interests, or institutional attachments of participants in interaction. By using the term *strategic* I do not mean that I take ideological communication as intentional or conscious in every instance; the most extreme cases of negative ideological communication are those instances where the institutional attachments of participants are unconsciously inscribed in their habitual behavior, particularly in their linguistic practices. In addition, it is tempting to view simpliciter and ideological communication as distinct activities that may occur separately in nature. In accordance with the view of critical linguists (e.g., Clegg, 1979, 1987; Fowler, 1986; Fowler, Hodge, Kress, & Trew, 1979; Kress, 1985), every instance of communicative behavior manifests both simpliciter and ideological aspects, and the struggle for every person engaged in communicative behavior is to look beyond the surface coherence of utterances to their inherent ideological implications.

The competence dialectic and the practice dialectic intersect where knowledge and action become manifest in individuals' formulations of meaning. A conceptual parallel exists between speakers' knowledge of ideological *performance* and the occurrence of ideological *communication*: Without knowledge of how to use language ideologically, communicative meanings that are based on implicatures and that are ideological will be unavailable. On the other hand, simpliciter communication is readily available to persons with high knowledge of canonical linguistic forms and behavioral performance, despite their having little competence and practice in implicative language.

The language model described here directs communication researchers' attention to the multiple forms of linguistic knowledge (competence dialectic) and communicative practices (practice dialectic) that must be evaluated in analyses of what occurs in intercultural interaction. The critical linguistics view of language use is compatible with this view on several points, besides agreeing that ideological performance is ubiquitous. First, critical linguistics generally holds that communication requires both linguistic and nonlinguistic knowledge. Fowler (1986) asserts that "all competent decoding of a text relies in large degree on the bringing of knowledge which is not *linguistic* knowledge" (p. 69). Second, language is seen as a practice that is used, consciously and unconsciously, both for advancing equality among interactants and, in other instances, for promoting asymmetries of power, privilege, status, and the like. Third, implicature and ambiguity are important notions in analyzing discourse. Finally, Fowler et al. (1979) have demonstrated that power is encoded in all features of language. Of the many linguistic features of power that have been identified, I have chosen one aspect of pronoun choice to illustrate the relationships among language, power, and intercultural understanding.

## THE CASE OF POWER PRONOUNS

The perspective on language just developed is relevant to understanding intercultural communication because it leads theorists and researchers to the site of communication—to *in situ* interaction involving participants from different cultural or ethnolinguistic backgrounds—and it focuses on meanings and understandings in instances of interaction, including meanings that involve power and institutional values. Recent work on the ideological implications of pronoun choice (Banks, 1987; Maitland & Wilson, 1987; Watson, 1987) suggests that pronouns are an apt case to illustrate this language model.

The classic work on the social dimensions of personal pronouns (Brown & Gilman, 1972) analyzed the ways in which speakers signal social solidarity or social superiority by their choice of second-person pronouns. Brown and Gilman's analysis focuses on the alternation of familiar and formal forms of *you* in various Indo-European languages (*tu/vous*, *tu/usted*, *du/Sie*, and so on, represented by T/V). Their work demonstrates convincingly that a "solidarity semantic," signaling intimacy and like-mindedness, and a "power semantic," signaling asymmetrical power and social status differences, are inscribed in speakers' choices of T versus V in specific circumstances. Moreover, they argue that the power and solidarity semantics are interarticulated, that is, there are circumstances in which participants must choose either the powerful or the solidary choice but not both. Relying on literary texts, Brown and Gilman then associate T/V choice with group "style," conceived as radicalism versus conservatism, and with speakers' transient attitudes.

More than a quarter century has passed since the first publication of this seminal work, but its rich implications and its shortcomings are just now being teased out. Among the problematic assumptions are its adherence to canonical systems of pronouns for interpreting possible meanings in pronoun choice. Another deficiency in the analysis is the obvious lack of T/V second-person pronouns in contemporary English. Both these shortcomings are addressed in the following treatment of English pronouns.

# NUMBER

| | | SINGULAR | | PLURAL | |
|---|---|---|---|---|---|
| | | Objective | Subjective | Objective | Subjective |
| | 1st | I | me | we | us |
| PERSON | 2nd | you | you | you | you |
| | 3rd | he/she/it | him/her/it | they | them |

Figure 9.2: Canonical system of English personal pronouns.

## *The English Pronoun System Reconsidered*

Every English-learner's textbook and virtually all nonlinguist speakers of English will, with greater or lesser difficulty, identify the canonical system of personal pronouns. The system is composed of pronouns that vary according to number (singular or plural) and "person" (i.e., first, second, third), and in some instances sex. In addition, a rudimentary case designation attaches to the pronoun system, indicating whether the person or thing referred to is a subject or an object relative to an action word. Thus the canonical system of personal pronouns can be arrayed as in Figure 9.2.

Maitland and Wilson (1987) have demonstrated that speakers deviate from this canonical system quite regularly and creatively. For example, the utterance

(1) One needn't stop trying just because we get older every day.

indicates that *one* needs to be added to one or more pronoun categories, conceivably to all objective case categories, depending on the context of interaction. Suppose that the speaker has been talking to her mother about her mother's reluctance to continue daily exercise walks; "one," taken in the context of her argument here, refers to "you, Mother." And "we" is best interpreted as "everyone" because it makes the argument in the situation in which the language use occurs. This example also points out that different dialects of English might make differential use of personal pronouns, such as the British tendency to use *one* (Rees, 1983; cited in Maitland & Wilson, 1987), or certain American English dialects that differentially employ *youse, y'all, we'ns,* and the like.[1]

The crucial point is not that the canon must be expanded to accommodate all possible uses of pronouns, but that the canon is used as a starting point from which more implicative reference can be made, using the pronouns that are available in the linguistic repertoire. Thus context of use becomes the sine qua non for interpreting pronoun reference. Watson (1987) describes this phenomenon as "the 'interrelation' between the grammatical [i.e., canonical] model and other interactional conventions" (p. 268). The interrelation depends on participants' knowing the possible referential domains of the canonical pronouns and being able to exploit their ambiguity in particular contexts. *Referential domain* means simply the possible things or person(s) to which a pronoun may refer, while "to refer" is simply to point out an object, action, or person within a text.

Speier (1969) notes that some pronouns, particularly *we,* have the property of partitioning referential domains into inclusive and exclusive groups. In particular stretches of talk and in particular situational contexts, the referential domain of a pronoun might separate hearers from a speaker; in other contexts it might consolidate them into a single unit. Consider, for example, an utterance asked by a committee member to an assembled group of other committee members who are waiting for their absent leader to return with an agenda:

(2) Can't we just make up an agenda?

This token of *we* almost certainly refers to both speaker and addressees, thereby conjoining them into a solidary aggregation who have a particular fate and concerns in common. On the other hand, the following utterance, taken from a transcript of an actual departmental meeting in a business establishment, partitions speaker from addressees:

03137:LAX:ING:GPP4

GM: *We've* (1) decided that we have made a=a special certification program for all you em*ploy*ees.

"We" in this case clearly does not include addressees, because the
audience for this utterance is the employees referred to at the end of
the utterance. Not only does the sentence logic preclude a conjoining
of speaker and addressees, but the inflection patterns (marked by
italics) indicate a counterposing of "we" and "employees," that is, the
audience. This awkward statement was uttered by a general manager
of a large hotel during a meeting with rank-and-file employees. The
meeting was held to introduce the employees to a new customer
incentive program, and the manager was reframing the customer incentive program as an employee incentive program to boost employee commitment to corporate objectives.

My focus on *we* is not accidental. Of all the pronouns, *we* has
greatest potential to be the most influential contemporary English
personal pronoun of power and solidarity (Fowler, 1986). It potentially carries a great deal of ambiguity apart from its canonical meanings of speaker plus addressee(s) or speaker plus some other per-
son(s). That ambiguity derives from the multiple referential domains
that language users can attach to *we* (see Banks, 1987). Using S to
stand for speaker, A for addressee, and O for other, with the paren-
thetical designator (N) for others who are not certifiably known to
addressees, the following logically constitute the possible referential
domains of *we*:

   (1) S
   (2) A
   (3) O
   (4) S + A
   (5) S + O
   (6) S + O (N)
   (7) S + A + O
   (8) S + A + O (N)
   (9) A + O
  (10) A + O (N)

The referential domains that commonly conjoin speaker and hearers are 4, 7, and 8; all others are more likely to partition the speaker

from the audience. The "power semantic" operates when the speaker is known to be in an institutionally more powerful position, has greater social status or prestige, or is in some way superior to the hearers. These circumstances inevitably obtain in organizational interaction between managers and rank-and-file employees, and the social effect of the choice to use *we* when a more precise choice would be *I* (referential domain 1) or *you* (referential domain 2) is to partition the interactants while obscuring the partitioning by using a pronoun that paradigmatically conjoins persons.

Clearly, the referential domain that emerges as operational in any instance of interaction is the one participants accept in the ongoing talk; consequently, it is not possible to specify in the abstract which referential domains of *we* effect a conjoining and which effect a separation. Moreover, Watson (1987) points out that the potential ambiguity in any pronoun deviating from the canonical system is not necessarily present in every token of that pronoun. It is present, however, if speakers choose to exploit it by matching their talk to the here-and-now circumstances of ongoing talk.

Not every language, however, has an equal or identical capacity for implicating power and solidarity through speakers' choices of pronouns. In Mandarin Chinese, for example, the first-person plural pronouns have more highly specified referential domains and thus less potential ambiguity than in English. In Beijing dialect, speakers commonly specify *we* in the sense of speaker and addressee(s) by one term, *zan-men*, and specify *we* in the sense of speaker and other by the term *wo-men*. *Zan-men* (and its variant, *zan*) is commonly used in Beijing Mandarin speech, and in all circumstances it directly or indirectly suggests intimacy between speaker and addressee. Zhao (1987) concludes that Mandarin Chinese therefore has a more highly specified system of pronoun reference than does English, particularly in the first-person plural slot. Zhao also notes that *zan* is not commonly found in dictionaries or textbooks published for learners of Chinese as a second/other language, and he attributes this omission to the written orientation of formal language learning in Chinese culture. While a case can be made for at least three referential domains for *zan/zan-men* (Zhao, 1987), the canonical slot for this pronoun is the intimate *we* in any of its contextual manifestations.

The point that needs to be made about the Chinese pronoun system, however, is that it provides more explicit means than does English for inscribing power and solidarity (partitioning and conjoining) in discourse. In addition, Chinese is a language that retains polite forms for pronouns of address and honorifics for other forms of reference. One consequence of these differences is that Chinese learners of English and English-speaking learners of Chinese must master new systems of pronominal reference; a more telling consequence, and the one that is most often overlooked, is the requirement to achieve a context-driven sensitivity to the meaning implicatures that are possible with the pronoun system in the new language. Going beyond the canonical forms is not textbook learning: A sophisticated grasp of acceptable ways to violate assumptions of cooperativeness demands extensive experience with specific interaction situations, since the possible meanings are only implicated in specific situations.

### *An Example of Power Pronouns*

The nonnative speaker will read all tokens of the pronoun in their canonical forms in the absence of requisite sensitivity to the ways in which the canonical pronoun system can be used to convey power and solidarity "without actually saying so" (as Grice would phrase it). As such, the addressee is precluded from fully understanding the ideological communication inscribed in the utterances of the speaker. Although every utterance potentially can be read as ideological communication, a speaker's values, motives, institutional attachments, and so on can be veiled in the implicative choices of pronouns in specific contexts.

This argument becomes more accessible when samples of real talk are examined. Consider the complexity of the following example. The hotel general manager is describing the guest incentive program to a group of nonmanagerial employees.

0313:LAX:TNG:GPP1/2

| | | |
|---|---|---|
| (1) | Manager: | As I say, what we're here to learn about |
| (2) | | our *new* frequent travellers program. |
| (3) | | A:nd difference between the new program |
| (4) | | the old is *now* we are awarding points on |
| (5) | | total dollars spent in the hotel, in |
| (6) | | rooms or food and *be*verage. It's no |
| (7) | | longer (.) based just on the amount of |
| (8) | | nights you *stay*. The reason we are |
| (9) | | *ma*king this change is=cause we want to |
| (10) | | encourage guests to *not* only sleep here |
| (11) | | but to *be* here as *well*. |

An addressee would avoid a conclusion that this speech is gibberish by simple interpretation based on canonical referential domains of the tokens of *we*. A paraphrase of the speech, using only canonical forms of *we*, would substitute "you and I" or "other person(s) and I" for "we" in every slot. It seems not unreasonable to assign either of these referential domains to the first token and last token of "we" at lines 1 and 9; however, the sense of the middle two tokens in this selection becomes a little strained because rank-and-file employees patently do not award points to guests, and the making of this change is news to those who are in the audience. Nonetheless, some sense can be made of these utterances without implicature if the addressees are not too critical about the referential domain, and the dense use of *we* conveys on its surface a warm solidarity between speaker and addressees. In the sense that linguistic cooperativeness in this instance is assumed and carried out in practice by the speaker, then, simpliciter communication occurs.

Ideological communication, however, requires a more refined evaluation of these tokens. The token in line 1, for example, does not include the speaker in its referential domain because the speaker is not attending the meeting to learn about the program; she is reporting it as news to the audience. "We" in this case refers instead to "you," the addressees. The use of *we* in place of *you* is reminiscent of the asymmetrical talk highly competent persons use toward much less competent persons, such as teachers or other adults interacting with small children.

Why would the manager wish to choose *we*, with its noncanonical domain of reference, instead of the more transparent *you* in this instance? Many scholars have noted the "warm" effect of using *we* in ambiguous discourse contexts (e.g., Maitland & Wilson, 1987; Watson, 1987); in all uses of *we* the pronoun at some level signals a conjoining of persons among whom one party is the speaker. *We* in this instance not only is a less direct partitioning of speaker from audience than would be the case if she had chosen *you*; it also suggests a warm, solidary attitude on the speaker's part. The partitioning, or separation, of powerful managers from less powerful addressees is hidden under the added meaning of solidarity that is carried over from the canonical form of the pronoun. Thus the choice of *we* implies on its surface that there is a community of interest shared by the manager and workers: They are together in the meeting to experience a joint embrace of the new program, which the manager labels "our" program; later on, all participants will reflect their implicit solidarity by their joint support for making the program a success. It is this need for the manager to "bring along" the workers in her quest for support of the new program that is served by invoking a solidary-sounding option for the pronoun in this slot; the ideological separation of the participants is veiled in the very choosing of the token.

Similar arguments apply to the analysis of the other three tokens of *we* in the manager's talk, although their probable domains of reference are different from that of the first token. The particular problem of language and intercultural understanding that is exemplified in this excerpt is the reduced likelihood that a nonnative speaker will detect the partitioning of manager and audience that is veiled by the speaker's pronoun choice. If a Chinese worker, for example, has learned only the canonical forms of English pronouns and understands that referential domains attached to *zan-men/zan* in Chinese are not differentiated in English, the Chinese speaker will be unlikely to challenge the implied solidarity of tokens of *we* in others' discourse. Without a highly developed sensitivity to the ideological implications of pronoun choice, developed through long experience in many contexts of interaction, ideological communication will be inaccessible to the nonnative speaker. In many cases, it is unlikely that native speakers are sufficiently sensitive to challenge the implied solidarity.

## CONCLUSION

My illustration has focused on choices of pronouns as features of language in which power is inscribed yet are likely to be problematic in intercultural communication. Just what can be problematic needs to be more clearly delineated, and longitudinal studies of intercultural interaction are needed to provide confirmatory data. As a beginning proposition, however, it appears that nonnative participants in interaction have less likelihood of discovering others' values, motives, sectional interests, and institutional attachments through ideological communication. One possible consequence of this problem is that nonnative speakers are more easily deceived, more easily persuaded, and more easily maintained in established positions within institutional hierarchies.

Pronoun choice, however, is only one of many aspects of language that carry power implications. Critical linguists, such as Fowler (1986) and his associates, have ambitious programs of research to identify and study them in both written and spoken discourse. This chapter is an argument that the goals and methods of critical linguists should be extended to research on the relation of language to intercultural communication, and that project begins with a pragmatics perspective on language.

## NOTE

1. Sample utterances that I have created to illustrate a point are marked by numbers in parentheses. All other transcribed utterances are taken from a corpus of transcribed talk recorded in various manager-employee meetings in two major hotels reported on in Banks (1987). Transcription conventions are based on the standard notations developed by Gail Jefferson. Relevant conventions used here are as follows: colon indicates elongated sound; brackets indicate overlapping talk; italics show vocal emphasis; falling slash indicates falling vocal tone; rising slash indicates rising vocal tone; and single parentheses contain speaker pauses, estimated to the nearest second.

## REFERENCES

Banks, S. P. (1987). *A critical analysis of ideology and discourse in two hotels.* Unpublished doctoral dissertation, University of Southern California.

Brown, R., & Gilman, A. (1972). The pronouns of power and solidarity. In P. Giglioli (Ed.), *Language and social context* (pp. 252–282). New York: Penguin.

Carbaugh, D. (1985). Cultural communication and organizing. In W. B. Gudykunst, L. P. Stewart, & S. Ting-Toomey (Eds.), *Communication, culture, and organizational processes.* Beverly Hills, CA: Sage.

Chilton, P. (1987). Co-operation and non-co-operation: Ethical and political aspects of pragmatics. *Language and Communication, 7,* 221–239.

Clegg, S. R. (1979). *The theory of power and organization.* London: Routledge & Kegan Paul.

Clegg, S. R. (1987). The language of power and the power of language. *Organization Studies, 8,* 61–70.

Clement R. (1986). Second language and acculturation: An investigation of the effect of language status and individual characteristics. *Journal of Language and Social Psychology, 5,* 271–294.

Coulmas, F. (1981). Introduction: The concept of native speaker. In F. Coulmas (Ed.), *A festschrift for native speaker* (pp. 1–28). The Hague: Mouton.

Edwards, J. (1985). *Language, society and identity*. Oxford: Basil Blackwell.

Fowler, R. (1986). *Linguistic criticism*. Oxford: Oxford University Press.

Fowler, R., Hodge, B., Kress, G., & Trew, D. (1979). *Language and control*. London: Routledge & Kegan Paul.

Gallois, C., Franklyn-Stokes, A., Giles, H., & Coupland N. (1988). Communication accommodation in intercultural encounters. In Y. Kim & W. Gudykunst (Eds.), *Theory in intercultural communication*. Newbury Park, CA: Sage.

Giles, H. (1977). Social psychology and applied linguistics: Towards an integrative approach. *ITL: Review of Applied Linguistics, 35*, 27–42.

Giles, H. (1979). Ethnicity markers in speech. In K. R. Scherer & H. Giles (Eds.), *Social markers in speech* (pp. 252–290). Cambridge: Cambridge University Press.

Giles, H., & Byrne, J. L. (1982). The intergroup model of second language acquisition. *Journal of Multilingual and Multicultural Development, 3*, 17–40.

Giles, H., & Johnson, P. (1987). Ethnolinguistic identity theory: A social psychological approach to language maintenance. *International Journal of the Sociology of Language, 68*, 69–99.

Giles, H., & Powesland, P. (1975). *Speech style and social evaluation*. London: Academic Press.

Gudykunst, W. W., & Kim, Y. Y. (1984). *Communicating with strangers: An approach to intercultural communication*. New York: Random House.

Gumperz, J. J. (1982). *Discourse strategies*. Cambridge: Cambridge University Press.

Haarmann, H. (1986). *Language in ethnicity: A view of basic ecological relations*. New York: Mouton de Gruyter.

Joseph, J. E. (1987). *Eloquence and power*. London: Frances Pinter.

Kim, Y. Y. (Ed.). (1986). *Interethnic communication: Current research*. Newbury Park, CA: Sage.

Kress, G. (1985). Ideological structures in discourse. In T. van Dijk (Ed.), *Handbook of discourse analysis: Vol. 4. Discourse analysis in society* (pp. 27–42). London: Academic Press.

Leech, G. N. (1983). *Principles of pragmatics*. London: Longman.

Levinson, S. C. (1983). *Pragmatics*. Cambridge: Cambridge University Press.

Maitland, K., & Wilson, J. (1987). Pronominal selection and ideological conflict. *Journal of Pragmatics, 11*, 495–512.

Nelde, P. H. (1987). Language contact means language conflict. *Journal of Multilingual and Multicultural Development, 8*, 33–42.

Paikeday, T. M. (1985). *The native speaker is dead*. Toronto: Paikeday.

Pateman, T. (1987). *Language in mind and language in society: Studies in linguistic reproduction*. Oxford: Clarendon.

Rees, A. (1983). *Pronouns of person and power: A study of personal pronouns in public discourse*. Unpublished master's thesis, University of Sheffield, England.

Romaine, S. (Ed.). (1982). *Sociolinguistic variation in speech communities*. London: Edward Arnold.

Ryan, E., & Giles, H. (Eds.). (1982). *Attitudes towards language variation: Social and applied contexts*. London: Edward Arnold.

Speier, M. (1969). *The organization of talk and socialization practices in family household interaction*. Unpublished doctoral dissertation, University of California, Berkeley.

Ting-Toomey, S. (1988). Intercultural conflict styles: A face-negotiation theory. In Y.
Y. Kim & W. B. Gudykunst (Eds.), *Theory in intercultural communication*. Newbury Park, CA: Sage.

Volosinov, V. N. (1986). *Marxism and the philosophy of language* (L. Matejka & I.
Titunik, Trans.). Cambridge, MA: Harvard University Press.

Watson, D. (1987). Interdisciplinary considerations in the analysis of pro-terms. In G.
Button & J. Lee (Eds.), *Talk and social organization*. London: Multilingual Matters.

Zhao, H. (1987). The Chinese pronoun *zan* and its person and social deictic features.
*Journal of Chinese Linguistics, 15*, 152–175.

# III

## LANGUAGE AND INTERGROUP COMMUNICATION

# 10

## The Contexts of Language Learning
### *Extending the Intergroup Model of Second Language Acquisition*

PETER GARRETT   ●   *University College of North Wales*

HOWARD GILES   ●   *University of Bristol*

NIKOLAS COUPLAND   ●   *University of Wales*

*This chapter updates Giles and Byrne's (1982) Intergroup Model, which seeks to outline the sociopsychological processes underpinning variable success in second language acquisition and its consequences. Recent data have provided modest support for the model, but some revisions are proposed here in response to evidence that language is not necessarily central to cultural identity, that groups may even promote their identity via second language acquisition, and that variable strategic responses to intergroup circumstances are possible. The model's central propositions are extended through further attention to outgroup as well as ingroup factors, and to dominant as well as minority group learners. Sociolinguistic factors are also considered, as well as pedagogically inclined factors relating to all components of communicative proficiency.*

The Intergroup Model (IGM) proposed by Giles and Byrne (1982) is one of several models in the social psychology of second language acquisition (SLA) (see Gardner, 1985; Schumann, 1986), each of which has evolved in response to the widely recognized (though by means undisputed) importance of attitudes and motivation as determining factors in the acquisition of a second language (L2). By focusing attention on interactions among social contexts, individual differences, and outcomes, these models aim at predicting the learner's competence in the L2. The IGM was proposed to counter what Giles and Byrne saw as significant shortcomings in the earlier models, namely, that they appeared to neglect the role of *intergroup* variables

AUTHORS' NOTE: *We are grateful to Richard Clément, Elite Olshtain, and Jane Zuengler for their useful comments on a previous version of this chapter.*

and processes, such as ethnic identification and social differentiation in SLA (see Turner & Giles, 1981). Fostering bilingualism is, of course, an important goal in the development of intercultural and international communication. Hence an understanding of factors promoting and inhibiting the learning of another cultural group's tongue seems of paramount importance to readers of this annual. Surprisingly, studies in intercultural communication rarely attend to such issues in much detail, and developments have emerged from theorists in *other* disciplines. The present chapter, then, is in many ways an attempt to alert scholars to the notion that SLA processes should be located squarely within the precincts of intercultural communication studies.

By no means underestimating the value of earlier models, Giles and Byrne set out to incorporate significant contributions from Gardner's (1985) and Clément's (1980) work into their IGM. In outlining it, Giles and Byrne stressed that it was embryonic and called for empirical research to test the validity of some of the basic premises. They also urged an integration of the approach with more linguistic, cognitive, and societally based perspectives on second and foreign language learning. With this in mind, and in the light of recent Canadian and other data and theory, a primary objective of this chapter is to make certain revisions to the IGM, in order to express more fully the sociopsychological conditions inhibiting and predisposing SLA. In particular, we consider both ingroup *and outgroup* perceptions, and the scope and applicability of the model in relation to variable goals and targets of SLA. In addition, we consider some sociolinguistic, pedagogically inclined processes with which intergroup processes interact, as we revise and develop concepts earlier proposed by Beebe and Giles (1984) and Giles, Garrett, and Coupland (1987).

## IGM ORIGINS

Giles and Byrne's (1982) model evolved out of speech accommodation theory, which in part seeks to explain the motivations and effects of speakers converging toward or diverging away from speech characteristics of interlocutors in interpersonal encounters (see review of Giles, Mulac, Bradac, & Johnson, 1987). The question arose as to whether similar sociopsychological forces were at work in intercultural contexts (see Gallois, Franklyn-Stokes, Giles, & Coupland,

1988) and what kinds of psychological conditions would precipitate ethnolinguistic differentiation in interethnic encounters (Giles, 1979; Giles & Johnson, 1981). Giles and Byrne argued that the socio-psychological conditions stimulating the widening of communicative "gaps" in (dyadic) interethnic encounters (i.e., divergences) would resemble those likely to lead to a subordinate group's setting up barriers to learning a dominant ethnic group's L2.

Thus what distinguishes the IGM from other models is that, unlike them, it predicts not only the conditions likely to promote SLA, but also those conducive to a preference *not* to acquire an L2. Empirical support for the occurrence of such hypothesized divergence-inducing conditions has been found in a (Welsh-English) study by Giles and Johnson (1981). The following are the *five sociopsychological propositions* Giles and Byrne saw as *inhibiting* SLA in *subordinate* groups where the language of acquisition is posed as a possible threat to the majority group. Inhibition is posited as emerging when *minority* group members

(a) identify strongly with their ethnic group and perceive the ingroup language (L1) as an important dimension of their cultural identity;

(b) construe "cognitive alternatives" to their subordinate intergroup status, such as feeling that their own relative position was *illegitimately* created historically by dominant group oppression (rather than its being part of the accepted order of nature), and that there is some possibility of the status hierarchy being changed now;

(c) perceive both their ingroup and the outgroup boundaries to be hard and closed;

(d) identify with few *other* social categories, each of which provides them with inadequate identities and low intragroup statuses, relative to their ethnic identification; and

(e) perceive their ingroup "ethnolinguistic vitality" to be high and compare it favorably with that of the outgroup.

These conditions are set out and discussed more comprehensively in the cited sources and are, in particular respects, revised in the following discussion.

### Ethnolinguistic Vitality

We would like to focus especially on the ethnolinguistic vitality proposition here because this has evoked some debate in the literature (e.g., Johnson, Giles, & Bourhis, 1983), and the literature allows us analytical access to the contextual conditions under which a second language is acquired or not. The concept of "ethnolinguistic vitality" originated as an attempt to incorporate individuals' construals of societal conditions as factors mediating individuals' interethnic attitudes and behaviors (see Bourhis & Sachdev, 1984). In this way, interethnic dynamics are viewed in their sociostructural context (Giles, Bourhis, & Taylor, 1977). It has been argued that the more vitality a group considers itself to have, the more likely it is that individual members will be disposed toward investing psychological energy in it, conceptualizing relevant situations in interethnic terms, and therein emphasizing their own ethnolinguistic identity. Vitality has three major components: status, demography, and institutional support (the constituent elements of which are shown in Figure 10.1). These components have been derived from sociological studies of factors contributing to language maintenance and decay (see Giles et al., 1977). Individual perceptions of the components can be measured by the 22-item SVQ devised by Bourhis, Giles, and Rosenthal (1981). A study of Anglo- and Greek-Australians in Melbourne (Giles, Young, & Rosenthal, 1985) confirmed that these three vitality components possess psychological reality. That is to say, people have corresponding subjective images (or social representations) of how their group stands in relation to relevant others that do, to greater or lesser extents, correspond with more objective measures (Sachdev, Bourhis, Phang, & D'Eye, 1987; Sachdev, Bourhis, D'Eye, & Phang, in press). On the other hand, as Clément (personal communication) points out, the relationship between vitality perception and SLA has yet to be demonstrated empirically (see also Clément, 1986; Labrie & Clément, 1985). The same Australian study showed that vitality may be affected by intergroup dynamics and loyalties. In Melbourne, although there is a large Greek community, institutional support, status, and demography are objectively in favor of Anglos. Our data suggest that while both groups recognize this reality, across some (notably language) scales, Anglos polarized the differences between ingroup and outgroup vitalities in their favor, whereas the Greeks significantly *attenuated* such discrepancies. Somewhat contrasting findings emerged in a recent study in the Francophone-dominant Canton of Neuchatel in Switzerland (Young, Bell, & Giles, in press). Although Swiss-German adolescents conceded (like the Greeks in Melbourne) much more vitality to the Swiss-French than to their own group on most ethnolinguistic

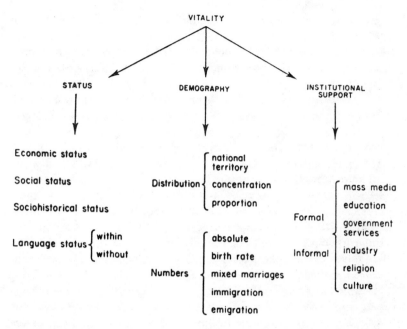

Figure 10.1: A taxonomy of the structural variables affecting ethnolinguistic vitality.

vitality items, they elevated the majority outgroup to a greater extent than even the Swiss-French themselves.

Vitality perception studies have also been carried out in Hong Kong during the current period of economic uncertainty and intense speculation about its future sovereignty. Pierson, Giles, and Young (1987) found that Western and local Cantonese students differed in their relative vitality perceptions to a far greater degree than manifested in the above-cited studies. Some ethnolinguistic vitality items revealed strong indications of "ingroup favoritism," where both Western and Chinese students saw their respective ingroups as having more vitality than the outgroup. However, the opposite profile emerged on other items, showing that each group felt that the other had more power and control. In another study, it was possible to embrace the effects of sociopolitical *change* on perceptions of vitality that were collected prior to the Sino-British Treaty of 1983 and compared with a matched group some 18 months later. Findings showed that Chinese subjective vitality increased, while Western subjective vitality diminished in parallel on some measures, even though there were no real changes in objective indices (Young, Giles, & Pierson, 1986).

The backdrop of social structure cannot be regarded as an immutable given. Its primary significance is as a multidimensional, sociopsychological construct for the individuals involved (see Allard & Landry, 1986) when operating through their particular social network (Clément, personal communication). Such factors as social category membership and sociopolitical climate will clearly have an impact on perceptions. Vitality, then, plays a crucial role in our understanding of language in society, and we feel it warrants much more theoretical and empirical attention, particularly with respect to SLA. To reiterate one productive pattern of association, the more vitality you perceive your group to possess—say, as a minority group under threat—the greater the psychological investment you are likely to make in ethnic attachment, and the less likely you are to sample or accommodate the ethnic routines (e.g., linguistic habits) of the relevant dominant outgroup.

In order to avoid confusion, it should be clarified that *conditions c and e* above are presented in a somewhat revised form compared to earlier formulations, owing to the fact that the original propositions referred to *ingroup* boundaries and vitality only (Giles, Mulac, Bradac, & Johnson, 1987). In line with Genesee, Rogers, and Holobow (1983), who point to the role of perceived motivational support from the L2 community in facilitating SLA, we wish to stress the value of acknowledging *outgroup* boundaries, too. As stated before, proposition c emphasizes that in- and outgroups may have their own perceived boundaries, *both* of which will impede or promote movement out of and into each other's group, thereby allowing, limiting, or preventing opportunities for SLA. Similarly, we have felt the need to recognize the importance of *outgroup* vitality with respect to proposition e above. *Relative* vitality in favor of the *L1* would predictably reduce the incentive for investing acquisition energy in SLA and, therefore, seems a theoretically more potent construct (Clément, 1980) than a mere theoretical reliance on any absolute value of ingroup vitality alone. These two modest revisions, then, enhance the "intergroup" character of the IGM.

Learning propensities and outcome performances can be seen to be *indirectly* predictable from group perceptions. Propositions a to e are, *in combination*, a consequence of *multiple* negative orientations. Not only is acquisition of the dominant outgroup language ideologically dispreferred (*proposition a* and especially in combination with *b*), but it is also difficult (in the sense of *c*) and possibly even unnecessary when it comes to *conditions d and e*. Those members of a minority group embracing perceptions and identifications a to e, we previously termed Subgroup A (Giles & Byrne, 1982; Giles, Mulac, Bradac, & Johnson, 1987). However, it is important to take account of the fact that ethnic groups are not homogeneous wholes, neither within Subgroup A nor certainly outside it. Accordingly, and in complete contrast, there may be other members of the same group with broadly *converse* identifications and perceptions (for example, identifying weakly with the ingroup and perceiving its vitality as low). Giles and Byrne (1982) regard these individuals as those most likely to achieve nativelike proficiency in the L2 and, in some circumstances, more likely to approximate the language patterns and communicative styles of outgroup members. Such individuals were provisionally termed Subgroup B (see also Ball, Giles, & Hewstone, 1984).

We would now wish to redefine the notion of Subgroups A and B, not solely in terms of concrete subcategory memberships, but rather, as alternative *learning orientations*. We see the conceptual merit in construing *conditions a-e* and their *converse* as a low or high propensity to learn the majority L2, respectively. This conceptual refinement not only acknowledges the fact that quite diverse and complex sociopsychological climates may underlie the *same learning orientation* (be it high or low), but also provides us with a more robust framework for modifying further the IGM as empirical work develops. Moreover, it is a moot point as to whether types A and B, as currently characterized, constitute significant proportions of a minority collectivity anyway (see Ball et al., 1984). That said, the proposed nomenclature does not belie the distinct possibility that in some contexts those who espouse high and low learning propensities may be socially distinguishable and labeled as discernible subcategories within the ethnic collectivity as well as by outsiders.

Using this terminology, then, those with a *low* propensity to accommodate the majority L2 will experience a "fear of assimilation" (see Clément, 1980) as a disincentive to learning the majority L2 and will see SLA, if it occurs, as "subtractive" of their identity (Lambert, 1974). Their learning orientation toward the L2 and its users will tend to be "segregative," or even "disintegrative." They will steer away from informal acquisition contexts (Gardner, 1985), particularly those involving personal encounters with members of the L1 community. Of course, learning contexts and pedagogic concerns will cut across any predictions made here (see below). Still, we might probably expect positive outcomes in narrowly linguistic areas such as course grades and grammar skills, but not along the dimensions of communicative competence in the L2. Intelligence and aptitude levels will mediate the extent of any of their achievements here (see Gardner, 1985).

On the other hand, those with a *high* propensity to accommodate the majority L2 will see SLA as "additive" to their identities and will have an "integrative" orientation toward the language and its speakers, seeking out informal learning contexts and opportunities, rather like Rubin's (1975) "good language learner." Individuals with such a learning orientation will work hard to compensate for, and transcend, the limitations of pedagogic practice by actively involving themselves in the acquisition process and maximizing its potential. They are likely to achieve not only high oral proficiency in the L2, but also additional nonlinguistic outcomes, such as an increased liking for L2 speakers and their culture. In turn, these gains will lead to their having greater confidence in using the L2 in public and their accomplishments will grow as their situational anxiety decreases.

### Consequences of SLA

Integral to the IGM are the social ramifications of performance (L2) *feedback* discerned by members of the ingroup and outgroup from those with the two learning orientations specified. Thus, to take those with a low propensity to accommodate the L2, their lack of proficiency in the L2 would be interpreted positively by those similarly inclined as the successful retention of their L1 in the face of threat imposed by the L2 and its concomitant culture. Those with a high propensity to accommodate the L2, on the other hand, would define the former's nonacquisition as "failure," but might explain it in terms of pedagogical limitations, poor supportive environments, and the like. Members of the dominant outgroup, however, who might not even consider the possibility that others have no desire to acquire their language or savor their culture, might well see this failure as confirmation of their preconceived ideas regarding the communicative and cognitive shortcomings of the particular ethnic group.

Those whose high propensity to accommodate the L2 is translated into actual mastery of it would be viewed very positively by others similarly inclined, and this would strengthen further their integrative orientation and desire. Those with a low propensity, however, would regard this "success" as cultural betrayal, and this could well aggravate their fears of assimilation as well as increase their reluctance to learn the L2. Indeed, this pattern reflects findings in Giles and Johnson (1981) in that a decrease in ingroup vitality can stimulate ethnic mobilization.

Finally, where sufficient numbers of those with a positive learning orientation attempt to "cross over" and adopt the primary linguistic ethnicity of the (former) L2, this will reduce the distinctiveness of the outgroup, especially if its members afford high value to their own distinctive L1. This may precipitate a "shift" in the L2 (see Joos, 1952, on the concept of "phonetic drift") so as to maintain its own advantages (Ulrich, 1971), thereby establishing "an ever-moving target to emulate" (Edwards, 1976). Individuals whose positive learning orientations have led them to proficiency in the L2 may nevertheless have adopted a speech style that can be stigmatized. They may then find themselves "between two stools" in terms of the outgroup and those members of their ingroup who have maintained a low propensity toward learning the dominant tongue.

Within the framework of the IGM and specifically with reference to minority group perceptions, bilingualism is a two-edged sword. It can bring positive cognitive gains and social benefits to those with a high propensity to learn the L2, whereas for those with a low propensity, where *non*competence is the goal, it may be deemed culturally suicidal. Furthermore, the IGM sees L2 as dynamic, changing entities, evolving in response to the sociohistorical fluctuations of intercultural relations and communication.

## THE IGM EXTENDED AND ELABORATED

Recently, some empirical data have been provided by Hall and Gudykunst (1986) that show some support for the IGM. Their study, in Arizona, employed a LISREL model-testing procedure and involved over 200 international students from a wide range of cultural and linguistic backgrounds. The IGM was found to provide a good and significant fit to their data for English language competency (as well as nonlinguistic outcomes). Since one of their groups was arguably nonsubordinate (the group's members were only temporarily in the United States), they might be better considered foreign than second language learners (Littlewood, 1984); thus these results suggest that the IGM may apply beyond subordinate groups on the one hand and second language learners on the other (see Hildebrandt & Giles, 1983). In fact, we have recently argued for the applicability of the IGM beyond subordinate group members learning a dominant group's L2 in relation to the learning of Euskaran among Basques unable to speak their own ingroup tongue (Giles, Garrett, & Coupland, 1987). More specifically, although *conditions a-e* are those likely to breed a low propensity toward learning a dominant group's language as previously discussed, they nonetheless may well be those necessary for fostering a *high* propensity for acquiring the minority language among those of the ingroup who cannot speak it. The successful maintenance of minority languages such as Catalan, Welsh, Frisian, and so forth (other macrocontextual forces notwithstanding) may then be dependent on the kinds of sociopsychological climates we have described in a to e before (see also Giles & Johnson, 1981).

Although the crux of the IGM can be usefully extended to encompass a wider variety of language learning settings than was originally envisaged, recent data from Lambert, Mermigis, and Taylor (1986) suggest that the propositions are severely limited in a manner that implies a biased underlying perspective with regard to our understanding of the complex interrelationships between language and ethnicity. These researchers have found some support for the "multiculturalism hypothesis" that suggests that the more secure and positive a minority group feels about its identity, the more tolerant the members will be toward the ethnic characteristics and activities of other nonmajority groups in the community. We feel that this has implications for the IGM in that strong ingroup identification and security can sometimes be an impoi.ant condition for embracing the L2 and other attributes of another (though, we assume, nonthreatening) group.[1] Interestingly, Bond and King (1985), again in relation to Hong Kong, have pointed to the fact that Chinese social identity actually incorporates the value of change, and that "modernization" does not necessarily equate with "Westernization." Thus the acquisition of English need not be regarded as "subtractive" of their cultural identity. Indeed, they may feel that, far from SLA leading to cultural assimilation, it could be invaluable in maintaining or bolstering their cultural resources in the face of sociotechnological advancements. This suggests, then, that SLA on occasion can actually be an intergroup strategy aimed at *preserving* ingroup identity, and adds to the observation that group identity can survive the disappearance of the original language (Anderson & Frideres, 1981).

Relatedly, Edwards (1985) has been vociferous in his questioning of the fundamental association between language and identity (see, for example, Fishman, 1977), claiming that loss of the former does not inevitably lead to a lessening of the latter (see Coupland, 1986). Indeed, Sawaie (1986) has shown how ethnicity can exist side by side with the disappearance of ethnic language maintenance when there is a socioeconomic need to learn the majority language, as with Arabs in the United States. Similarly, San Antonio (1987), in an ethnographic study of the use of English and associated communicative norms in an American corporation in Japan—the acquisitive use of which is a prerequisite of improving one's status in the organization—does not involve a commensurate loss in Japanese identity. Pak, Dion, and Dion (1985), in like fashion, found among Chinese students in Toronto that self-rated confidence in English did not necessarily constitute any corresponding loss to their cultural identity.

Edwards (1988) also has shown evidence of Scottish cultural continuity in Nova Scotia, where Gaelic language loyalty is not very much in evidence. Other groups having low ethnolinguistic vitality have been shown to adopt particularly *creative* (and *non*linguistic) strategies for maintaining their group identities (see Giles, 1979; Giles & Johnson, 1981). In studying the Valdotans (a French-speaking community in Northern Italy), Saint-Blancat (1985) found that they try to achieve socioeconomic parity with the dominant group by speaking Italian (their L2), yet still "perpetuate traditional values by maintaining family land property and securing its survival by handing on religious beliefs and a sense of work and duty" (p. 22). Finally, in this respect, Edwards and Shearen (1987), in their study of ethnolinguistic relations in Brussels, make the salutary point that "language issues can be manipulated for political ends, and need not always imply grassroot priorities" (p. 147).

In recognition of the role of nonlinguistic factors as valued aspects of cultural identity, and the claims that L2 gains are not commensurate with identity loss in all cases, we have set out *propositions f to j* below (Giles, Mulac, Bradac, & Johnson, 1987). These are revisions to Giles and Byrne (1982) insofar as they modify the earlier reliance on the *converse* of *propositions a to e* as learning orientations conducive to SLA. Hence a *high propensity* to accommodate the dominant L2 may exist when minority group members

(f) identify weakly with their ethnic group, and their language is not a salient dimension of ethnicity; *or*, if L1 is a salient dimension, it is not perceived to be threatened by SLA; *or*, if seen as threatened, there are alternative *non*linguistic salient dimensions deemed satisfactory for preserving ethnic identity;

(g) construe no cognitive alternatives to their subordinate status to the extent that it is attributed as legitimate and there is little likelihood of change; *or*, when aware of alternatives, these are realizable only through SLA;

(h) perceive ingroup and outgroup boundaries to be soft and open;

(i) identify with many other social categories, each of which provides adequate group identities and a satisfactory intragroup status; and

(j) perceive ingroup vitality as low and neglected relative to outgroup vitality; *or*, it is judged that SLA will maintain or promote satisfying nonlinguistic aspects of ingroup vitality.

## SOCIOLINGUISTIC FACTORS AND THE IGM

In circumstances where *propositions f to j* pertain, what kinds of *sociolinguistic* climates will promote SLA? Beebe and Giles (1984) explored this issue and suggested, along with several other conditions, that learners might need to (a) promote the use of simplified L2 inputs from native speakers and others, and (b) attempt communicative strategies to compensate for their limited proficiency.

As regards the first, included under the heading "simplified codes" were foreigner talk, teacher talk, and interlanguage talk. Some modification to this proposal is required, however, in the light of claims that such inputs may at times serve to *hinder* SLA (e.g., Krashen, 1985; Prabhu, 1987; Snow & Hoefnagel-Hohle, 1982). Indeed, Valdman (1981, p. 42) has even suggested that foreigner talk "is sometimes used to prevent foreign speakers acquiring the language," and this would actually be in accord with intergroup theory. Simplified talk from native speakers who experience a threat to their group distinctiveness can thus reduce or deny access to the target language for learners and thereby restrict them to simple codes, which have traditionally been awarded low social prestige (James, 1986). Some caution is also required with the second condition, since it could be argued, after all, that the more effectively learners are able to compensate through L2 communicative strategies for the gap between their communicative needs and their L2 linguistic competence, the less need they have for acquiring more of the L2. In turn, this could precipitate fossilization.

To some extent, the difficulties with these and other (e.g., language background, status, environment, repertoire) IGM "sociolinguistic riders" formulated by Beebe and Giles (1984) stem from a static/dynamic ambiguity in the term *acquisition.* We may attempt to identify factors reflecting a particular stage in the process of acquisition, and therefore the quality of performance and capacity for accommodation at a given time. These, however, do not necessarily contribute to predicting *whether* acquisition to a level approaching nativelike proficiency is more or less likely to occur over a given period, and this was the question the IGM originally addressed.

Apart from this, the very assumption that learners are capable of achieving "nativelike" proficiency is questionable. Precious few, it is claimed, ever reach this level (Johansson, 1978; Selinker, 1972). More important, the concept of nativelike proficiency begs at least three further questions. First, is the learner in fact aiming at any identifiable native variety (e.g., for English, see Kachru, 1986; also see the discussion of regional standards in Trudgill & Hannah, 1985), and, if so, which? Second, what is meant by *proficiency, communicative competence,* and so on (e.g., see Yalden, 1987)? Third, what level of proficiency does our model native speaker actually have? Such questions clearly need to be kept in mind as we develop our ideas on SLA, even if it is beyond our immediate concerns to examine them in depth in this context.

Our emendations lead us to the following broad propositions portraying at least some of the contextual features supportive of SLA:

(1) The L2 and culture are fairly *similar* in their components of communicative proficiency to the L1 and its culture.
(2) There is facilitative *exposure* to the L2.
(3) There is facilitative *use* of the L2.

To elaborate on these, we would hesitate to make the seemingly plausible assertion that the closer two languages are, the more likely will be successful SLA. It is possible that the most difficult L2s to master are those either closest to or most distant from the L1

(Corder, 1978). Facilitative exposure will be partly dependent on the opportunities that exist for exposure and contact (see Hewstone & Brown, 1986). Foreign language learners may be confined to one native or nonnative speaker source in the classroom, but for second language learners, the perception of ingroup and outgroup boundaries may well have a profound impact on their learner orientations (as above). Such exposure is important quantitatively and qualitatively; that is, in both degree and variety (Rubin, 1975). The development of stylistic variation, for example, will occur only if there is exposure to it. Learners may then constantly "match" their output against input (Klein, 1986). Indeed, it is the essential role of output and interaction that brings us to the importance of use (Ervin-Tripp, 1970; Hatch, 1983; Long, 1983; Porter, 1986; Soh, 1987). Facilitative use will also depend partly on the availability of opportunities, and restrictions similar to the above will apply for foreign and second language learners. Learners will require opportunities to use a variety of styles and to operate in a range of social contexts equivalent to those in which a native speaker would perform.

How then do learners themselves raise their levels of competence within these conditions, narrowing the gap between input and intake, expanding and improving their output? Pedagogical factors play a part, of course, though these may not always have the intended outcome. Some programs may stress one or another component of "communicative proficiency" (Bachman & Palmer, 1982), for example, grammatical at the expense of pragmatic and sociolinguistic competence. This, in turn, may precipitate infelicities, or "pragmatic failure" (Thomas, 1983), or various kinds of incongruities or hypercorrection (see Labov, 1972) as learners battle to master a particular (standard or nonstandard) variety. Resulting "overaccommodation" (see Coupland, Coupland, Giles, & Henwood, in press) may then simply be socially downgraded by native recipients (Garrett, 1984).

Cummins and Swain (1986) suggest that the improvement of competence in sociolinguistic and discourse areas is closely linked to the learner's cognitive processes (see also Gale & Brown, 1985). We therefore endorse Faerch and Kasper's (1986) proposition that input leads to more learning when the learner "assumes responsibility" for, and so aims to reduce, knowledge gaps as they occur in interaction. Marton (1987) feels that competence increases not simply through volumes of input, with learners focusing on meaning alone, but when learners in addition pay conscious attention to formal features (e.g., grammatical signals, phraseology, collocations) of the input and adopt a "mental set" to retain as much new input as possible for future production. Somewhat comparable intervention to draw attention to formal L2 properties has been proposed by Sharwood Smith (1981) and Rutherford (1987).

We are reminded, however, that such attention alone is not a sufficient condition for SLA. Shapira's (1978) *Zoila*, though clearly aware of her underuse of such features, made no attempt to use them more frequently. We return, then, ultimately, to the inclination to "assume responsibility," where acquirers avail themselves of, and even seek out, opportunities for facilitative exposure and use (see Rubin, 1975).

The *learning contexts* characterized in terms of our three sociolinguistic propositions, whether they be immutably and structurally constrained or open to creative construction, are obviously an important component to our model. They are hereby acknowledged as such and elevated to a formal status in the revised schema of the IGM as portrayed in Figure 10.2, which provides a summary of the foregoing discussion. It should be emphasized, however, that the model here directs itself explicitly to the processes underlying minority individuals' learning of a dominant group's language.

## CONCLUSIONS

All in all, we feel that we have infused some robustness into the IGM, particularly with respect to adopting a less rigid stance than previously on the nature of the relationship between language and cultural identity. The exploration of learner processes and their interaction with intergroup processes still has far to go. While we are attracted to fleshing out *common* sociopsychological processes underlying different SLA contexts, we are nonetheless not blind to the fact that each has its own particularities (a perspective apparent to us from Mick Billig's recent work with prejudice among different social categories; personal communication). In other words, the variabilities among language learning contexts—and their associated intercultural dynamics, pedagogical resources, and unique vitality properties—may raise far more issues and problems than hitherto appreciated in the development of SLA theory. Hence the IGM should be utilized analytically in any setting with due caution and

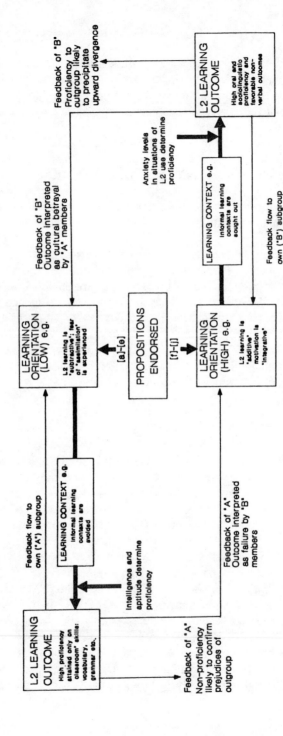

**Figure 10.2: The (revised) Intergroup Model of second language learning.**

L2 LEARNING OUTCOME

High oral and sociolinguistic proficiency and favorable non-verbal outcomes

Anxiety levels in situations of L2 use determine proficiency

Feedback of 'B' Proficiency to outgroup likely to precipitate upward divergence

LEARNING CONTEXT e.g. informal learning contexts are sought out

Feedback flow to own ('B') subgroup

LEARNING ORIENTATION (HIGH) e.g. L2 learning is "additive"; motivation is "integrative"

Feedback of 'B' Outcome interpreted as cultural betrayal by 'A' members

PROPOSITIONS ENDORSED

[a]–[e]

[f]–[j]

LEARNING ORIENTATION (LOW) e.g. L2 learning is "subtractive"; fear of "assimilation" is experienced

LEARNING CONTEXT e.g. informal learning contexts are avoided

Intelligence and aptitude determine proficiency

Feedback flow to own ('A') subgroup

L2 LEARNING OUTCOME

High proficiency attained only on classroom' skills: vocabulary, grammar etc.

Feedback of 'A' Non-proficiency likely to confirm prejudices of outgroup

Feedback of 'A' Outcome interpreted as failure by 'B' members attention to the particular historical, ideological, and political forces that impinge upon, and sometimes may fundamentally mold, the SLA processes operating. Hence not only do different ethnic groups attach varying social meanings to their ingroup cultural identities (see Brown & Williams, 1984), but they also attach different values to them in terms of importance, emotion, and stability (Garza & Herringer, 1987), to name but a few. In addition, the emotive climate associated with interacting with different target outgroups can be of crucial importance. Dijker (1987) has shown that different emotional dimensions, such as positive mood, anxiety, and irritation, are associated differentially by the host community with various immigrant groups in the Netherlands and can affect communicative outcomes accordingly. In sum, the multidimensional meanings associated with acquiring an L2 will be highly variable.

We are then just beginning to face the complexity inherent in understanding factors that promote *and* impede SLA among minority groups. That said, the IGM model does allow us to pinpoint how SLA is just as much a sociopsychological process as it is a linguistic or an educational one. Put another way, the failures of bilingual educational programs cannot always be located in peculiarities of pedagogy alone. We recognize, of course, that the IGM is still lacking in specifications of interrelationships among its propositions and in considering factors mediating group orientations and individual predispositions. However, we regard the IGM as still very much evolving, and see a need for further contributions and elaborations to attempt to combine these sociopsychological processes with sociolinguistic and cognitive mechanisms in different cultural settings.

## NOTE

1. We feel there might be some theoretical value in distinguishing between what could be termed "neutral" and "defensive" identifications. Strong *neutral* ingroup identification may occur where a thriving group does not feel threatened by an outgroup (or outgroups); strong *defensive* ingroup identification would occur where a group does feel its identity is threatened by the outgroup. The ingroup identification referred to in Giles and Byrne's (1982) IGM, then, is implicitly defensive in its identification character. Where this is weak or absent, SLA will be less impeded; where strong, it will be more impeded. We would propose that strong neutral identification, on the other hand, will not create barriers to SLA.

# REFERENCES

Allard, R., & Landry, R. (1986). Subjective ethnolinguistic vitality viewed as a belief system. *Journal of Multilingual and Multicultural Development, 7,* 1–12.

Anderson, A., & Frideres, J. (1981). *Ethnicity in Canada.* Toronto: Butterworths.

Bachman, L. F., & Palmer, A. S. (1982). The construct validation of some components of communicative proficiency. *TESOL Quarterly, 16,* 449–464.

Ball, P., Giles, H., & Hewstone, M. (1984). The intergroup theory of second language acquisition and catastrophic dimensions. In H. Tajfel (Ed.), *The social dimensions* (Vol. 2). Cambridge: Cambridge University Press.

Beebe, L., & Giles, H. (1984). Speech accommodation theories: A discussion in terms of second language acquisition. *International Journal of the Sociology of Language, 46,* 5–32.

Bond, M. H., & King, A.Y.C. (1985). Coping with the threat of Westernization in Hong Kong. *International Journal of Intercultural Relations, 9,* 351–364.

Bourhis, R. Y., Giles, H., & Rosenthal, D. (1981). Notes on the construction of a "Subjective Vitality Questionnaire" for ethnolinguistic groups. *Journal of Multilingual and Multicultural Development, 2,* 144–155.

Bourhis, R. Y., & Sachdev, I. (1984). Vitality perceptions and language attitudes: Some Canadian data. *Journal of Language and Social Psychology, 3,* 97–126.

Brown, R., & Williams, J. (1984). Group identification: The same thing to all people? *Human Relations, 37,* 547–564.

Carroll, J. B. (1965). The prediction of success in intensive foreign language training. In R. Glazer (Ed.), *Training research and education.* New York: John Wiley.

Clément, R. (1980). Ethnicity, contact and communicative competence in a second language. In H. Giles, W. P. Robinson, & P. M. Smith (Eds.), *Language: Social psychological perspectives.* Oxford: Pergamon.

Clément, R. (1986). Second language and acculturation: An investigation of the effect of language status and individual characteristics. *Journal of Language and Social Psychology, 5,* 271–294.

Corder, S. P. (1978). Language distance and the magnitude of the language learning task. In *Proceedings, VII Colloquium on Applied Linguistics.* Berne: University of Berne.

Coupland, N. (1986). [Review of J. R. Edwards, *Language, identity and society.*] *Journal of Language and Social Psychology, 5,* 63–70.

Coupland, N., Coupland, J., Giles, H., & Henwood, K. (in press). Accommodating the elderly: Invoking and extending a theory. *Language in Society.*

Cummins, J., & Swain, M. (1986). *Bilingualism in education.* London: Longman.

Dijker, A.J.M. (1987). Emotional reactions to ethnic minorities. *European Journal of Social Psychology, 17,* 305–325.

Edwards, A. D. (1976). *Language, culture and class.* London: Heinemann.

Edwards, J. R. (1985). *Language, identity, and society.* Oxford: Basil Blackwell.

Edwards, J. R. (1988). Gaelic in Nova Scotia. In C. H. Williams (Ed.), *Geolinguistic essays.* Clevedon: Multilingual Matters.

Edwards, J. R., & Shearn, C. (1987). Language and identity in Belgium. *Ethnic and Racial Studies, 10,* 135–148.

Ervin-Tripp, S. M. (1970). Structure and process in language acquisition. In J. E.

Atlatis (Ed.), *21st Annual Round Table*. Washington, DC: Georgetown University Press.

Faerch, C., & Kasper, G. (1986). The role of comprehension in second language learning. *Applied Linguistics, 7*, 257–274.

Fishman, J. A. (1977). Language and ethnicity. In H. Giles (Ed.), *Language, ethnicity and intergroup relations*. London: Academic Press.

Gale, L. E., & Brown, B. L. (1985). A theory of learning and skill-acquisition applied to interactive video: Activities at the David O. McKay Institute, Brigham Young University. *Studies in Language Learning, 5*, 105–114.

Gallois, C., Franklyn-Stokes, A., Giles, H., & Coupland, N. (1988). Communication accommodation theory and intercultural encounters: Intergroup and interpersonal considerations. In Y. Kim & W. B. Gudykunst (Eds.), *Theories in intercultural communication*. Newbury Park, CA: Sage.

Gardner, R. C. (1985). *Social psychology and second language learning*. London: Arnold.

Garrett, P. (1984). *Judgements of French and Spanish speakers of English: What accentedness communicates*. Unpublished master's thesis, University College, Bangor, North Wales.

Garza, R. T., & Herringer, L. G. (1987). Social identity: A multidimensional approach. *Journal of Social Psychology, 127*, 299–308.

Genesee, F., Rogers, P., & Holobow, N. (1983). The social psychology of second language learning: Another point of view. *Language Learning, 33*, 209–224.

Giles, H. (1979). Ethnicity markers in speech. In K. R. Scherer & H. Giles (Eds.), *Social markers in speech*. Cambridge: Cambridge University Press.

Giles, H., Bourhis, R. Y., & Taylor, D. M. (1977). Towards a theory of language in ethnic group relations. In H. Giles (Ed.), *Language, ethnicity and intergroup relations*. London: Academic Press.

Giles, H., & Byrne, J. L. (1982). The intergroup model of second language acquisition. *Journal of Multilingual and Multicultural Development, 3*, 17–40.

Giles, H., Garrett, P., & Coupland, N. (1987, August). *Language acquisition in the Basque Country: Invoking and extending the intergroup model*. Paper presented at the Second World Basque Congress, San Sebastian.

Giles, H., & Johnson, P. (1981). The role of language on ethnic group relations. In J. C. Turner & H. Giles (Eds.), *Intergroup behavior*. Chicago: Chicago University Press.

Giles, H., Mulac, A., Bradac, J. J., & Johnson, P. (1987). Speech accommodation theory: The first decade and beyond. In M. L. McLaughlin (Ed.), *Communication yearbook 10*. Newbury Park, CA: Sage.

Giles, H., Rosenthal, D., & Young, L. (1985). Perceived ethnolinguistic vitality: The Anglo- and Greek-Australian setting. *Journal of Multilingual and Multicultural Development, 6*, 256–269.

Hall, B. J., & Gudykunst, W. B. (1986). The intergroup theory of second language ability. *Journal of Language and Social Psychology, 5*, 291–302.

Hatch, E. M. (1983). *Psycholinguistics: A second language perspective*. Rowley, MA: Newbury House.

Hewstone, M., & Brown, R. (Eds.). (1986). *Intergroup contact*. Oxford: Basil Blackwell.

Hildebrandt, N., & Giles, H. (1983). The Japanese as subordinate group: Ethnolinguistic identity theory in a foreign language context. *Anthropological Linguistics, 25,* 436–466.

James, C. (1986). Welsh foreigner talk: Breaking new ground. *Journal of Multilingual and Multicultural Development, 7,* 41–54.

Johansson, S. (1978). *Studies in error gravity.* Gothenburg: Acta Universitatis Gothoburgensis.

Johnson, P., Giles, H., & Bourhis, R. Y. (1983). The viability of ethnolinguistic vitality: A reply to Husband and Khan. *Journal of Multilingual and Multicultural Development, 4,* 255–269.

Joos, M. (1952). The medieaval sibilants. *Language, 28,* 222–231.

Kachru, B. B. (1986). *The alchemy of English.* Oxford: Pergamon.

Klein, W. (1986). *Second language acquisition.* Cambridge: Cambridge University Press.

Krashen, S. D. (1985). *The input hypothesis: Issues and implications.* London: Longman.

Labov, W. (1972). *Sociolinguistic patterns.* Philadelphia: University of Pennsylvania Press.

Labrie, N., & Clément, R. (1985). Ethnolinguistic identity, self-confidence and second language proficiency: An investigation. *Journal of Multilingual and Multicultural Development, 7,* 269–282.

Lambert, W. E. (1967). A social psychology of bilingualism. *Journal of Social Issues, 23,* 91–109.

Lambert, W. E. (1974). Culture and language as factors in learning and education. In F. E. Abound & R. D. Meads (Eds.), *Cultural factors in learning and education.* Bellingham: Western Washington College Press.

Lambert, W. E., Mermigis, L., & Taylor, D. M. (1986). Greek Canadians' attitudes toward own group and other Canadian ethnic groups: A test of the multiculturalism hypothesis. *Canadian Journal of Behavioral Science, 18,* 35–51.

Littlewood, W. T. (1984). *Foreign and second language learning.* Cambridge: Cambridge University Press.

Long, M. H. (1983). Native speaker/non-native speaker conversation and the negotiation of comprehensible input. *Applied Linguistics, 4,* 126–141.

Marton, W. (1987). The communicative approach and the three language learning/teaching strategies. *Tromso Working Papers on Language and Linguistics, 13,* 23–69.

Pak, A. W-P., Dion, K. L., & Dion, K. K. (1985). Correlates of self-confidence with English among Chinese students in Toronto. *Canadian Journal of Behavioral Science, 17,* 369–378.

Pierson, H., Giles, H., & Young, L. (1987). Intergroup vitality perceptions during a period of political uncertainty: The case of Hong Kong. *Journal of Multilingual and Multicultural Development, 8,* 541–460.

Porter, P. (1986). How learners talk to each other: Input and interaction in task-centered discussions. In R. Day (Ed.), *Talking to learn: Conversation in second language acquisition.* Rowley, MA: Newbury House.

Prabhu, N. S. (1987). *Second language pedagogy.* Oxford: Oxford University Press.

Rubin, J. (1975). What the "good language learner" can teach us. *TESOL Quarterly, 9,* 41–51.

Rutherford, W. E. (1987). *Second language grammar: Learning and teaching.* London: Longman.

Sachdev, I., Bourhis, R. Y., D'Eye, J., & Phang, S-W. (in press). Cantonese vitality in London. In H. Giles & H. D. Pierson (Eds.), *First Pacific Rim annual on language and communication worldwide.* Clevedon: Multilingual Matters.

Sachdev, I., Bourhis, R. Y., Phang, S-W., & D'Eye, J. (1987). Language attitudes and vitality perceptions: Intergenerational effects amongst Chinese Canadian communities. *Journal of Language and Social Psychology, 6.*

Saint-Blancat, C. (1985). The effect of minority group vitality upon its sociopsychological behavior and strategies. *Journal of Multilingual and Multicultural Development, 6,* 31–44.

San Antonio, P. M. (1987). Social mobility and language use in an American company in Japan. *Journal of Language and Social Psychology, 6.*

Sawaie, M. (1986). The present and future status of a minority language: The case of Arabic in the United States. *Journal of Multilingual and Multicultural Development, 7,* 31–40.

Schumann, J. H. (1986). Research on the acculturation model for second language acquisition. *Journal of Multilingual and Multicultural Development, 7,* 379–392.

Selinker, L. (1972). Interlanguage. *International Review of Applied Linguistics, 10,* 201–231.

Shapira, R. G. (1978). The non-learning of English: Case study of an adult. In E. M. Hatch (Ed.), *Second language acquisition: A book of readings.* Rowley, MA: Newbury House.

Sharwood Smith, M. (1981). Consciousness-raising and the second language learner. *Applied Linguistics, 2,* 159–169.

Snow, C. E., & Hoefnagel-Hohle, M. (1982). School-age second language learners' access to simplified linguistic input. *Language Learning, 32,* 411–427.

Soh, K-C. (1987). Language use: A missing link? *Journal of Multilingual and Multicultural Development, 8,* 443–449.

Thomas, J. (1983). Cross-cultural pragmatic failure. *Applied Linguistics, 4,* 91–112.

Trudgill, P., & Hannah, J. (1985). *International English.* London: Arnold.

Turner, J. C., & Giles, H. (Eds.). (1981). *Intergroup behavior.* Chicago: University of Chicago Press.

Ulrich, H. E. (1971). Linguistic aspects of antiquity: A dialect study. *Anthropological Linguistics, 13,* 106–113.

Valdman, A. (1981). Sociolinguistic aspects of foreigner talk. *International Journal of the Sociology of Language, 28,* 41–52.

Yalden, J. (1987). *Principles of course design for language teaching.* Cambridge: Cambridge University Press.

Young, L., Bell, N., & Giles, H. (in press). Perceived vitality and context: A national majority in a minority setting. *Journal of Multilingual and Multicultural Development.*

Young, L., Giles, H., & Pierson, H. D. (1986). Sociopolitical change and perceived vitality. *International Journal of Intercultural Relations, 10,* 459–469.

# 11

## Cultural Variability in Ethnolinguistic Identity

WILLIAM B. GUDYKUNST  •  *Arizona State University*

*Cross-cultural research on social identity and ethnolinguistic vitality indicates that both influence intergroup behavior across cultures. The same research, however, suggests that both may vary across cultures. The present study examines the influence of Hofstede's (1980) dimensions of cultural variability on the ethnolinguistic identity of sojourners in the United States. The results are discussed in terms of Hofstede's (1980) theory of cultural differentiation and Giles and Johnson's (1988) ethnolinguistic identity theory.*

Social identity theory was developed in an individualistic culture, but research suggests that it is generalizable to collectivistic cultures (Bond & Hewstone, 1986; Ghosh & Huq, 1985; Hewstone, Bond, & Wan, 1983; Majeed & Ghosh, 1982). Cross-cultural research on social identity and ethnolinguistic vitality indicates that both influence intergroup behavior across cultures. The same research, however, suggests that both may vary across cultures. To date no research has compared social identity or ethnolinguistic identity systematically across cultures. Linking cultural variability to intergroup processes such as ethnolinguistic identity is necessary for different levels of analysis to be articulated (Doise, 1986). The purpose of this exploratory study is to begin to fill the void in previous research by examining how dimensions of cultural variability influence the ethnolinguistic identity of sojourners in the United States.

## CULTURE AND ETHNOLINGUISTIC IDENTITY

### Ethnolinguistic Identity

One of the major cognitive tools individuals use to define themselves vis-à-vis the world in which they live is social categorization, "the ordering of social environment in terms of groupings of persons in a manner which makes sense to the individual" (Tajfel, 1978, p.

61); for example, men and women, Blacks and Whites. Individuals, therefore, perceive themselves as belonging to social groups, and recognition of membership in these groups carries with it a knowledge of the values, positive and negative, attached to these groups. A social group is "two or more individuals who share a common social identification of themselves or . . . perceive themselves to be members of the same social category" (Turner, 1982, p. 15). Once individuals become aware of belonging to social groups, their social identities begin to form. Social identity, according to Tajfel (1978), is defined as "that *part* of an individual's self-concept which derives from his [or her] knowledge of his [or her] membership in a social group (or groups) together with the value and emotional significance attached to that membership" (p. 63). Language use plays a major role in the development of social identities (Eastman, 1985).

Giles and Johnson (1981) argue that language is a vital aspect of any group's, but particularly an ethnic group's, identity. Ethnic identity is a function, at least in part, of perceived ethnolinguistic vitality (Bourhis, Giles, & Rosenthal, 1981; for recent studies of vitality see Bourhis & Sachdev, 1984; Giles, Rosenthal, & Young, 1985). *Perceived ethnolinguistic vitality* refers to individuals' subjective perception of the status, demographic characteristics, and institutional support of the language community. Status involves economic, political, sociohistorical, and language status variables. Demographic characteristics include such items as population of those speaking the language, their distribution, birthrate, and migrations. Institutional support considers representation of the ethnic group and use of the language in government, education, industry, and the mass media. Recent research indicates that perceived ethnolinguistic vitality is related highly to self-reports of assimilative linguistic behavior (Allard & Landry, 1986).

Perceived group boundaries are also an important part of ethnic identification (Giles & Johnson, 1981). Boundaries are a function of the type of interaction that occurs between the two ethnic groups and can be perceived as either hard or soft. Hard boundaries are viewed as closed, and mobility in and out of the group is seen as difficult. Soft boundaries, in contrast, are seen as open, allowing easy movement and acceptance between groups.

The more social groups to which individuals belong, the less they are dependent upon one group for their social identity (Giles &

Johnson, 1981). Individuals' status within a group also influences the group's salience in their social identity, with those groups where status is high being more prominent. Individuals with few group memberships are less inclined to use the dialect of other groups or learn their language since it is perceived as a threat to their social identities. Those who belong to many groups, in contrast, should be more open to code-switching and second language acquisition, since the identification with a specific group is of less overall importance. Further, individuals who feel there is little chance for a change in the dominant/subordinate language relationship that exists are less likely to use language as a salient comparison point between groups, and it would, therefore, facilitate, not impede, second language proficiency.

Drawing together research on ethnolinguistic vitality, group boundaries, interethnic comparisons, status, and social identity, Giles and Johnson (1981) argue:

> Individuals are more likely to define an encounter with an outgroup person in interethnic terms and to adopt strategies for positive linguistic distinctiveness when they:
>
> 1 identify with their ethnic group which considers language an important dimension of its identity;
> 2 make insecure interethnic comparisons (for example, are aware of cognitive alternatives to their own group's status position);
> 3 perceive their ingroup to have high ethnolinguistic vitality;
> 4 perceive their ingroup boundaries to be hard and closed;
> 5 identify strongly with few other social categories;
> 6 perceive little overlap with the outgroup person in terms of other social category memberships;
> 7 consider that the social identities derived from other social category memberships are relatively inadequate;
> 8 perceive their status with the ethnic group to be higher than their intragroup status in their other social category memberships. (p. 240; italics omitted)

While Giles and Johnson (1981) originally outlined the theory, Beebe and Giles (1984) were the first to use the label *ethnolinguistic identity theory*. More recently, Giles and Johnson (1988) have elaborated the theory, linking it systematically to speech accommodation, language attitudes, and second language acquisition.

### Research on Culture and Social/Ethnolinguistic Identity

While there is little, if any, research theoretically linking culture and social or ethnolinguistic identity, there are several studies that have been conducted in cultures other than where the theories originated. Majeed and Ghosh (1982), for example, examined social identity in three ethnic groups in India, discovering differential evaluations of self, ingroup, and outgroups in High Caste Hindus, Muslims, and Scheduled Castes. Their research also indicated that the more attributes were shared, the less differentiation between ingroups and outgroups. Ghosh and Huq (1985) found similar results for Hindu and Muslim evaluations of self and ingroup in India and Bangladesh. Brewer and Campbell's (1976) study of ingroup-outgroup evaluations in Africa and Peabody's (1985) research in Europe supports these findings. Bond and Hewstone (1986) found that British high school students in Hong Kong perceived social identity and intergroup differentiation to be more important than Chinese high school students. The British students also perceived group membership to be more important and had a more positive image of the ingroup than the Chinese.

Closely related to work on social identity theory is research on ethnolinguistic identity in general and ethnolinguistic vitality in particular. Giles, Bourhis, and Taylor (1977) argue that ethnolinguistic vitality influences the degree to which individuals will act as members of a group in intergroup situations. Several studies comparing different ethnic groups' perceptions of ethnolinguistic vitality within cultures have been conducted. Bourhis and Sachdev (1984) examined Italian and English Canadians in both majority/minority and equal situations. They found that both groups had more realistic perceptions in the majority than in the equal setting. English Canadians, however, were more biased against the Italian language in the equal than in the majority setting. Giles et al. (1985) studied Greek- and Anglo-Australian perceptions of ethnolinguistic vitality. Both groups agreed about some aspects of each other's vitality, but disagreed about each other's position in Australian society. The Anglos accentuated perceived differences between ingroup and outgroup vitalities, while the Greeks attenuated the differences. In a related study, Young, Pierson, and Giles (in press) found that perceptions of ingroup vitality are associated with the amount of exposure to the outgroup language in Hong Kong. Finally, recent research found that spoken language is the most salient feature of the social identity of Mauritian immigrants in South Africa (Leclezio, Louw-Potgieter, & Souchon, 1986).

Given the factors that contribute to ethnolinguistic identity and the research cited here, it appears reasonable to argue that ethnolinguistic identity should vary systematically across cultures. Ethnolinguistic identity should be influenced particularly by those dimensions of cultural variability that deal with relations between groups in a society. It is therefore necessary to examine dimensions of cultural variability and their relationship to ethnolinguistic identity.

*Cultural Variability*

Differences in ethnolinguistic identity between specific cultures are not of theoretical interest. Rather, specific cultures are of theoretical interest only when they are used to operationalize dimensions of cultural variability. Foschi and Hales (1979) succinctly outline the issues involved in treating cultural differences as a theoretical variable: "A culture X and a culture Y serve to operationally define a characteristic *a*, which the two cultures exhibit to different degrees" (p. 246). Hofstede (1980, 1983) isolated four dimensions of culture: power distance, uncertainty avoidance, individualism, and masculinity. Differences along these dimensions can be used to operationalize cultural variability in order to examine its influence on ethnolinguistic identity. The major dimension that should influence ethnolinguistic identity is individualism-collectivism.

Individualism-collectivism is the major dimension of cultural variability isolated by theorists across disciplines (e.g., Bellah, Madsen, Sullivan, Swindler, & Tipton, 1985; Hofstede, 1980; Hsu, 1981; Hui & Triandis, 1986; Kluckhohn & Strodtbeck, 1961; Marsella, DeVos, & Hsu, 1985; Parsons & Shils, 1951; Tonnies, 1963; Triandis, 1988; Westin, 1985). Individualistic cultures emphasize individual goals, while collectivistic cultures stress that group goals have precedence. In individualistic cultures, "people are supposed to look after themselves and their immediate family only," while in collectivistic cultures, "people belong to ingroups or collectivities which are supposed to look after them in exchange for loyalty" (Hofstede & Bond, 1984, p. 419). Members of individualistic cultures form specific friendships, while members of collectivistic cultures form friendships that are predetermined by stable relationships formed early in life (Hofstede,

1980). People in individualistic cultures tend to be universalistic and to apply the same value standards to all. People in collectivistic cultures, in contrast, tend to be particularistic and to apply different value standards for members of their ingroups and outgroups.

Triandis (1988) sees the key distinction between individualistic and collectivistic cultures as the focus on the ingroup in collectivistic cultures. Collectivistic cultures emphasize goals, needs, and views of the ingroup over those of the individual; the social norms of the ingroup, rather than individual pleasure; shared ingroup beliefs, rather than unique individual beliefs; and a value on cooperation with ingroup members, rather than maximization of individual outcomes. Triandis goes on to argue that the number of ingroups, the extent of influence for each ingroup, and the depth of the influence must be taken into consideration in the analysis of individualism-collectivism. He contends that the larger the number of ingroups, the narrower the influence and the less the depth of influence. Since individualistic cultures have many specific ingroups, they exert less influence on individuals than ingroups do in collectivistic cultures. Some, for example, put family ahead of all other ingroups, while others put their company ahead of other ingroups.

Triandis's (1988) conceptualization further suggests that members of collectivistic cultures draw sharper distinction between members of ingroups (e.g., those with whom they go to school or work) and outgroups and perceive ingroup relationships to be more intimate than do members of individualistic cultures. Research indicates that members of collectivistic cultures use the equality norm (i.e., divide resources equally, rather than based on equity) more than members of individualistic cultures with ingroup members (Bond, Leung, & Wan, 1982; Leung & Bond, 1982, 1984; Mann, Radford, & Kanagawa, 1985). Members of collectivistic cultures also use the equity norm as much as or more than members of individualistic cultures with members of outgroups (Leung & Bond, 1984; Mahler, Greenberg, & Hayashi, 1981; Marin, 1981).

Triandis and his associates argue that there is a personality dimension, idiocentrism-allocentrism, that corresponds to cultural variability in individualism-collectivism, respectively (Triandis, Bontempo, Betancourt, et al., 1986; Triandis, Bontempo, Villareal, et al., 1986; Triandis, Leung, Villareal, & Clack, 1985). Triandis et al. (1985) found that allocentric tendencies involved three factors: subordinating individual goals to group goals, viewing the ingroup as an extension of the self, and possessing a strong ingroup identity. Allocentrics reported greater social support than idiocentrics, while idiocentrics reported being more lonely than allocentrics. This finding was corroborated by Triandis et al. (1986) in Puerto Rico.

Given that individualism influences ingroup-outgroup relations, it should affect several aspects of ethnolinguistic identity. Specifically, it would be expected that there is greater identification with ingroups and multiple-group memberships in collectivistic cultures than in individualistic cultures. Research on the use of the equity and equality norms further suggests that individuals should make more secure intergroup comparisons in collectivistic cultures than in individualistic cultures because of secure multiple-group membership identity.

Hofstede's (1980) second dimension of cultural variability, uncertainty avoidance, is "the extent to which people feel threatened by ambiguous situations and have created beliefs and institutions that try to avoid these" (Hofstede & Bond, 1984, p. 419). This dimension is related to how people deal with conflict and aggression, how they release energy and use formal rules, and the tolerance they have for ambiguity. Members of high uncertainty avoidance cultures try to avoid uncertainty, but at the same time they show their emotions more than members of low uncertainty avoidance cultures. People in low uncertainty avoidance cultures frown on aggressive behavior, while those in high uncertainty avoidance cultures see aggressive behavior as acceptable. Since intergroup situations involve greater uncertainty and ambiguity than nonintergroup situations (Thibaut & Kelley, 1959), variability in uncertainty avoidance should affect ethnolinguistic identity in general and the intergroup comparisons that are made in particular. Uncertainty avoidance also should influence perceived ethnolinguistic vitality. Specifically, it would be expected that more vitality would be perceived by members of high uncertainty than low uncertainty avoidance cultures, because of the tendency of high uncertainty cultures to avoid ambiguous situations.

Hofstede's (1980) third dimension relevant to the present discussion also is a bipolar continuum, masculinity-femininity. Masculinity predominates in countries where the dominant values "are success, money, and things," while femininity predominates where "caring for others and quality of life" are dominant values (Hofstede & Bond, 1984, pp. 419–420). Cultures high in masculinity differentiate sex roles clearly, while cultures low in masculinity (high in femininity) tend to have fluid sex roles. Given the emphasis on people in feminine cultures, members of feminine cultures should perceive softer boundaries between groups than members of masculine cultures.

Hofstede's (1980) final dimension is power distance, "the extent to which less powerful members of institutions and organizations accept that power is distributed unequally" (Hofstede & Bond, 1984, p. 418). This dimension relates to social inequality and the amount of authority one person has over others. Members of high power distance cultures see power as a basic part of life and believe there is latent conflict between the powerful and the powerless, while members of low power distance cultures think that power should be used only when it is legitimate and that there is latent harmony between the powerful and the powerless. Since power difference is one of the major factors influencing intergroup relations (see Taylor & McKirnan, 1984), power distance should affect the group boundaries and/or intergroup comparison dimensions of ethnolinguistic identity.

Eight hypotheses emerge from the preceding analysis:

*H1:* Members of collectivistic cultures identify more strongly with the ingroup than do members of individualistic cultures.

*H2:* Members of collectivistic cultures identify more with multiple groups than do members of individualistic cultures.

*H3:* Members of collectivistic cultures make more secure intergroup comparisons than do members of individualistic cultures.

*H4:* Members of high uncertainty avoidance cultures make less secure intergroup comparisons than do members of low uncertainty avoidance cultures.

*H5:* Members of high uncertainty avoidance cultures perceive greater ethnolinguistic vitality than do members of low uncertainty avoidance cultures.

*H6:* Members of feminine cultures perceive softer boundaries between groups than do members of masculine cultures.

*H7:* Members of high power distance cultures perceive harder boundaries between groups than do members of low power distance cultures.

*H8:* Members of high power distance cultures make less secure intergroup comparisons than do members of low power distance cultures.

Predictions regarding the influence of Hofstede's (1980) dimensions of cultural variability on the five dimensions of ethnolinguistic identity were tested using data from sojourners in the United States from 29 of the 50 countries and all three regions for which Hofstede (1983) presents scores. Data on sojourners allow the predictions to be tested, but at the same time may yield results different from those that would be obtained when examining individuals' ethnolinguistic identity in their native cultures because of what is defined as the major relevant ingroup. Japanese respondents, for example, would utilize their company as the number one ingroup if studied in their native culture, but would use their country as the major ingroup when living in a foreign culture. The implications of studying this respondent group are examined in the discussion section.

## METHODS

### Respondents

Data were collected from 237 (166 males and 71 females) international students at a large southwestern university in the United States who volunteered to participate in the research. Respondents completed a questionnaire in English containing measures of the dependent variable and their cultural backgrounds, as well as questions for another study (Gudykunst, Chua, & Gray, 1987). The other study concerned a specific relationship respondents had with a person in the United States.

A total of 122 of the males responded about relationships with other males, while 44 responded about relationships with females in this study. Of the females, 15 responded about relationships with males and 55 reported on relationships with other females. Because the instructions asked the respondents to answer the questions about a relationship with a member of the *same sex*, participants who responded about opposite-sex relationships were dropped from analysis; this left 177 usable responses (122 males and 55 females). Of these 177, 19 of the respondents were from cultures for which there are no data on Hofstede's (1983) four dimensions and they, therefore, were dropped, leaving 158 respondents. While the same-sex/opposite-sex issue is not directly relevant to the present research, it was decided that failure to follow the initial instructions warranted dropping those who responded about opposite-sex relationships. The average Test of English as a Foreign Language (TOEFL) score for the respondents included was 585.

## *Measurement*

Scores for individualism, power distance, uncertainty avoidance, and masculinity were assigned to respondents based on Hofstede's (1980, 1983) scores for their native cultures. The range of scores for individualism were from 8 to 89, with a mean of 39 and a median of 38 (Hofstede's range 8–91, mean = 50). Power distance scores ranged from 13 to 104, with a mean of 66 and median of 64 (Hofstede's range 11–104, mean = 52). The range for uncertainty avoidance was 29–112, and the mean was 65 and the median was 68 (Hofstede's range 8–112, mean = 64). Masculinity scores ranged from 8 to 95, with a mean of 53 and median of 52 (Hofstede's range 5–95, mean = 50). Responses for each dimension were dichotomized using Hofstede's mean as the dividing point.

Respondents were from 29 of the 50 countries and all three regions in Hofstede's (1983) analysis. In an effort to determine if there was anything unique about this subset of cultures in terms of their scores on Hofstede's dimensions, the correlations between each pair of dimension scores were examined; these are presented in Table 11.1 (note that the scores were *not* dichotomized when the correlations were computed). Hofstede's data yielded only one moderately strong correlation between the power distance and individualism dimensions (−.67, −.68). This correlation was also moderate in the present sample (−.49). The correlation between power distance and uncertainty avoidance was in the opposite direction from that in Hofstede's data, but similar to that found in Hofstede and Bond's (1984) analysis (−.17), which was not considered problematic. No other correlation

TABLE 11.1  Comparison of the Correlations Among the Dimensions in the Present Sample with Hofstede's Samples[a]

| Pair of Dimensions | Present Sample | Hofstede (1980) | Hofstede (1983) |
|---|---|---|---|
| Power distance × uncertainty avoidance | −.26 | .28 | .23 |
| Power distance × individualism | −.49 | −.67 | −.68 |
| Power distance × masculinity | .14 | .10 | .06 |
| Uncertainty avoidance × individualism | −.03 | −.35 | −.33 |
| Uncertainty avoidance × masculinity | .37 | .12 | −.03 |
| Individualism × masculinity | −.04 | .00 | .08 |

a. Hofstede (1980) correlations for 40 countries in original analysis (p. 316). Hofstede (1983) correlations for 50 countries and three regions (p. 343).

was significantly different from those in Hofstede's data. The subset of cultures represented in the present sample, therefore, appears to be a reasonable subset of the total set for which Hofstede's scores are available.

The five components of ethnolinguistic identity were assessed by combining the responses for two items for each. Response scales for all items were 7-point semantic differentials. The specific items used (and the end points of the scales) were as follows: *ingroup identification*—(1) "To what extent do you identify with your native culture?" (not at all-totally) and (2) "How important is being a member of your native culture?" (unimportant-important); *multiple group membership*—(1) "How important is being a male/female to you?" (unimportant-important) and (2) "How important is being a member of your religion to you?" (unimportant-important); *intergroup comparisons*—(1) "In relation to the United States, my culture is" (inferior-superior) and (2) "In the United States, my status is" (low-high); *group boundaries*—(1) "To what extent does this person [the specific person about whom respondents had answered other questions] try to bridge the cultural gap between you?" (not at all-as much as possible) and (2) "When this person tries to use your language and bridge the cultural gap between you, to what extent is his/her intent positive or negative?" (negative-positive); and *vitality*—(1) "How highly regarded is your native language in the city in which you live in the United States?" (very low-very high) and (2) "How highly regarded is your native language internationally?" (very low-very high). All five measures of ethnolinguistic identity resulted in reliable indices (i.e., alpha > .70).

## RESULTS

The influence of cultural variability on ethnolinguistic identity was examined by treating qualitative variations in the four dimensions of culture (e.g., low or high) as the independent variables in a four-way multivariate analysis of variance (MANOVA), and treating each of the five dimensions of ethnolinguistic identity as the dependent variables. Bartlett's test of sphericity (42.42, 10df, $p < .001$) indicated that multivariate analysis was warranted. Significant multivariate effects emerged for individualism (Wilks's lambda = .89, $F[5, 139]$ = 3.17, $p < .01$), uncertainty avoidance (Wilks's lambda = .86, $F[5,$

139] = 4.54, p < .001), and masculinity (Wilks's lambda = .92, F[5, 139] = 2.48, p < .05). Only power distance did not yield a significant effect (Wilks's lambda = .94, F[5, 139] = 1.78, ns). Power for the MANOVA was at least .72 for a small effect size (Stevens, 1980). Two-way and higher-order interactions were omitted because of empty cells.

Univariate tests were examined for those analyses where the multivariate tests were significant. Following Cramer and Bock's (1966) suggestion, significant univariate tests and those that approached significance were interpreted. Power for the univariate tests was approximately .88 for a small effect size of .15 (Cohen, 1977). Individualism had a significant univariate effect on two variables: multiple-group memberships (F[1, 143] = 4.57, p < .05, $eta^2$ = .03) and ethnolinguistic vitality (F[1, 143] = 8.02, p < .01, $eta^2$ = .06). The data, therefore, support Hypothesis 2, but not Hypotheses 1 and 3. Multiple-group memberships were higher in collectivistic cultures ($\bar{X}$ = 4.89) than in individualistic cultures ($\bar{X}$ = 4.43), while ethnolinguistic vitality was higher in individualistic cultures ($\bar{X}$ = 4.09) than in collectivistic culture ($\bar{X}$ = 3.58). Means and standard deviations for each dependent variable are presented in Table 11.2.

Uncertainty avoidance had a significant effect on two dependent variables: intergroup comparisons (F[1, 143] = 5.12, p < .05, $eta^2$ = .04) and vitality (F[1, 143] = 8.16, p < .01, $eta^2$ = .06). The data, therefore, support Hypotheses 4 and 5. More positive intergroup comparisons were made in low uncertainty avoidance cultures ($\bar{X}$ = 4.96) than in high uncertainty avoidance cultures ($\bar{X}$ = 4.65). Ethnolinguistic vitality was lower in low uncertainty avoidance cultures ($\bar{X}$ = 3.11) than in high uncertainty avoidance cultures ($\bar{X}$ = 4.03).

Masculinity had a univariate effect on three variables: ethnolinguistic vitality (F[1, 143] = 8.98, p < .01, $eta^2$ = .06), group boundaries (F[1, 143] = 2.53, p = .11, $eta^2$ = .02), and ingroup identification (F[1, 143] = 2.41, p = .12, $eta^2$ = .02). The data, therefore, support Hypothesis 6. Vitality was lower in feminine cultures ($\bar{X}$ = 3.30) than in masculine cultures ($\bar{X}$ = 3.38). Boundaries and ingroup identification also were lower in feminine cultures (boundaries, $\bar{X}$ = 4.29; ingroup identification, $\bar{X}$ = 5.29) than in masculine cultures (boundaries, $\bar{X}$ = 4.95; ingroup identification, $\bar{X}$ = 5.64).

Since the multivariate effect for power distance was not significant,

TABLE 11.2 Means and Standard Deviations by Dimensions of Culture

| Dependent Variables | Individualism | | | | Power Distance | | | | Uncertainty Avoidance | | | | Masculinity | | | |
|---|---|---|---|---|---|---|---|---|---|---|---|---|---|---|---|---|
| | Low | | High | | Low | | High | | Low | | High | | Low | | High | |
| | $\bar{X}$ | SD | $\bar{X}$ | SD | $\bar{X}$ | SD | $\bar{X}$ | SD | $\bar{X}$ | SD | $\bar{X}$ | SD | $\bar{X}$ | SD | $\bar{X}$ | SD |
| Ingroup identification | 5.50 | 1.24 | 5.43 | 1.45 | 5.55 | 1.32 | 5.48 | 1.27 | 5.46 | 1.31 | 5.51 | 1.26 | 5.29 | 1.30 | 5.64 | 1.24 |
| Multiple-group membership | 4.89 | 1.65 | 4.43 | 1.75 | 4.59 | 1.64 | 4.84 | 1.68 | 4.68 | 1.80 | 4.88 | 1.58 | 4.56 | 1.57 | 5.00 | 1.73 |
| Group boundaries | 4.73 | 1.61 | 5.06 | 1.60 | 5.07 | 1.72 | 4.74 | 1.59 | 5.01 | 1.43 | 4.65 | 1.70 | 4.59 | 1.79 | 4.95 | 1.44 |
| Intergroup comparisons | 4.70 | .89 | 5.13 | 1.06 | 5.09 | 1.03 | 4.72 | .91 | 4.96 | .80 | 4.65 | .99 | 4.77 | .92 | 4.78 | .95 |
| Ethnolinguistic vitality | 3.58 | 1.59 | 4.09 | 2.01 | 3.64 | 1.95 | 3.68 | 1.63 | 3.11 | 1.70 | 4.03 | 1.57 | 3.30 | 1.60 | 3.98 | 1.68 |

the univariate effects were not examined. The data, therefore, do not support Hypotheses 7 and 8.

## DISCUSSION

The present data suggest that Hofstede's (1980) dimensions of cultural variability influence the ethnolinguistic identities of sojourners in the United States. The multivariate tests indicate that individualism, uncertainty avoidance, and masculinity affect ingroup identification, multiple-group memberships, group boundaries, intergroup comparisons, and ethnolinguistic vitality. The univariate tests reveal that individualism influences multiple-group memberships and vitality, uncertainty avoidance affects intergroup comparisons and vitality, and masculinity is related to ingroup identification, group boundaries, and vitality. The consistency of the present findings with Hofstede's theory of cultural differentiation and the effect studying sojourners in the United States had on the results, including the lack of significant effect for power distance, need to be discussed. The two issues are interrelated and, therefore, are assessed together.

Initially, it was expected that individualism would influence three of the five dimensions of ethnolinguistic identity: ingroup identification (H1), multiple-group memberships (H2), and intergroup comparison (H3). It was argued that since individualism affects the ingroup-outgroup distinction, it should influence both ingroup identification and multiple-group memberships. Also, since individualism has been found to be related to the use of the equity and equality norms, it was predicted that it would influence intergroup comparisons. The present data, however, reveal that, of the three, individualism-collectivism only influences multiple-group memberships and that, in addition, it influences vitality.

In part, the findings for Hypotheses 1 and 3 may be due to the particular respondents studied. Since the respondents were sojourners in the United States, the major ingroup with which they identify is the group of sojourners sharing the same cultural background (i.e., co-nationals). Members of collectivistic cultures, therefore, should have higher multiple-group memberships than members of individualistic cultures because the "other-groups" include their ingroup within their native cultures. Previous research suggests that regardless of cultural background, sojourners identify with members of their own cultures while in a foreign culture (e.g., Selltiz, Christ, Havel, & Cook, 1963). If individuals from individualistic and collectivistic cultures were studied in their native cultures, however, the degree of individualism present in the culture should influence ingroup identification, with members of collectivistic cultures identifying more highly with the ingroup than members of individualistic cultures.

The results for individualism's influence on intergroup comparisons also may be due to studying sojourners. Individualism may not influence sojourners' comparisons of their culture with the host culture (i.e., the United States). Such a comparison is more likely to be influenced by the perceived status of the native and host culture (see, e.g., Morris, 1960). Individualism, however, should influence the intergroup comparisons sojourners make within their native cultures. This effect would be expected given the relationship between individualism and the use of the equity/equality norms (e.g., Leung & Bond, 1984).

The finding that individualism and masculinity influenced ethnolinguistic vitality was unexpected. It was predicted that uncertainty avoidance would influence vitality (H5), and it did have a univariate effect in the present study. It appears that there may be an interaction among the three dimensions that influences vitality that the present data were not able to isolate. Vitality was lower in collectivistic cultures than in individualistic cultures, lower in low uncertainty avoidance cultures than in high uncertainty avoidance cultures, and lower in feminine cultures than in masculine cultures. Based upon these findings, it would be predicted that the highest amount of vitality would be perceived by sojourners from relatively individualistic cultures that are high in uncertainty avoidance and are also masculine.

Uncertainty avoidance influenced intergroup comparisons as predicted (H4). Specifically, more secure intergroup comparisons were made by sojourners from low uncertainty avoidance cultures than by sojourners from high uncertainty avoidance cultures. Thibaut and Kelley (1959) point out that intergroup encounters involve greater uncertainty than nonintergroup encounters. Members of high uncertainty avoidance cultures try to avoid uncertainty and anxiety, which also are associated with intergroup encounters (Stephan & Stephan, 1985). It follows, therefore, that members of high uncertainty avoidance cultures should feel less secure in making intergroup comparisons than should members of low uncertainty avoidance cultures.

While it was not expected initially, the finding that masculinity influences ingroup identification appears consistent with Hofstede's (1980) conceptualization of this dimension. The present data reveal that ingroup identification is lower in feminine than in masculine cultures. Hofstede (1980) argues that feminine cultures focus on people, quality of life, and service, and that they have sympathy for "the unfortunate." Masculine cultures, in contrast, focus on things, performance, and achievement, and have sympathy for "the successful achiever." Given these societal norms, it appears reasonable that members of feminine cultures would identify less with their ingroup and perceive softer boundaries between groups than members of masculine cultures. This logic was used to generate Hypothesis 6, regarding perceived boundaries, but was not applied to ingroup identification because theoretically this component of ethnolinguistic identity appeared to be related only to individualism.

Power distance did not influence perceived boundaries (H7) or intergroup comparisons (H8) for sojourners in the United States. Sojourners' stay in the host culture is temporary and therefore they may not use equality as a factor influencing their interactions with host nationals. If individuals from low and high power distance cultures are studied in their native cultures, however, the degree of power distance present in the culture should influence group boundaries and/or the intergroup comparisons made. Specifically, it would be expected that members of minority groups in high power distance cultures would see group boundaries as harder and make more insecure intergroup comparisons than would minorities in low power distance cultures.

Taken together, the findings suggest that cultural variability influences ethnolinguistic identity. Given the present results and plausible explanations for lack of significant findings due to studying sojourners, nine specific hypotheses for future research emerge:

*H1:* Members of collectivistic cultures identify more highly with the ingroup than do members of individualistic cultures.

*H2:* Members of collectivistic cultures identify more with multiple groups than do members of individualistic cultures.

*H3:* Members of collectivistic cultures make more favorable intergroup comparisons than do members of individualistic cultures.

*H4:* Members of high uncertainty avoidance cultures make less secure intergroup comparisons than do members of low uncertainty avoidance cultures.

*H5:* Members of feminine cultures identify less with the ingroup than do members of masculine cultures.

*H6:* Members of feminine cultures perceive softer boundaries between groups than do members of masculine cultures.

*H7:* Members of minority groups in high power distance cultures perceive harder boundaries between groups than do members of minority groups in low power distance cultures.

*H8:* Members of minority groups in high power distance cultures make more insecure intergroup comparisons than do members of minority groups in low power distance cultures.

*H9:* Perceived ethnolinguistic vitality is higher in individualistic cultures that are also high in uncertainty avoidance and masculinity than in collectivistic cultures that are low in uncertainty avoidance and masculinity.

Hypotheses 2, 4, 5, 6, and 9 were supported in the present study. Hypotheses 1, 3, 7, and 8 were not supported, but their lack of support may be due to the fact that sojourners were studied rather than individuals' ethnolinguistic identities in their native cultures. The first eight hypotheses are not mutually exclusive, and future research may reveal that (a) individualism and masculinity interact to influence ingroup identification; (b) individualism, uncertainty avoidance, and power distance interact to influence intergroup comparisons; and (c) masculinity and power distance interact to influence perceptions of group boundaries.

In addition to variations across cultures, within-culture differences can be hypothesized based on Triandis and his associates' (1985, 1986; Marin & Triandis, 1985) work on idiocentrism and allocentrism, the personality correlates of individualism and collectivism, respectively. Extending Hypotheses 1–3 to the individual level, three additional hypotheses can be proffered:

*H10:* Allocentrics identify more strongly with the ingroup than do idiocentrics.

*H11:* Allocentrics identify more with multiple groups than do idiocentrics.

*H12:* Allocentrics make more favorable intergroup comparisons than do idiocentrics.

Hypothesis 10 is supported by Triandis and his associates' research in the United States and Puerto Rico. Hypothesis 11 and 12, in contrast, do not appear to have been tested to date, but appear to be plausible extensions of Hypotheses 2 and 3.

The present results and the hypotheses for further research suggest that culture can be linked theoretically to ethnolinguistic identity, thereby articulating Doise's (1986) ideological (i.e., culture) and positional (i.e., intergroup) levels of analysis. While the present data indicate that culture influences ethnolinguistic identity, they do not address whether or not the relationship between ethnolinguistic identity and the maintenance of linguistic distinctiveness varies across cultures. Future research ideally will examine variations in ethnolinguistic identity across cultures and, at the same time, assess the impact of ethnolinguistic identity on the degree to which interethnic situations are defined in terms of ethnicity and the degree to which individuals attempt to maintain their distinctive language features in their interactions with members of other ethnic groups. Only when such comparisons are made and theoretically linked to culture can the scope and boundary conditions regarding culture be specified for ethnolinguistic identity theory.

Before concluding, two methodological issues need to be discussed. First, international students in the United States are not the "best" respondents to test the theory. Ideally, respondents in many different cultures would be used. There is, however, no reason to rule out the use of international students. Since international students have many other factors (such as income and social status) in common, there is a built-in control for these factors. Also, there is no reason to expect experiences in the United States to affect students from different countries in different ways. While the respondents may not be totally representative of the respective cultures, the unrepresentativeness should be relatively systematic across cultures. Hofstede (1980) makes a similar observation regarding the use of employees of a multinational corporation in his study. While the use of international students should not affect cultural variability, it may have had an impact upon the major ingroup with which the respondents identified, as pointed out above, thereby influencing the present results.

The second methodological issue involves measurement. The specific measures for the dependent variables were only two-item indices, not specifically designed to assess ethnolinguistic identity. They are all plausible, reliable indicators, but future research ideally should utilize multiple-item scales designed specifically to measure these constructs. Also, the measures were administered in English. The average TOEFL score of the respondents was 585 and, therefore, there should have been no problem with their understanding the questionnaire. Further, since all respondents answered the questions in their second language, there should have been no major problems due to the language of the questionnaire (e.g., the use of second language should have had a systematic effect across respondents). Future research on cross-cultural variations in ethnolinguistic identity, however, should utilize research instruments in the respondents' native languages in order to rule out any potential bias that may be caused by the use of second language.

To conclude, an initial study of the influence of cultural variability on ethnolinguistic identity has been presented and hypotheses for future research proffered. Linking culture to ethnolinguistic identity begins to articulate the two levels of analysis and lays the groundwork for an integrated theory of interpersonal-intergroup behavior.

## REFERENCES

Allard, R., & Landry, R. (1986). Subjective ethnolinguistic vitality viewed as a belief system. *Journal of Multilingual and Multicultural Development, 7*, 1–12.

Beebe, L. M., & Giles, H. (1984). Speech accommodation theories: A discussion in terms of second-language acquisition. *International Journal of the Sociology of Language, 46*, 5–32.

Bellah, R. N., Madsen, R., Sullivan, W. M., Swindler, A., & Tipton, S. M. (1985). *Habits of the heart: Individualism and commitment in American life*. Berkeley: University of California Press.

Bond, M., & Hewstone, M. (1986). *Social identity theory and the perception of intergroup relations in Hong Kong*. Unpublished manuscript, Chinese University of Hong Kong.

Bond, M. H., Leung, K., & Wan, K. C. (1982). How does cultural collectivism operate? The impact of task and maintenance contributions on reward distribution. *Journal of Cross-Cultural Psychology, 13*, 186–200.

Bond, M. H., Wan, K. C., Leung, K., & Giacalone, R. A. (1985). How are responses to verbal insults related to cultural collectivism and power distance? *Journal of Cross-Cultural Psychology, 16*, 111–127.

Bourhis, R. Y., Giles, H., & Rosenthal, D. (1981). Notes on the construction of a "Subjective Vitality Questionnaire" for ethnolinguistic groups. *Journal of Multilingual and Multicultural Development, 2*, 145–155.

Bourhis, R., & Sachdev, I. (1984). Subjective vitality perceptions and language attitudes: Some Canadian data. *Journal of Language and Social Psychology, 3*, 97–126.

Brewer, M. B., & Campbell, D. T. (1976). *Ethnocentrism and intergroup attitudes: East African evidence*. Washington, DC: Halstead.

Cohen, J. (1977). *Statistical power analysis for the behavioral sciences* (rev. ed.). New York: Academic Press.

Cramer, E. M., & Bock, R. D. (1966). Multivariate analysis. *Review of Educational Research, 36*, 604–617.

Doise, W. (1986). *Levels of explanation in social psychology*. Cambridge: Cambridge University Press.

Eastman, C. M. (1985). Establishing social identity through language use. *Journal of Language and Social Psychology, 4*, 1–26.

Foschi, M., & Hales, W. H. (1979). The theoretical role of cross-cultural comparisons in experimental social psychology. In L. H. Eckensberger, W. J. Lonner, & Y. H. Poortinga (Ed.), *Cross-cultural contributions to psychology*. Lisse, The Netherlands: Swets & Zeitlinger.

Ghosh, E., & Huq, M. (1985). A study of social identity in two ethnic groups in India and Bangladesh. *Journal of Multilingual and Multicultural Development, 6*, 239–251.

Giles, H., Bourhis, R. Y., & Taylor, D. M. (1977). Towards a theory of language in ethnic group relations. In H. Giles (Ed.), *Language, ethnicity and intergroup relations*. London: Academic Press.

Giles, H., & Johnson, P. (1981). The role of language in ethnic group relations. In J. Turner & H. Giles (Eds.), *Intergroup behavior*. Chicago: University of Chicago Press.

Giles, H., & Johnson, P. (1987). Ethnolinguistic identity theory: A social psychological approach to language maintenance. *International Journal of the Sociology of Language, 68*, 69–99.

Giles, H., Rosenthal, D., & Young, L. (1985). Perceived ethnolinguistic vitality: The Anglo- and Greek-Australian setting. *Journal of Multilingual and Multicultural Development, 6*, 253–269.

Gudykunst, W. B., Chua, E., & Gray, A. (1987). Cultural dissimilarities and uncertainty reduction processes. In M. McLaughlin (Ed.), *Communication yearbook 10*. Newbury Park, CA: Sage.

Hewstone, M., Bond, M. H., & Wan, K.-C. (1983). Social facts and social attributions: The explanation of intergroup differences in Hong Kong. *Social Cognition, 2*, 142–157.

Hofstede, G. (1980). *Culture's consequences*. Beverly Hills, CA: Sage.

Hofstede, G. (1983). Dimensions of national cultures in fifty countries and three regions. In J. Deregowski, S. Dziurawiec, & R. Annis (Eds.), *Expiscations in cross-cultural psychology*. Lisse, The Netherlands: Swets & Zeitlinger.

Hofstede, G., & Bond, M. (1984). Hofstede's culture dimensions: An independent validation using Rokeach's value survey. *Journal of Cross-Cultural Psychology, 15*, 417–433.

Hsu F. L. K. (1981). *American and Chinese: Passage to difference* (3rd ed.). Honolulu: University of Hawaii Press.

Hui, C. H., & Triandis, H. C. (1986). Individualism-collectivism: A study of cross-cultural researchers. *Journal of Cross-Cultural Psychology, 17*, 225–248.

Kluckhohn, F., & Strodtbeck, F. (1961). *Variations in value orientations*. New York: Row, Peterson.

Leclezio, M., Louw-Potgieter, J., & Souchon, M. (1986). The social identity of Mauritian immigrants in South Africa. *Journal of Social Psychology, 126*, 61–69.

Leung, K., & Bond, M. H. (1982). How Chinese and Americans reward task related contributions: A preliminary study. *Psychologia, 25*, 32–39.

Leung, K., & Bond, M. H. (1984). The impact of cultural collectivism on reward allocation. *Journal of Personality and Social Psychology, 47*, 793–804.

Mahler, I., Greenberg, L., & Hayashi, H. (1981). A comparative study of rules of justice: Japanese versus Americans. *Psychologia, 24*, 1–8.

Majeed, A., & Ghosh, E.S.K. (1982). A study of social identity in three ethnic groups in India. *International Journal of Psychology, 17*, 455–463.

Mann, L., Radford, M., & Kanagawa, C. (1985). Cross-cultural differences in children's use of decision rules: A comparison between Japan and Australia. *Journal of Personality and Social Psychology, 49*, 1557–1564.

Marin, G. (1981). Perceiving justice across cultures: Equity vs. equality in Colombia and the United States. *International Journal of Psychology, 16*, 153–159.

Marin, G., & Triandis, H. C. (1985). Allocentrism as an important characteristic of the behavior of Latin Americans and Hispanics. In R. Diaz Guerrero (Ed.), *Cross-cultural and national studies in social psychology*. Amsterdam: Elsevier.

Marsella, A. J., DeVos, G., & Hsu, F.L.K. (Eds.). (1985). *Culture and self: Asian and Western perspectives*. New York: Tavistock.

Morris, R. T. (1960). *The two-way mirror: National status in foreign students' adjustment*. Minneapolis: University of Minnesota Press.

Parsons, T., & Shils, E. A. (1951). *Toward a general theory of action*. Cambridge, MA: Harvard University Press.

Peabody, D. (1985). *National characteristics*. Cambridge: Cambridge University Press.

Selltiz, C., Christ, J., Havel, J., & Cook, S. W. (1963). *Attitudes and social relations of foreign students in the United States*. Minneapolis: University of Minnesota Press.

Stephan, W. G., & Stephan, C. W. (1985). Intergroup anxiety. *Journal of Social Issues, 41*, 157–166.

Stevens, J. (1980). Power of the multivariate analysis of variance test. *Psychological Bulletin, 88*, 728–737.

Tajfel, H. (1978). Social categorization, social identity, and social comparison. In H. Tajfel (Ed.), *Differentiation between social groups*. London: Academic Press.

Taylor, D. M., & McKirnan, D. (1984). A five-stage model of intergroup relations. *British Journal of Social Psychology, 23*, 291–300.

Thibaut, J. W., & Kelley, H. H. (1959). *The social psychology of groups*. New York: John Wiley.

Tonnies, F. (1963). *Community and society*. New York: Harper & Row.

Triandis, H. C. (1988). Collectivism vs. individualism: A reconceptualization of a basic concept in cross-cultural psychology. In C. Bagley & G. Verma (Eds.), *Personality, cognition and values: Cross-cultural perspectives of childhood and adolescence*. London: Macmillan.

Triandis, H. C., Bontempo, R., Betancourt, H., Bond, M., Leung, K., Brenes, A., Georgas, J., Hui, H., Marin, G., Setiadi, B., Sinha, J., Verna, J., Spangenberg, J., Touzard, H., & de Montmollin, G. (1986). The measurement of the etic aspects of individualism and collectivism across cultures. *Australian Journal of Psychology, 38*, 257–267.

Triandis, H. C., Bontempo, R., Villareal, M., Asai, M., Lucca, N., Betancourt, H., Bond, M., Leung, K., Brenes, A., Georgas, J., Hui, H., Marin, G., Sinha, J., Verna, J., Setiadi, B., Spangenberg, J., Touzard, H., & de Montmollin, G. (1986). *Individualism and collectivism: Cross-cultural perspectives on self-ingroup relationships.* Unpublished manuscript, University of Illinois.

Triandis, H. C., Leung, K., Villareal, M., & Clack, F. (1985). Allocentric vs. idiocentric tendencies. *Journal of Research in Personality, 19,* 395–415.

Turner, J. (1982). Towards a cognitive redefinition of the social group. In H. Tajfel (Ed.), *Social identity and intergroup relations.* Cambridge: Cambridge University Press.

Westin, D. (1985). *Self and society: Narcissism, collectivism, and the development of morals.* Cambridge, MA: Harvard University Press.

Young, L., Pierson, H., & Giles, H. (in press). The effects of language and academic specialization on perceived group vitalities. *Linguistic Berichte.*

# 12

## Bilingual Communication in Organizational Settings: Aspects of the Canadian Case

RICHARD Y. BOURHIS • *Université du Quebec à Montréal*

*The aim of this chapter is to present an analysis of important factors that influence language choice strategies in bilingual work settings. It represents an attempt to integrate two hitherto independent fields of research, namely, intercultural communication and organizational communication. The case study used to introduce this integration deals with the issue of bilingual language use among Francophone and Anglophone co-workers within the Canadian work setting. Five factors are identified as important in accounting for speaker's language choice strategies in bilingual settings. The chapter also introduces the linguistic work environment (LWE) survey as a new research tool for the study of communication in bilingual organizations.*

As the privileged tool of human communication, the vehicle of culture, and often the distinctive symbol of "peoplehood," it is not surprising that language has become the frequent target of state planning by policymakers around the world (Cobarrubias & Fishman, 1983; Laforge, 1987; Maurais, 1988; Weinstein, 1983). A common premise of state intervention in language matters is that "free" market forces are not sufficient to solve perceived language problems in multilingual societies. Canada is one example of a country that has devoted much energy to promoting and implementing language policies designed to address language tensions between its two major linguistic communities: the Anglophone majority and the Francophone minority (Bourhis, 1984a; Breton, Reitz, & Valentine, 1980; Wardhaugh, 1983).

Though the focus of the present work is on language problems encountered in the Canadian setting, it is hoped that the issues raised

AUTHOR'S NOTE: *I gratefully acknowledge the helpful comments of Uus Knops (Catholic University of Nijmegen, the Netherlands), Yan Carbon (Office of the Commissioner of Official Languages), Stella Ting-Toomey (Arizona State University), and Margaret Weiser (McMaster University) on earlier drafts of this chapter.*

in this chapter will have relevant implications for those concerned with multilingual issues in the United States (Gray, 1987). It is indeed the case that bilingualism is more the rule than the exception in numerous parts of the United States, including the Southwest, where Hispanophones make up a substantial proportion of the population (Ferguson & Heath, 1981). In the United States, as elsewhere in the world, the way linguistic majorities treat linguistic minorities is of considerable relevance for all those involved in issues related to language rights and linguistic pluralism (Bourhis, 1984a; Cummins, 1986).

In 1969, the Canadian federal government adopted the Official Language Act, which declared both French and English as equal-status official languages of Canada. The act was adopted by the federal government as a partial response to the rise of the Québécois Francophone independence movement (Coleman, 1984). This bilingualism policy was promulgated to demonstrate that "being Francophone" was possible not only within the Francophone majority province of Quebec but also throughout Anglo-Canada, thanks to federally sponsored bilingual services and schooling introduced since the act took effect (Mallae, 1984). One of the immediate goals of the policy was to increase the presence of Francophone speakers in the federal administration, which in turn would sustain the provision of more adequate French language services to Francophone citizens across Canada (Breton et al., 1980). After almost two decades of implementation, it is acknowledged that the provision of French language services to Francophone minorities across Canada has improved as a result of this policy (Canadian Ministry of Supply and Services, 1987).

Another goal of the policy was to create work environments within the federal administration that would allow Francophone civil servants to envisage the possibility of a successful career conducted not solely through the medium of English, as in the past, but also through the use of the French language. Despite years of implementation and the sustained efforts of the Office of the Commissioner of Official Languages, much concern still remains regarding the lack of French language use within the Canadian public administration (Canadian Ministry of Supply and Services, 1987; Mackay, 1983). This lack of French language use has prevailed despite the government's relative success in increasing the proportion of Francophones employed at different levels of the federal administration (Breton et al., 1980).

Furthermore, the implementation of extensive French language training programs for Anglophone public servants did not result in greater
use of French in the federal administration as originally anticipated
by policymakers (Mackay, 1983). Thus, despite the implementation
of numerous organizational measures, the use and status of French as
a language of work has remained far below targeted goals among
both Anglophone and Francophone civil servants within the Canadian federal administration. Therefore, the following question remains relevant for policymakers today: How can language policies be
designed to increase the status and use of a minority language, like
French in Canada, without necessarily decreasing the status and use
of a majority language such as English, which has enjoyed a dominant
status in Canada for so long? Though this question is formulated
specifically for the Canadian context, the challenge of developing
successful language policies designed to increase the status of one
language relative to other more established ones remains quite pertinent for policymakers in numerous bilingual and multilingual states
of the world (Maurais, 1988; Weinstein, 1983).

## DETERMINANTS OF LANGUAGE CHOICE IN BILINGUAL
## ORGANIZATIONS

One aim of the present case study is the identification of factors
likely to account for French and English language use among Francophone and Anglophone civil servants working in the Canadian federal administration. This issue remains important, because language
choices made by Anglophone and Francophone civil servants may
have a substantial impact on work-related matters such as job produc-
tivity, the maintenance of effective interpersonal communication, job
satisfaction, the smooth flow of cross-cultural encounters, and pride
in belonging to one of Canada's official language groups.

Research in the areas of social psychology and intercultural communication has identified important factors that help account for language
choice strategies in numerous types of cross-cultural encounters
(Bourhis, 1979, 1985; Giles, Bourhis, & Taylor, 1977; Gudykunst,
1986). Research within the organizational communication literature
has also identified important factors that account for communication
patterns within complex organizational settings (Drake & Moberg,
1986; McPhee, 1985). Taking these research traditions together, it is

possible to identify the following five factors as important elements that help account for the language choice strategies of speakers working within bilingual organizational settings:

(1) the communicator's *linguistic skills* in the relevant working languages of the region or country

(2) motivational and cognitive factors related to *speech accommodation*

(3) the relative power and status of interlocutors in terms of their *organizational position* as supervisors, colleagues, and subordinates within the work setting

(4) the relative *group vitality* of the linguistic communities present in the immediate vicinity of the work location or region

(5) the *linguistic work environment* (LWE) of interlocutors in terms of the ethnic and linguistic backgrounds of the individuals interacting in the organizational setting

The above elements interact with one another in complex ways to influence the language choice strategies of Francophones and Anglophones in bilingual work settings. Since factors such as linguistic skills, speech accommodation, organizational position, and group vitality have already received attention in the literature, these elements will be discussed first, but only briefly as they relate to bilingual organizational settings.

(1) A communicator's *linguistic skills* in the other's official language is a basic requirement for more effective communication between Francophones and Anglophones in everyday life and in organizational settings such as the Canadian federal administration. However, despite extensive French language training, it remains that many Anglophone civil servants just don't make use of their French language skills in their work settings (Mackay, 1983). In contrast, Francophone civil servants are more likely to be bilingual and to use English as their language of work in the federal administration (Mackay, 1983). It would seem that motivational factors related to speech accommodation may help account for the lack of French language use in bilingual work settings (Taylor & Simard, 1975; Taylor, Simard, & Papineau, 1978).

(2) Social psychological studies using the *speech accommodation* framework have shown that speakers often adapt, or "accommodate," their speech toward that their interlocutors (see Garrett, Giles, & Coupland, this volume; Giles, Mulac, Bradac, & Johnson,

1987). Such switches, known as speech *convergence*, not only allow for more efficient communication, but may also reflect speakers' conscious or unconscious need for social integration with their interlocutors. Thus, in a bilingual work setting, an Anglophone may converge to French with a Francophone colleague not only for the sake of communicative effectiveness but also as a strategy for promoting interpersonal liking and for enhancing the climate of cross-cultural encounters, where linguistic dissimilarities may otherwise be a serious stumbling block to intercultural harmony (Bourhis, 1979). Mutual language convergence between Francophone and Anglophone bilinguals was demonstrated in empirical studies conducted in the Quebec setting and supported the notion that convergence could be used as a language strategy to bridge the cultural gap between speakers of contrasting ethnolinguistic groups (Giles, Taylor, & Bourhis, 1973).

Although speakers from different language groups may wish to converge linguistically toward each other, there may be circumstances where speakers wish to *maintain* their own language or *diverge* linguistically from their interlocutors (Bourhis, 1979). Speakers may use speech maintenance and speech divergence sometimes because they dislike their interlocutors as individuals or because speakers wish to assert their group identity vis-à-vis outgroup interlocutors. So far, experimental evidence depicting language divergence and language maintenance has been obtained in bilingual settings such as Belgium (Bourhis, Giles, Leyens, & Tajfel, 1979) and Quebec (Bourhis, 1984b). For instance, in the Quebec setting, language maintenance was demonstrated in a series of Montreal field studies in which it was found that, overall, 30% of the English Canadian pedestrians sampled in the study maintained English in their responses to a plea for directions voiced in French by a French Canadian interlocutor (Bourhis, 1984b). These language-maintenance responses were obtained even though the Anglophone respondents had sufficient linguistic skills to utter a few words of French in their replies to the French Canadian interlocutor. Given the anonymity of these casual encounters, indications were that, indeed, English language maintenance was being used by Anglophones as a dissociative response aimed against the Francophone simply because the French Canadian was categorized as an outgroup speaker. Within bilingual organizational structures such as the Canadian federal administration, speech accommodation may account for language maintenance on the part of bilingual civil servants who wish to assert their group distinctiveness, or who don't care enough about their outgroup colleagues to make an effort to speak their language.

(3) A third element influencing language choice strategies is *organizational position*. Research in the organizational and interpersonal communication literature has shown that social power is related to the ways in which interpersonal communication is structured and perceived in a broad range of social relationships (Berger, 1985; Drake & Moberg, 1986). Within organizational settings, studies have shown that conversations between superiors and subordinates can be used to maintain or assert the power and status differentials that exist between superiors and subordinates (Molotch & Boden, 1985). Recent studies have also shown that conversational resources can be shared or not, depending on the nature of the power relationship that exists between supervisors and their subordinates (Fairhurst, Chandler, & Rogers, 1988).

Within bilingual organizations where one language is ascribed more status than the other, language choice can also be used as a conversational resource among superiors, subordinates, and colleagues of contrasting ethnolinguistic backgrounds. Thus language choices in the work setting may reflect not only the power differentials that exist among superiors, subordinates, and colleagues within the organization, but also the status and power differentials that exist between speakers of contrasting linguistic communities. Language choice strategies can also be used to renegotiate the power and status differentials that exist between speakers not only by virtue of their superior/subordinate position within the work setting but also by virtue of their relative position as ethnolinguistic group members within the social structure.

In organizations such as the Canadian administration, where English has long dominated as the language of authority and upward mobility, French/English language choices in conversations can be used to accentuate or attenuate the power distance that exists between Francophone and Anglophone civil servants. Thus language choice strategies can be used as conversational resources that define the nature of the relationship between speakers who differ not only by virtue of their power position within the organization, but also by virtue of their status as ethnolinguistic group members within the intergroup setting.

(4) Research in both the sociolinguistic (Hudson, 1980) and the social psychology of language literature (Bourhis, 1979) has shown

that the relative position of language groups in the social structure does affect the use of language choice strategies in cross-cultural encounters. Giles et al. (1977) propose a framework for assessing the *group vitality* of language communities in terms of sociostructural factors such as demographic strength, institutional control (power), and the social status enjoyed by members of contrasting language groups. These researchers assert that each of the factors mentioned can contribute to the strength and vigor of language groups in multilingual settings. Using such a framework, language groups can be roughly classified as possessing low, medium, or high vitality. Bourhis and Sachdev (1984) show that language choices made by speakers of contrasting language groups differ according to whether speakers belong to high-, medium-, or low-vitality groups. The literature shows that more often than not, it is the language of the high-vitality group that emerges as the dominant language of use in cross-cultural communication between speakers of high- and low-vitality groups.

As regards to the Canadian intergroup situation, the Francophone minority has long occupied an economically inferior position relative to the dominant Anglophone majority (Breton et al., 1980). Consequently, the English language has dominated over the French language in status value and as the privileged language of business and economic advancement in Canada (Bourhis, 1984a). The substantial anglicization of Francophone minorities across Canada attests to the weak vitality position of French Canadians relative to English Canadians (Breton et al., 1980). Thus, despite federal governments efforts to declare English and French to be equal-status official languages in Canada, it remains that English is seen as the higher-status language of economic advancement, not only in Canada but in North America as a whole. Thus the pressure to use English in a federal administration serving a population that is predominantly Anglophone remains very strong for both Anglophone and Francophone civil servants.

(5) The *linguistic work environment* is one aspect of what is known as the social network of individuals. A social network consists of all the persons with whom an individual comes in contact on a regular basis in settings such as the home, the community, and the work world (Milroy, 1980). The ethnic and linguistic background of individuals participating in such networks should have an impact on the language choice strategies adopted by speakers involved in specific settings, such as the home and the work world. The power and status of individuals occupying different positions within such networks will

also have an impact on the language-use patterns adopted by speakers in these settings. A way to measure a respondent's ethnic and linguistic network of co-workers within the work setting is to use the linguistic work environment (LWE) survey.

## THE LINGUISTIC WORK ENVIRONMENT (LWE) SURVEY

The linguistic work environment survey (LWE) is a research tool designed to address the question of how linguistic work environments combine with the factors described above to affect language choice in bilingual organizations. At this early stage of research, it seems appropriate to devote the rest of this chapter to a discussions of the key conceptual and methodological aspects of the LWE survey as an instrument for conducting research in bilingual work environments. At this point of development the LWE survey is made up of three components. The first consists of questions concerning respondents' linguistic work environments proper. The second part of the LWE survey deals with respondents' self-reports of bilingual language use within their organizational settings. The third part of the survey deals with information concerning respondents' demolinguistic backgrounds. Taken together, these three components of the LWE survey are designed to relate the LWE to patterns of language use within bilingual organizations.

On a day-to-day basis at work, civil servants come in contact with a regular number of co-workers such as colleagues, subordinates, and supervisors. This social network of peers has a linguistics component in bilingual organizations such as the Canadian federal administration, where both Francophones and Anglophones hold civil service positions. The LWE of a civil servant can be assessed by taking into consideration the mother tongue (English or French) and linguistic skills (unilingual/bilingual) of each civil servant found in that person's immediate work environment. The linguistic work environment itself constitutes the first component of the LWE survey; it is to this part of the survey instrument that much of the rest of this chapter will be devoted.

The linguistic work environment of a civil servant can be quite important in determining patterns of French/English language use within bilingual organizational settings. The second component of the LWE survey is specifically designed to explore this relationship and is made up of numerous questions dealing with respondents' self-reports of bilingual language use in different domains of organizational communication, including language choices with supervisors, subordinates, and colleagues. This second component of the LWE survey, along with the third part, which deals with respondents' demolinguistic backgrounds, will be discussed following the presentation of how to calculate the linguistic work environment of respondents working in bilingual organizations.

### LWE Survey, Part 1: Measuring the Linguistic Work Environment

To assess the LWE of a civil servant, one must classify each relevant co-worker in terms of the following attributes:

A: Anglophones, persons whose mother tongue is English
F: Francophones, persons whose mother tongue is French
U: unilinguals in French or English
B: bilinguals in French and English

These language background and linguistic skills data are needed to arrive at an accurate picture of civil servants' linguistic work environments. Though these data could be obtained from existing government data banks, such sources are often out of date and sometimes inexact due to frequent transfers of civil service personnel and changes in organizational structure within and between different units of government departments. A feature of the present approach is to obtain these LWE data *directly* through self-reports from respondents who participate in the LWE survey.

In addition to ethnic and linguistic data, one must also consider the status and role relationships that exist among different civil servants. The status and power differentials that exist among supervisors, colleagues, and subordinates can have quite an impact on patterns of French/English use among individuals occupying these various organizational positions. For instance, supervisors are often in a stronger position than subordinates to dictate which language should be used to discuss a certain topic in a given conversation. In contrast, colleagues may negotiate more freely regarding which language should be used to conduct a particular conversation, given their equal status position within the work environment.

Table 12.1 represents a version of the first component of the LWE

TABLE 12.1  Linguistic Work Environment Described by a Hypothetical
Anglophone Bilingual Respondent on Part 1 of the LWE Survey

*Linguistic Work Environment (LWE) Survey: Part 1*

(1)  From the four items below choose the one which best describes YOURSELF:

———— Anglophone (A) unilingual (U)    √ Anglophone (A) bilingual (B)
———— Francophone (F) unilingual (U)    ———— Francophone (F) bilingual (B)

Now think about the supervisors, colleagues, and subordinates with whom you deal habitually and currently in your immediate work environment.

(2)  Please indicate the number of your immediate SUPERVISORS who can best be described by the following terms:

__0__ Anglophone (A) unilingual (U)    __1__ Anglophone (A) bilingual (B)
__0__ Francophone (F) unilingual (U)    __0__ Francophone (F) bilingual (B)

(3)  Please indicate the number of your immediate COLLEAGUES who can best be described by the following terms:

__6__ Anglophone (A) unilingual (U)    __1__ Anglophone (A) bilingual (B)
__0__ Francophone (F) unilingual (U)    __1__ Francophone (F) bilingual (B)

(4)  Please indicate the number of your immediate SUBORDINATES who can best be described by the following terms:

__6__ Anglophone (A) unilingual (U)    __1__ Anglophone (A) bilingual (B)
__0__ Francophone (F) unilingual (U)    __4__ Francophone (F) bilingual (B)

survey. The responses presented below are hypothetical ones designed to illustrate the workings of this first part of the survey. In completing this chart, respondents begin by indicating in the "yourself" section which of four categories best describes their ethnic and linguistic backgrounds. These four ethnic and linguistic categories are as follows:

Anglophone (A) unilinguals (U)

Anglophone (A) bilinguals (B) in English and French

Francophone (F) unilinguals (U)

Francophone (F) bilinguals (B) in English and French

As before, Anglophones are defined as persons whose mother tongue is English, while Francophones are defined as persons whose mother tongue is French. After checking only one of these items, respondents then proceed to enumerate the number of individuals in their immediate work unit who fit the different ethnic and linguistic categories of supervisors, colleagues, and subordinates listed in the chart.

TABLE 12.2 Linguistic Work Environment Scores Summarizing Table 12.1 Data

|   | A | F |   |
|---|---|---|---|
| U | 12 | 0 | tU = 12 |
| B | 4 | 5 | tB =  9 |
|   | tA =16 | tF = 5 | tN = 21 |

The hypothetical civil servant whose answers are illustrated Table 12.1 chose *Anglophone bilingual* to represent his or her self-identification in the "yourself" part of the survey. The linguistic work environment described by this hypothetical Anglophone (A) bilingual (B) is best summarized in the $2 \times 2$ matrix presented in Table 12.2. Note that the total score obtained in each quadrant of the matrix is obtained by adding the total number of co-workers represented in the corresponding section of each role position in Table 12.1, including colleagues, supervisors, subordinates, and the respondent included in the "yourself" section. These totals are then added to calculate the total number of Anglophones, Francophones, unilinguals, and bilinguals present in the respondent's linguistic work environment.

The total scores presented in Table 12.2 can be described as follows:

tA = 16: represents the total number of Anglophones in the respondent's work environment, including unilinguals and bilinguals as well as, in this case, the respondent him- or herself

tF = 5: represents the total number of Francophones in the respondent's work environment, including unilinguals and bilinguals

tU = 12: represents the total number of unilinguals in the respondent's work environment, including both Francophone and Anglophone unilinguals

tB = 9: represents the total number of bilinguals in the respondent's work environment, including both Francophone and Anglophone bilinguals

tN = 21: represents the total number of co-workers in the respondent's work environment, including the respondent him- or herself

These scores can now be used to calculate two important aspects of the linguistic work environment of civil servants in the federal administration, namely, the intensity of Francophone presence (IFB) and the intensity of bilingualism (IB) scores.

*(1) Intensity of Francophone presence.* This ratio score depicts the numerical presence of Francophones (tF) relative to the total number of co-workers (tN) present in the respondent's linguistic work environment. Thus the IFP score of a given linguistic environment is calculated by dividing the total Francophone presence (tF) by the total number of co-workers (tN) reported in the respondent's work environment.

The *total IFP* score obtained from the linguistic work environment summarized in Table 12.2 is calculated as follows:

$$tF \div tN = IFP$$
$$5 \div 21 = .24$$

This score reflects a relatively weak presence of Francophones in this particular linguistic work environment. Indeed, the IFP score for a linguistic work environment can range from 1.00 to 0.00 such that an *IFP score of 1.00* would indicate that all the individuals listed in the work environment are Francophone, none are Anglophone; an *IFP score of 0.50* would indicate that half the individuals in the work environment are Francophone and the other half are Anglophone; and an *IFP score of 0.00* would indicate that no individuals in the work environment are Francophone, all are Anglophone. Note that an IFP score of .26 would indicate that the Francophone presence in a particular linguistic work environment matches the Francophone demographic presence in the Canadian population as a whole (Breton et al., 1980).

*(2) Intensity of bilingualism.* The intensity of bilingualism (IB) in the linguistic work environment is the ratio of co-workers identified by the respondent as being bilingual (in English and French) relative to the total number of co-workers present in the respondent's work environment. Thus the IB score of a given linguistic environment is calculated by dividing the total bilingual presence (tB) by the total number of co-workers (tN) reported in the respondent's work environment.

The total IB score obtained from the linguistic work environment summarized in Table 12.2 is calculated as follows:

$$tB \div tN = IB$$
$$9 \div 21 = .43$$

This score reflects a moderate level of bilingualism within the respondent's linguistic work environment. Indeed, the IB score for a particular linguistic work environment can range from 1.00 to 0.00 such that an *IB score of 1.00* would indicate that all individuals listed in the work environment are bilingual in French and English (F + E); an *IB score of 0.50* would indicate that half the individuals in the work environment are bilingual in F + E, while half the others are unilingual in French or English; and an *IB score of 0.00* would indicate that no individual in the work environment is bilingual, all are unilingual in French or English.

Note that the IFP and IB scores of a number of respondents surveyed within the *same* department or branch can be *averaged* to obtain an overall picture of the intensity of Francophone presence (IFP) and intensity of bilingualism (IB) that prevails within the particular organizational branch or department under study. The progress of bilingualism and of the Francophone presence within the organization can be monitored in more detail by comparing IB and IFP scores obtained at different points in time within the same department or branch of the federal administration.

Though the total IFP and IB scores of a particular linguistic work environment can be related to patterns of French/English language use within a particular department or branch as a *whole*, finer-tuned IFP and IB scores may be needed to account for the actual language strategies adopted by *individual* civil servants surveyed in the study.

Three additional IFP and IB scores can be scored on the basis of the data presented in Table 12.1. The total linguistic environment can be broken down into its constituent parts, which are the linguistic environments created by (a) the respondent's interactions with his or her *subordinate(s)*, (b) the respondent's interactions with his or her *colleague(s)*, and (c) the respondent's interactions with his or her *supervisor(s)*. As can be seen in parts a, b, and c of Table 12.3, each of these linguistic environments can be summarized by $2 \times 2$ matrix tables. These linguistic environments are depicted in table form using the same nomenclature and calculations as those used in Table 12.2 except that in this case the respondent him- or herself is excluded from the calculations.

The linguistic work environment scores presented in Table 12.3 can be used to calculate IFP and IB scores for each of these three linguistic environments using the calculation procedures described previ-

**TABLE 12.3 Linguistic Work Environment Scores Obtained from Table 12.1 for Relations with Subordinates, Colleagues, and Supervisors, Excluding the Respondent in Each Case**

|   | A | F |         |
|---|---|---|---------|
| U | 6 | 0 | $tU = 6$ |
| B | 1 | 4 | $tB = 5$ |
| $tA = 7$ | $tF = 4$ | $N = 11$ |

(3a) Subordinates

|   | A | F |         |
|---|---|---|---------|
| U | 6 | 0 | $tU = 6$ |
| B | 1 | 1 | $tB = 2$ |
| $tA = 7$ | $tF = 1$ | $N = 8$ |

(3b) Colleagues

|   | A | F |         |
|---|---|---|---------|
| U | 0 | 0 | $tU = 0$ |
| B | 1 | 0 | $tB = 1$ |
| $tA = 1$ | $tF = 0$ | $N = 1$ |

(3c) Supervisors

257

ously. The IFP and IB scores calculated for the three linguistic environments are as follows:

(3a) The IFP and IB scores of subordinates:

$$tF \div tN = IFP \qquad tB \div tN = IB$$
$$4 \div \phantom{11} = .36 \qquad 5 \div 11 = .45$$

(3b) The IFP and IB scores of colleagues:

$$tF \div tN = IFP \qquad tB \div tN = IB$$
$$1 \div 8 = .13 \qquad 2 \div 8 = .25$$

(3c) The IFP and IB scores in relations with supervisors:

$$tF \div tN = IFP \qquad tB \div tN = IB$$
$$0 \div 1 = 0.00 \qquad 1 \div 1 = 1.00$$

Note that these "organizational position" IFB and IB scores differ from the IFP and IB scores obtained for the linguistic work environment as a *whole*. For instance, whereas the intensity of Francophone presence reaches only .24 for the *total* linguistic work environment, the IFP scores obtained for the linguistic environment with *subordinates* did reach a .36 score, while IFP scores dropped to .13 in the linguistic work environment of *colleagues*. Used in conjunction with IB scores, these finer measures of IFP may help better account for the French/English language-use strategies reported by Anglophone and Francophone civil servants in their dealings with subordinates, colleagues, and supervisors.

Note that organizational position IFB and IB scores obtained from a number of individuals surveyed within the same department or branch can be *averaged* to obtain overall picture of the intensity of Francophone presence (IFP) and intensity of bilingualism (IB) in the different occupational ranks of a particular branch or department of the organization. Thus, while two federal administration departments may have very similar *total IFP* scores, one of the two may have strong IFP scores in the *subordinate* linguistic environments but weak ones in the *supervisor* linguistic environments and in the other department the converse may be the case. Average IFP and IB scores calculated at different points in time within the same department for each of the three organizational position environments can also be used to monitor the progress of bilingualism and Francophone presence within the different echelons of the department concerned.

### LWE Survey, Parts 2 and 3: Self-Reports of Language Use and Demolinguistic Data

LWE results can be used optimally when they are obtained from respondents who also complete sociolinguistic questions dealing with their use of French and English during different activities at work and while speaking with the various interlocutors they encounter in their work environment. Thus self-reports of percentage use of French and English at work as well as preferred degree of language use can be related to LWE results such as IB and IFP scores. So, for instance, Part 2 of the LWE survey would include Francophone and Anglophone respondents' self-reports of language use in the following work activities:

percentage of time speaking in French and English at work
percentage of time writing in French and English at work
percentage of time listening in French and English at work
percentage of time reading in French and English at work

The above ratings would be complemented by respondents' ratings of how much they prefer using French and English in each of these activities.

Francophone and Anglophone respondents would also provide in percentage terms the amount of time they speak in French and in English with the following types of interlocutors within their immediate work setting: Francophone supervisors, Anglophone supervisors, Francophone colleagues, Anglophone colleagues, Francophone subordinates, Anglophone subordinates, members of the Francophone public, and members of the Anglophone public. Such ratings would also be supplemented by respondents' ratings of how much they prefer using French and English with each of the above types of interlocutors within their organizational settings.

Finer-tuned measures of language-use strategies can be obtained by asking Francophone and Anglophone respondents to provide self-reports of language use depending on the language choice of each of the above types of interlocutors present in the respondents' work environments. From a speech accommodation perspective, such data could reveal interesting patterns of convergence or maintenance among Francophone and Anglophone supervisors, colleagues, and subordinates.

The premise underlying this approach is that the immediate LWE of individual workers should play an important role in determining overall French/English language use within bilingual organizations. Linguistic work environments in which the intensity of Francophone presence is high should result in greater French language usage than environments in which the IFP is low. French language usage should be further improved in settings where high IFP scores co-occur with high intensity of bilingualism. Results of the LWE survey may reveal that the intensity of Francophone presence is a stronger determinant of French language use in the federal administration than the intensity of bilingualism.

In some work settings the relative importance of IFP and IB scores may also shift depending on whether one is considering communication between supervisors and subordinates or communication between colleagues. Thus the impact of IB and IFP scores on French/English language use should also be affected by the status and power differentials that exist among co-workers within the organizational setting. For instance, by virtue of their power and status, supervisors can be in a better position than subordinates to choose the language they wish to use in their communication with subordinates. However, as noted earlier, superiors whose linguistic community has a strong group vitality may be in a better position to exert their authority through language choice vis-à-vis outgroup subordinates than supervisors whose linguistic community has less vitality as a collectivity than that of the outgroup members who happen to be their subordinates within the organization.

The LWE survey can be used in many departments and branches of a given administration to determine which levels of IFP and IB scores best correlate with achieved or desired levels of French or English language use among civil servants. Thus LWE results can be used as a tool to identify the IB and IFP rates needed to promote French and/or English language use in different branches of the civil administration. Such information can then be used by policymakers to create linguistic work environments that are more likely to foster desired intensities of French/English language use in targeted organizational settings.

Part 3 of the LWE survey consists of questions about demolinguistic information concerning the background of the Anglophone and Francophone civil servants taking part in the study. Information about respondents' mother tongue, age, sex, educational background, and linguistic skills in the first and second language, as well as self-reports of language use at home and with friends, can be used to explore further the links between linguistic work environments and bilingual language use in family and organizational settings.

The relationship between LWE and language use in bilingual organizations may also be affected by the broader sociocultural settings in which the intercultural encounters take place. Indeed, recent research conducted in both Montreal and Quebec city has shown that the relative group vitality of the linguistic communities present in a given intergroup environment can affect the evaluation of language choice strategies of Francophone and Anglophone interlocutors in client-clerk encounters (Genesee & Bourhis, 1982, 1988). Regarding language choice strategies in the federal administration, the relative power and status enjoyed by the Francophone majority in Montreal may encourage Francophone civil servants working in predominantly Anglophone federal government branches in that city to be more assertive in French language use with their Anglophone supervisors than they would be in cities such as Ottawa, where the Francophone minority is weaker as a collectivity relative to the Anglophone majority.

Ongoing research should indicate the usefulness of the current version of the LWE survey as a tool for identifying key factors that limit or promote French/English language use in bilingual organizations such as those found in the Canadian setting. Results from studies combining linguistic work environment data with language-use and language-proficiency data should help further explore the determinants of language choice strategies in bilingual organizations.

Effective public policy options regarding language use in bilingual work settings can best be formulated and implemented when they are based on the most relevant empirical and conceptual framework available in the field. The present conceptualization of how the LWE framework relates to both language use and elements such as speech accommodation, organizational communication, and group vitality remains tentative. Current development in the areas of communication studies, sociolinguistics, and the social psychology of language should be useful in further developing and refining public policy tools such as the linguistic work environment survey. Given the inevitable constraints put on research activity conducted within public and private sector work settings, it is believed that currently the LWE survey constitutes an instrument quite apt to address the conceptual, empirical, and applied problems often encountered in bilingual organizations not only in Canada, but also in other settings such as the United States, Mexico, and numerous nation-states of Western and Eastern Europe. As such, the linguistic work environment survey represents a conceptual and methodological tool that helps to bridge two important areas of research in communication studies: intercultural communication and organizational communication. In a world where bilingualism and multilingualism are more the rule than the exception within national and international organizations, it is time to devote more research efforts to what Albert (1988) has called the "emerging new frontier"—cross-cultural and intercultural perspectives on organizational communication.

## REFERENCES

Albert, R. (1988). *The emerging new frontier: Cross-cultural and intercultural perspectives on organizational communication*. Paper presented at the 38th annual meeting of the International Communication Association, New Orleans.

Berger, C. R. (1985). Social power and interpersonal communication. In M. L. Knapp & G. R. Miller (Eds.), *Handbook of interpersonal communication*. Beverly Hills, CA: Sage.

Bourhis, R. Y. (1979). Language and ethnic interaction: A social psychological approach. In H. Giles & B. Saint-Jacques (Eds.), *Language and ethnic relations*. Oxford: Pergamon.

Bourhis, R. Y. (1984a). Language policies in multilingual settings. In R. Y. Bourhis (Ed.), *Conflict and language planning in Quebec*. Clevedon, Avon, England: Multilingual Matters.

Bourhis, R. Y. (1984b). Cross-cultural communication in Montreal: Two field studies since Bill 101. *International Journal of the Sociology of Language, 46*, 33–47.

Bourhis, R. Y. (1985). The sequential nature of language choice in cross-cultural communication. In R. L. Street & J. N. Cappella (Eds.), *Sequence and patterns in communicative behavior*. London: Edward Arnold.

Bourhis, R. Y., Giles, H., Leyens, J. P., & Tajfel, H. (1979). Psycholinguistic distinctiveness: Language divergence in Belgium. In H. Giles & R. St. Clair (Eds.), *Language and social psychology*. Oxford: Basil Blackwell.

Bourhis, R. Y., & Sachdev, I. (1984). Vitality perceptions and language attitudes. *Journal of Language and Social Psychology, 3*, 97–126.

Breton, R., Reitz, J., & Valentine, V. (1980). *Cultural boundaries and the cohesion of Canada*. Montreal: Institute for Research on Public Policy.

Canadian Ministry of Supply and Services. (1987). *Commissioner of Official Languages annual report, 1986*. Ottawa: Author.

Cobarrubias, J., & Fishman, J. A. (Eds.). (1983). *Progress in language planning*. Berlin: Mouton.

Coleman, W. (1984). *The independence movement in Quebec: 1945–1980*. Toronto: University of Toronto Press.

Cummins, J. (1986). Empowering minority students: A framework for intervention. *Harvard Educational Review, 56*, 18–36.

Drake, B. H., & Moberg, D. (1986). Communicating influence attempts in dyads: Linguistic sedatives and palliatives. *Academy of Management Review, 11*, 567–587.

Fairhurst, G. T., Chandler, T., & Rogers, L. E. (1988). *Leader-member exchange in situ: The accomplishing of social structure in communication*. Paper presented at the annual meeting of the International Communication Association, New Orleans.

Ferguson, C. A., & Heath, S. B. (Eds.). (1981). *Language in the USA*. Cambridge: Cambridge University Press.

Genesee, F., & Bourhis, R. Y. (1982). The social psychological significance of code switching in cross-cultural communication. *Journal of Language and Social Psychology, 1*, 1–27.

Genesee, F., & Bourhis, R. Y. (1988). Evaluative reactions to language choice strategies: The role of sociostructural factors. *Language and Communication, 8*, 229–250.

Giles, H., Bourhis, R. Y., & Taylor, D. M. (1977). Towards a theory of language in ethnic group relations. In H. Giles (Ed.), *Language, ethnicity and intergroup relations*. London: Academic Press.

Giles, H., Mulac, A. Bradac, J., & Johnson, P. (1987). Speech accommodation theory: The first decade and beyond. In M. McLaughlin (Ed.), *Communication yearbook 10* (pp. 8–34). Newbury Park, CA: Sage.

Giles, H., Taylor, D. M., & Bourhis, R. Y. (1973). Toward a theory of interpersonal accommodation through speech: Some Canadian data. *Language in Society, 2*, 177–192.

Gray, T. (1987). Language policy and educational strategies for language minority and majority students in the United States. In L. Laforge (Ed.), *Proceedings of the International Colloquium on Language Planning*. Quebec City: International Center for Research of Bilingualism, Les Presses de l'Université Laval.

Gudykunst, W. (1986). Towards a theory of intergroup communication. In W. B. Gudykunst (Ed.), *Intergroup communication*. London: Basil Blackwell.

Hudson, R. A. (1980). *Sociolinguistics*. Cambridge: Cambridge University Press.

Laforge, L. (Ed.). (1987). *Proceedings of the International Colloquium on Language Planning*. Quebec City: International Center for Research on Bilingualism, Les Presses de l'Université Laval.

Mackay, W. F. (1983). U.S. language status policy and the Canadian experience. In J. Cobarrubias & J. A. Fishman (Eds.), *Progress in language planning*. Berlin: Mouton.

Mallae, J. (1984). Minority-language education in Quebec and Anglophone Canada. In R. Y. Bourhis (Ed.), *Conflict and language planning in Quebec*. Clevedon, Avon, England: Multilingual Matters.

Maurais, J. (Ed.). (1988). *Politique et aménagement linguistique*. Quebec: Conseil de la langue française.

McPhee, R. D. (1985). Formal structure and organizational communication. In R. D. McPhee & P. K. Tompkins (Eds.), *Organizational communication*. Beverly Hills, CA: Sage.

Milroy, L. (1980). *Language and social network*. Oxford: Basil Blackwell.

Molotch, H. L., & Boden, D. (1985) Talking social structure: Discourse, domination and the Watergate hearings. *American Sociological Review, 50*, 273–288.

Taylor, D. M., & Simard, L. M. (1975). Social interaction in a bilingual setting. *Canadian Psychological Review, 16*, 240–254.

Taylor, D. M., Simard, L., & Papineau, D. (1978) Perceptions of cultural differences and language use: Field study in a bilingual environment. *Canadian Journal of Behavioural Science, 10*, 181–191.

Wardhaugh, R. (1983). *Language and nationhood: Canadian experiences*. Toronto: New Star.

Weinstein, B. (1983). *The civic tongue*. New York: Longman.

# Index

# About the Authors

STEPHEN P. BANKS is an Assistant Professor of Communication at Arizona State University. He completed his Ph.D. at the University of Southern California in an interdisciplinary communication program that embraced organizational communication, sociolinguistics, and critical theory. His current research investigates the relation of linguistic practices and institutional relationships, conversation and discourse analysis, and critical theory of work organizations.

RICHARD Y. BOURHIS is a Professor in the Psychology Department at l'Université du Quèbec à Montréal. Of Breton and Québécois origin, he was educated in both French and English in Montreal. After completing a B.Sc. in psychology at McGill University, he pursued his interest in cross-cultural communication and intergroup relations by obtaining a Ph.D. in social psychology at the University of Bristol, England. He has published numerous papers in scientific journals and in 1984 edited a volume titled *Conflict and Language Planning in Quebec*. He has also taught at McGill University and McMaster University in Ontario.

DONAL CARBAUGH received his Ph.D. from the University of Washington in 1984. He is an Assistant Professor of Communication at the University of Massachusetts, Amherst. His special interests include the development of communication theory through cross-cultural study, with a special focus on American patterns. His current projects attempt to explore and analyze comparatively how communication constructs social and cultural models of personhood, sociality, emotion, and communication itself. He is the author of *Talking American: Cultural Discourses on DONAHUE*.

NIKOLAS COUPLAND obtained his Ph.D. in sociolinguistics in 1981 from the University of Wales and is now Director of the Center for Applied English Language Studies at the University of Wales, Cardiff. He is author of *Dialect in Use* (University of Wales Press,

1988), editor of *Styles of Discourse* (Routledge & Kegan Paul, 1988), and coauthor or coeditor of several forthcoming books, including *Sociolinguistics and Style, The Handbook of Miscommunication and Problematic Talk, Contexts of Accommodation,* and *Communication, Health and Aging.* With Howard Giles, he codirects an interdisciplinary research program on communication and the elderly.

NADA KOLEILAT DOANY is a Ph.D. candidate and Assistant Instructor of Speech Communication at the University of Texas at Austin. She has taught at American University in Beirut. Her skills in Arabic and French made the research reported in this volume possible. Her research has considered message forms across languages, including telephone conversation, dramatic performance, and graffiti.

PETER GARRETT has been for several years a teacher and teacher trainer in ESL and EF, working in Austria, Britain, Gambia, Sudan, and Sweden. He has an M.A. in applied linguistics from the University College of North Wales, Bangor, where he is Lecturer in ESFL Methodology and English Grammar, and is Course Director for the master's in ESFL. His current research interests are in the areas of native and nonnative reactions to interlanguage, language awareness, and the teaching of writing.

HOWARD GILES is Professor of Social Psychology and Director of the Center for the Study of Communication and Social Relations at the University of Bristol, England. He is founding editor of the *Journal of Language and Social Psychology* as well as coeditor of a forthcoming annual series on Pacific Rim language and communication issues, and is general editor of three other book series. He has published widely in the areas of ethnic language attitudes and intercultural accommodation and currently has interests in intergenerational communication from a cultural perspective.

YOUSUF GRIEFAT is a graduate student at the School of Education, University of Haifa, and teaches at the Arab Teachers' College in Haifa as well as the Teachers' Seminary, Nahalal. He is working on a study concerned with traditional storytelling forms and their role in the socialization of children within a Bedouin community.

WILLIAM B. GUDYKUNST is a Professor of Communication at Arizona State University. His research focuses on explaining uncertainty reduction processes across cultures and between members of different groups. His most recent books include *Intergroup Communication* (Edward Arnold) and *Cross-Cultural Adaption*, coedited with Y. Y. Kim (Sage). He recently completed *Culture and Interpersonal Communication*, with S. Ting-Toomey and E. Chua, and *Theories in Intercultural Communication*, coedited with Y. Y. Kim (both for Sage). He is currently working on *Strangeness and Similarity: A Theory of Interpersonal and Intergroup Communication* (Multilingual Matters), as well as coediting the *Handbook of International and Intercultural Communication*, with M. Asante (Sage).

BETH HASLETT is a Professor of Communication at the University of Delaware. She has published numerous articles on developmental communication, and her majc. research interests are in developmental communication, conversational and discourse analysis, and interpretive analyses of organizations. She is the author of *Communication: Strategic Action in Context*, and is currently working on a book in developmental communication.

ROBERT HOPPER is Charles Sapp Centennial Professor of Communication at the University of Texas at Austin. His studies of discourse and conversation consider a variety of sociolinguistic issues involving dialects, speech evaluation, and language universals.

BARBARA JOHNSTONE received her Ph.D. in Linguistics from the University of Michigan in 1981. She is Assistant Professor of English at Texas A&M University. Her work on Arabic linguistics, persuasive styles and strategies, forms and functions of repetition, and personal experience narrative has appeared in such journals as *Anthropological Linguistics, Linguistics, Text, General Linguistics*, and *Studies in Language*.

TAMAR KATRIEL is a Senior Lecturer at the School of Education, University of Haifa. She is the author of *Talking Straight: "Dugri" Speech in Israeli Sabra Culture* (Cambridge University Press, 1986), and has published in the areas of sociolinguistics and cultural studies in such journals as *Communication Monographs, Quarterly*

*Journal of Speech, Language in Society, Anthropological Linguistics*, and *Language Arts*.

FELIPE KORZENNY is Professor of Communication and Coordinator of Graduate Studies at the Department of Speech and Communication Studies, San Francisco State University. He was born in Mexico City and has worked in many Latin American countries on development projects dealing with health, nutrition, agriculture, and education. His consulting activities over the past five years have been concentrated on communication research and strategies relevant to U.S. Hispanics. He has served as Chairperson of the Intercultural and Development Communication Division of the International Communication Association. His publications include numerous research articles in communication journals. His current work includes a book on Mexican Americans and the mass media, and articles and research projects on communication discrimination, communication and drug usage across cultures, effects of international news, ethnicity as a factor in communicating with strangers, and AIDS communication.

GERRY PHILIPSEN is an Associate Professor of Speech Communication at the University of Washington. His research interests focus on the relationship between speech and the communal function in different cultures. His work has appeared in such journals as *Communication Monographs, Language in Society*, and *Quarterly Journal of Speech*.

THOMAS M. STEINFATT received his Ph.D. from Michigan State University in 1971. He is Professor and Director of Speech Communication at the University of Miami. In addition to linguistic relativity, his research interests include statistics and research design, the effects of personality variables on communication, and communication in organizations, in situations of conflict, and in love and intimate relationships. He is the author of two books and numerous articles and chapters in scholarly journals and books.

STELLA TING-TOOMEY is an Associate Professor of Communication at Arizona State University. Her research focuses on cross-cultural conflict styles and face-negotiation in interpersonal relationships. Her most recent books include *Culture and Interpersonal Communication*, with W. Gudykunst and E. Chua, and *Communication*,

*Culture, and Organizational Processes*, coedited with W. Gudykunst and L. Stewart. Her publications have appeared in *American Behavioral Scientist, Communication Monographs, Human Communication Research,* and *International Journal of Intercultural Relations*. She is the Chair of the Speech Communication Association's International and Intercultural Communication Division.